Journal of Research
of the
American Federation
of Astrologers

2015

Copyright 2015 by American Federation of Astrologers
All rights reserved.

No part of this book may be reproduced or transcribed in any form or by any means, electronic or mechanical, including photocopying or recording or by any information storage and retrieval system without written permission from the author and publisher, except in the case of brief quotations embodied in critical reviews and articles. Requests and inquiries may be mailed to: American Federation of Astrologers, Inc., 6535 S. Rural Road, Tempe, AZ 85283.

ISBN-13: 978-0-86690-656-2

Cover Design: Jack Cipolla

Published by:
American Federation of Astrologers, Inc.
6535 S. Rural Road
Tempe, AZ 85283

Printed in the United States of America

Contents

From the Editor	v
Letter to the Editor	ix
Hybris Syndrome: An Astrological Approach By Ana Andrade and Silvia Méndez	1
Islamic Astrology: A History By Joe Simon	31
The Impact of Astrology on Carl Jung By José Luis Belmonte	47
The Influence of the Tropical and Sidereal Zodiacs on Personal Transits By Peter Meyer	61
How Midpoints Feature in 2014 World Political Trials and Health Issues By Pamela Rowe, LPMAFA, FMFAA	69
Astrology as a Ten-Dimensional Science By Pamela J. Fernsler	97
The Astrology Code By Michael Bergen	113
Tidy Vesta Can Warn Us of Messy Disasters By Sue Kientz	131
Yods in Suicide and Homicide Charts By Arlene DeAngelus	149
9/56 Year Cycle: U.S. Presidential Assassinations By David McMinn	175

Wind Direction By Kris Brandt Riske	193
Biodynamics Agriculture: An Earth Astrology Glen Atkinson	197
Homosexuality Signature in Vedic Astrology By Indranil Ray	217
AntiKythera Mechanism: A 2000-year-old Astro-Computer By Demetra George	231
About the Authors	241

From the Editor

We want to honor James H. Holden, FAFA for his many years of service as the Director of Research for the American Federation of Astrologers. With his passing in 2013, the wise counsel and scholarly expertise that he shared so generously will be missed by everyone. He set a bar that inspires us for the pursuit of excellence in astrology.

Education and research are two of AFA's most important missions. Research serves to stabilize the "body of knowledge" that provides a foundation for the practice of astrology. It leads to revelations of ancient wisdom teachings as well as new discoveries that move the field toward expanding vistas of the future. In collaboration with the Ernest and Catharine Grant Trust provided by our founding members, AFA is sponsoring several research grants beginning in 2015. Future plans include educational seminars on how to conduct astrological research.

We are pleased to present you with the 2015 Journal of Research and thank each of the contributors not only for their efforts in research but even more so for sharing the results of their investigations. We hope you enjoy the wide variety of papers that span quantitative, qualitative and historical approaches to the research of astrology from a broad spectrum of international authors in both the Western and Eastern traditions.

Several papers take an in-depth look at specific personality traits. Ana Andrade and Silvia Mendez (Argentina) explore the role of asteroids associated with overweening ambition, retribution and justice in the charts of political figures, tracking their rise to power and subsequent fall. Indrinal Ray (India) referring to ancient Vedic texts and contemporary Indian sources, investigates the signatures of homosexuality in the birth chart. Arlene DeAngelus (New York) takes a close look at the role of critical degrees and yods in the charts of suicide victims. Sue Kientz (Southern California) focuses on the placement and aspects of the asteroid Vesta, goddess of household, in the charts of civic leaders faced with a catastrophe that requires extensive cleanup or other recovery work.

In the Medieval era, the two acceptable and uncontroversial uses of the stars were for the purposes of weather and farming. Kris Brandt Riske (Arizona) presents an analysis of wind direction in astrometeorology and Glen Atkinson (New Zealand) gives an overview of the correlations between astrology and the work of Rudolph Steiner regarding land, plant, and animal management. Pamela Fernsler (Pennsylvania) takes us on a futuristic journey exploring the interface between astrology, cosmology, and the new science of noetics.

Technical accuracy and use of statistical analysis in the determination of significant factors are important directions for astrological research. Peter Meyer (international nomadic traveler) explains the differences between the tropical and sidereal zodiacs and shows how each system yields different timing of transits to personal points in the birth chart. Michael Bergen summarizes the findings of his extensive research using a statistical analysis of over 12,000 birth charts to distinguish the dominant zodiacal trend of a range of study groups. David McMinn (Australia) examines various Sun-Moon cycles in the timing of successful and attempted assassinations of U.S. presidents and vice presidents.

Scholarly research into ancient history, primary source texts, and the biographies of astrologers and thinkers illuminates the how the mutual influences between astrology and philosophy, religion, and politics shapes subsequent astrological practice. Jose Luis Belmonte (Florida and Spain) documents how Carl

Jung was indirectly exposed to astrology through his investigations into gnosticism, hermetism, mithraism, and alchemy and how this influence returned back to astrology enriching it with new transpersonal psychological approaches. Joe Simon (Ohio) reaches back into the medieval era and traces how the mystical stream of Islamic religion provided a philosophical foundation for the development of Arabic astrology. Demetra George (Oregon) summarizes the recent discovery and findings concerning the antikythera mechanism, a 2000-year-old astro-computer, and speculates how this invention may have contributed to the quantum of leap of astrological techniques during the Hellenistic era.

Demetra George
AFA Director of Research

Letter to the Editor

In the course of researching a set of 122 Chiron interpretations for natal reports, I made some breakthroughs in understanding what Chiron is all about. First of all, Chiron is just as important in reading a natal chart as are the rest of the planets. Second, when I was researching the sextile interpretations, I became aware that Chiron is not just about the concept of healing, it actually covers the whole concept of growth in general. It may not be physical growth, but it is the kind of internal growth to which ability, fortitude, and generosity of the spirit refers. The inharmonious aspects to Chiron may provoke growth by setting up barriers or obstacles that must be overcome, but the overall effect is the same as with the harmonious aspects to Chiron, namely that the organism expands its range of capabilities, it becomes more competent and more compassionate.

With this new understanding that Chiron is about general growth of the spirit, that Chiron is not just the asteroid of wounds and healing, it is time to think about Chiron as the higher octave of Jupiter. Astrologers know that Jupiter is the planet of assimilation and expansion in the external world. The other three outer planets, Uranus, Neptune, and Pluto, the higher octaves of Mercury, Venus, and Mars, each involves the spirit rebelling in its own way against the limitations of the day-to-day world ruled by Saturn. Chiron is similar to Uranus, Neptune, and Pluto in that it too is about the spirit working to overcome limitations, but this time the limitations are upon growth, such as from sickness, injuries, misfortune, bigotry and prejudice— all lower manifestations of this Saturn-ruled world.

I first saw the extent of the limitations ruled by Chiron, which include prejudice, when I was researching the biographies of individuals in whom Chiron is the focus planet of an aspect configuration, such as a Yod or a T-Square. Chiron's more general function as a planet of higher growth only became clear to me when I was researching the sextile aspects from each of the planets to Chiron. In these biographies I saw only positive growth, without the need to have it be provoked by setbacks or limitations.

Probably the most surprising thing about proposing Chiron to be the higher octave of Jupiter is that Chiron does not lie outside the orbit of Pluto, where we would physically expect it. Chiron orbits in between Saturn and Uranus. Our culture, however, did discover Chiron forty-seven years after it discovered Pluto. I personally think that our culture has been growing through stages corresponding to each of the planets, such as a stage devoted to Jupiter during the expansion of the Renaissance and a stage devoted to Saturn during the time of the scientific revolution and Puritanism, followed of course by stages corresponding to Uranus, Neptune, Pluto, and Chiron.

John Halloran
Los Angeles, California

Hybris Syndrome: An Astrological Approach

By Ana Andrade and Silvia Méndez

ABSTRACT: History is full of stories written by leaders engaged in power struggles and responsible the loss of lives. These people have transcended death, remembered for events and dramatic consequences, including the loss of their own lives. The objective of this study is the hybris syndrome, whose essence is the understanding of the need for power, along with an exaggerated self-confidence, and its application in the natal charts of seven leaders in three different events in their lives: start, apogee, and downfall. These leaders are: Adolf Hitler, Benito Mussolini, and Rafael Trujillo. In addition, the research includes the asteroids Hybris, Ate, and Nemesis—intertwined in the Greek concept of hybris—that clearly illustrate the dynamism of this syndrome. The astrological symbolism reflects the facts as transits and progressions indicate events through hard and soft aspects.

The history of mankind has been characterized by constant power struggles, conflicts, disagreements, and pacification agreements, where many lives have been lost, many territories conquered, new nations born, and ethnic cleansing used as a tool that generated countless consequences on immigration issues, displaced persons, and refugees.

These social phenomena remain an interesting subject of study and research in human and collective psychology. However, it is one of those social phenomena that the authors studied.

British neurologist David Owen studied hubris or hybris syndrome, a common disorder in long-term periods of power. It is characterized by symptoms easily recognized, among which are an exaggerated self-confidence, refusal of the advice given by those around them, and progressive distance from reality. There is a moment in which those who govern stop listening, become reckless, and make decisions on their own without sharing information since they think that their ideas are correct. So, although their ideas finally demonstrate that these ideas were inappropriate, they do not acknowledge their mistakes and continue thinking about the good job they did, adding a feeling that they were called by destiny to great deeds.

This usually happens when a person enters the world of politics, not necessarily in this unique context, but it is a more visible arena. The individual reaches power, although he can feel insecure about his ability to handle the position.

But as the syndrome progresses, it is common for followers to appear—unconditional or sycophants—to congratulate the leadership style so that the initial uncertainty of power suddenly becomes a certainty of merit for the person who has earned this position. The followers (unconditional or sycophants) greet him, seeking contact with him, and in return he gets thousands of compliments.

But this continues. The individual starts to receive comments such as "how good you fit with us" and "what would we do without you?" Such comments feed the ego of the person reaffirming the idea that he is "the best" and it then creates a sense of being infallible and irreplaceable. Upon reaching this point, the person plans and acts to perpetuate his power, to be "hooked" in the job as if it will never be lost.

Consequently, the person plans titanic projects (much better if they take his name) and can even talk about issues that are not in his entire domain, revealing some inconsistency in his message and causing confusion to listeners. However, to the individual, what he is saying or doing is totally correct for him.

This process does not end here. Those affected by hubris or hybris are susceptible of what is psychopathologically known as "paranoid development," when those who oppose the individual or his ideas are considered personal enemies. And it is possible that he might suspect that the entire world is his enemy. This phenomenon, at the end, leads people who experience this syndrome to be isolated, depressed, or even dead.

Greeks were the first to use the word Hubris to define the hero that sought glory and was drunk on success, that would start to behave like a god, capable of anything. This feeling led him to make one mistake after another. Nemesis appears as a consequence of hubris, returning the individual to reality through a failure.

As noted earlier, this syndrome is commonly seen in politics because of, on one hand, the needed networks and loyalties between the members of a group to climb the ladder of power; on the other hand, it is known that power is not always in the most capable hands, but those who assume leadership roles think they are the perfect ones and start behaving with narcissistic traits. These two factors make them susceptible to the syndrome.

The definition of Hybris is:

> The hubris or hybris is a Greek concept that can be translated as "excess" and now refers to a pride or self-confidence greatly exaggerated, especially when it holds power. In ancient Greece referred to a reckless disregard to the personal space of others coupled with the lack of control over one's impulses, being a violent feeling inspired by the exaggerated passions, both considered diseases because of an irrational and unbalanced character, specifically by Ate (anger or pride). As the famous old proverb says, erroneously attributed to Euripides: "He, whom the gods wish to destroy, they first drive you crazy."

The person that commits hubris is responsible for desiring more than the part assigned to him in the division of destination. The excess designates the fact of wanting more what fate assigns him. The punishment for Hubris is Nemesis, which is the punishment of the gods that has the effect of returning the individual to reality when limits were crossed.

In consequence, the concept of hubris is a breach of restraint, of moderation and sobriety; it is the effect when not measuring all things, or even better, "never too much" or "it is not long enough." So those who were affected by hubris ended up being punished by the gods.

To define hybris, it is necessary to study Ate in Greek mythology (or Atheist: ancient Greek "ruin," "folly," "deception"). She was the goddess of fate and personified thoughtless actions and their consequences. This refers to the mistakes made by both mortals and gods, usually due to excessive pride or hubris that brought them to destruction or death.

In the Iliad, Homer relates that Atea or Ate, is the eldest daughter of Zeus, but her mother is not mentioned at all. Instigated by Hera, Atea used her influence with Zeus for him to swear that the day a mortal descendant of him was born, he would be a great leader. Hera immediately delayed the birth of Heracles and instead she provoked the premature birth of Eurystheus, with the intention to be the first in getting power. Angered, Zeus sent Atea or Ate to Earth forever, forbidding her to return to heaven or Olympus.

Atea or Ate then wandered through the world, stepping on the heads of men rather than walking on the soil, causing chaos among mortals. In that sense, Ate or Atea is symbolized as pride and anger, as a "bad advisor" whose consequence is being banished from Olympus.

And finally, Nemesis, mentioned in previous lines. In Greek mythology, Nemesis is the goddess of retributive justice, solidarity, revenge, and fortune. She punished those under her command who did not follow her and especially those children disobedient to their parents. It is a sort of justice applied to those who are out of bounds, a justice that restrains and punishes Hybris.

Astrologically, the asteroids corresponding with these three concepts or goddesses are:
- (430) Hybris, asteroid discovered on December 18, 1897 by A. Charlois in Nice, France. Wherever Hybris is placed in the chart, there are options for excess and overflow. Naturally this asteroid is interpreted by sign and house as well as the aspects with planets.
- (111) Ate, asteroid discovered August 14, 1870 by CHF Peters in the United States. As explained in mythology, where Ate is placed in the chart it is possible to be a bad advisor or to be misguided, and the consequence of "exile" is possible. In addition, it could be interpreted as the easiness for advice of followers or sycophants to feed the narcissism of those who experience hybris. Another interpretation is the advice provided to perpetuate the plans or ideas once invaded by hybris. As always, this asteroid is analyzed by sign and house and its aspects with planets.
- (128) Nemesis, asteroid discovered November 25, 1872 by J. C. Watson in Ann Arbor, Michigan. As stated in mythology, she brings revenge and order. Wherever the asteroid Nemesis is placed in the chart, it can indicate the possibility of justice in terms of the characteristics of the sign and the house where it is located. This justice is to repair the order altered and to serve as a reminder that all humans are simple mortals.

The authors considered adding Lilith (Mean Lilith) to this analysis as a signifier of resolution or enforcement of what is repressed through expression of feelings of rejection or anger manifested from within or coming from the outside. Lilith does not always manifest in the best terms and it can take different shapes.

The reason to incorporate Lilith is to tune her meaning with the topic of this article, with some similarities in the core of the interpretation, especially in the case of historical figures who have had to deal with issues of power that could have served as a "ground line" of feelings and resentments from childhood and adulthood and family psychological underlying rules and traumas that arise. In sum, all these factors help to highlight a more sensitive Lilith when interconnected with the asteroids mentioned.

This article presents three people in history whose passage through life and actions have changed the destiny of their countries and left their mark in the annals of mankind: Adolf Hitler, "Der Führer"; Benito Mussolini, "Il Duce"; and Rafael Trujillo, President of the Dominican Republic (aka "The Goat"—"El Chivo" in Spanish).

The authors have chosen three events to reflect Hybris syndrome. The first event is about the beginning of the race or power that makes the individual famous, such as a presidential inauguration date. The second event has to do with the peak time, which is not necessarily a positive event for the population; it may be a point of exaggeration or a moment identified by the use of unlimited power, where a natural feeling of invulnerability can be seen. These moments are crucial when Hybris is ready to leave room to Nemesis. The third event is related to the downfall or declination moment of the leader, the end of his government, either physical or political death.

With these sequences of events, the performance of Hybris can be noted as a power; when not well used, it exacerbates the need to take over everything. For the leader seduced by Hybris, Ate—considered as a wrong counselor or unhealthy advice—can go two ways: on one hand, Ate can reaffirm the vision of the leader or, on the other hand, the leader simply does not want to hear anyone's advice so the same person is self-advised ("self-Ate," so to speak); and Nemesis, goddess of revenge and order, comes to destroy everything that prevents from equitable justice.

These three mythological concepts will be incorporated through the asteroids and it will be seen how they perform in three different events, more prominent in some moments than in others.

The three individuals and the events to be studied are:
Adolf Hitler
    Start: Leader of the Nazi Party
    Apogee: Invasion of Poland

Downfall: Suicide

Benito Mussolini
Start: Creation of the Fasci Italiani de Combattimento
Apogee: Founding of the Italian Socialist Republic
Downfall: Execution

Rafael Trujillo, "El Chivo"
Start: First Presidential Inauguration
Apogee: Million Parade
Downfall: Assassination

The analysis is presented in this way: birth chart of the leader, the birth chart in a tri-wheel with transits and progressions for the date of the event, and comments with the most important observations. It is amazing how the additional information defines the aspects of the event in combination with transits and natal chart.

Adolf Hitler

Natal Chart

Asteroid Hybris at 4 Virgo is trine the natal Moon, Nemesis, and Jupiter in the third house, and completes a grand trine with the Sun in the seventh house. (See chart on next page.)

These points show a natural disposition for a lush and critical power, expressed through extensive and plentiful communication. Hybris is in an animated conversation with the Sun (ruler of his Midheaven), which brings to mind the natural association with power, hubris, and arrogance, in spite of the Sun in the seventh house, where the mission would have been agreement or harmonious relationships with others.

Nemesis is conjunct the Moon and Jupiter in the third house (in detriment and in fall, respectively) completing a grand trine with the luminaries, Jupiter, and Hybris, as well as a quincunx to Pluto, linking the eighth house to this interaction.

Several books discuss the effect of the strong maternal influence of his mother and his authoritarian father. Cancer is intercepted

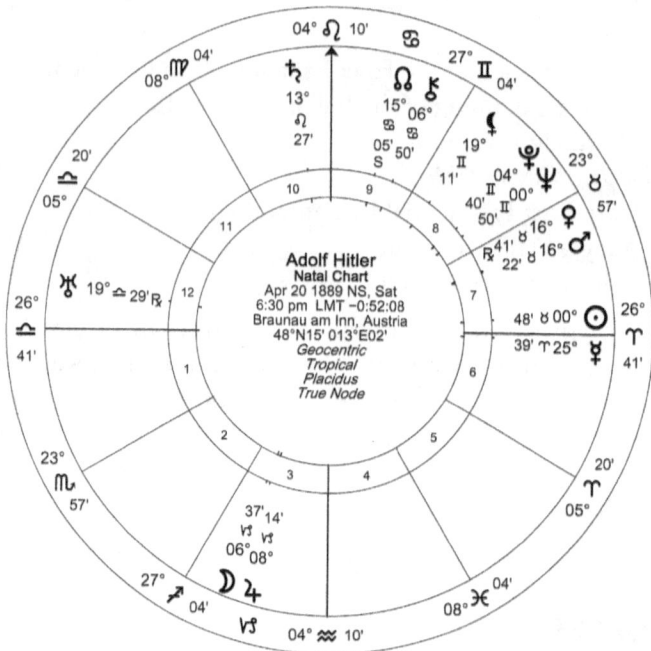

Hybris, 4 Virgo 08; Nemesis, 4 Capricorn 56; Ate, 28 Cancer 24

in the ninth house and its ruler, the Moon, manifested through the mind, communication of the concepts of "justice" combined with his excessive ambition for power. The ninth house symbolizes religious, ethical, and political concepts, and notice that the Moon in this house reflects Hitler's ideas of racial and religious persecution.

Ate in the ninth house square the Ascendant/Descendant axis and natal Mercury ratifies the wrong advice by exalting nationalism with fiery speeches.

Pluto (co-ruler of the first house) is in the eighth house conjunction Neptune, so Hitler might have been inclined to the esoteric and occultism. On the other hand, Lilith in the eighth house deploys all its fury and vengeance toward anything different, and is trine Uranus.

Leader of the Nazi Party, July 29, 1921

- Transiting Neptune conjunction natal Saturn
- Transiting Nemesis, 29 Sagittarius, possibly conjunct natal Nemesis
- Transiting Lilith opposition natal Saturn
- Transiting Saturn square transiting Venus
- Progressed Ascendant activated natal Lilith-Uranus trine

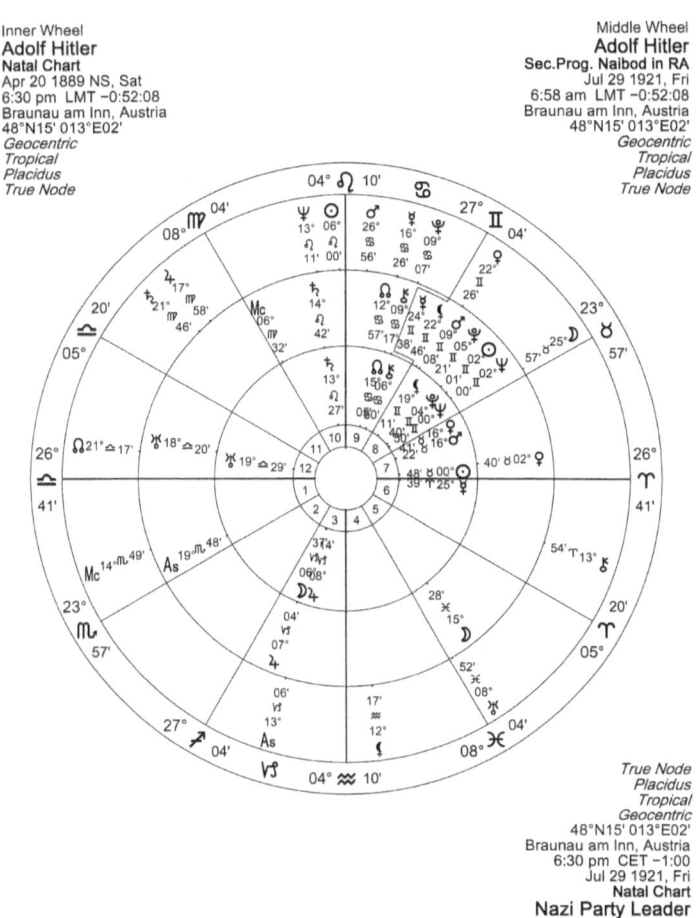

- Progressed Venus, Ascendant ruler, trine progressed Nemesis
- Progressed Hybris, 7 Virgo, conjunction progressed Midheaven
- Progressed Jupiter trine progressed Hybris and Midheaven

When analyzing the planets and asteroids in the progressed chart related to Hitler's leadership of the Nazi Party, the Ascendant at 19 Scorpio activated the natal Lilith-Uranus trine.

His progressed Midheaven was conjunct progressed retrograde Hybris, symbolizing how fate had put him in touch with excess.

His retrograde progressed Jupiter formed a trine with this combination, pointing to a relevant and important event in his life.

With regard to transits, the most prominent was Hybris aspecting natal Neptune, exacerbating the lack of limits in the house of power and death. It was also conjunct the Moon-Ate in aspect to the natal Venus-Mars conjunction in the house of declared or known enemies. In addition, Nemesis was retrograde that day, so it might have transited the degree of natal Nemesis some time before the event.

Invasion of Poland, September 1, 1939
- Transiting Saturn conjunction natal Sun, opposition progressed Moon
- Transiting Hybris, 13 Capricorn, opposition natal North Node, trine natal Venus-Mars conjunction
- Transiting Ate, 12 Virgo, trine natal Venus-Mars conjunction
- Transiting Jupiter square natal Nemesis
- Progressed Midheaven quincunx natal Mercury
- Progressed Sun trine natal Lilith-Uranus
- Progressed Moon opposition natal Sun
- Progressed Saturn square natal Mars; progressed Nemesis trine natal Sun
- Progressed Jupiter approaching quincunx to natal Pluto
- Progressed Lilith trine natal Ascendant
- Progressed Chiron sextile progressed Hybris, 11 Virgo

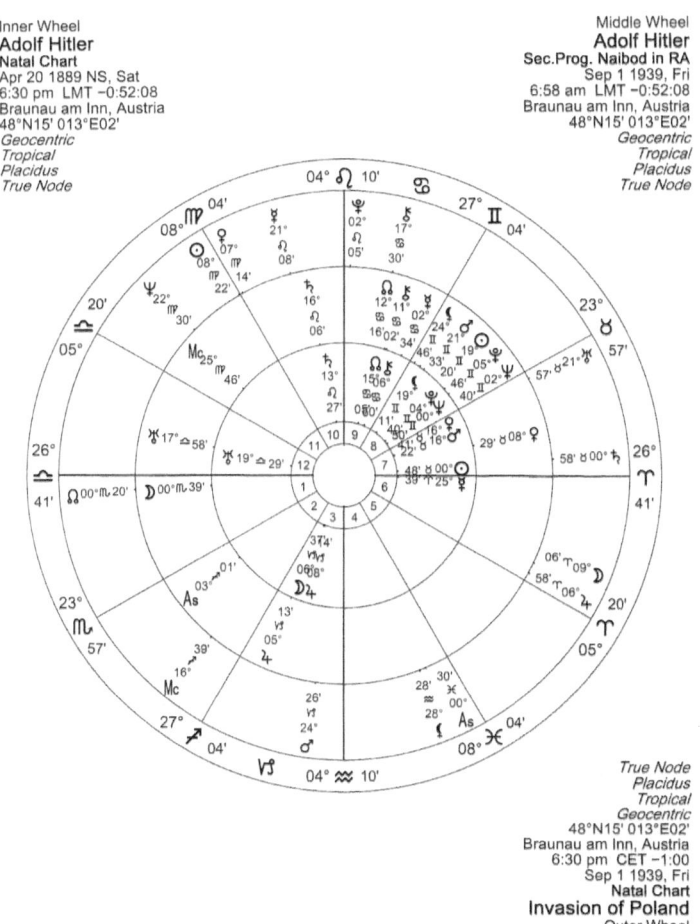

- Progressed Ate, 16 Leo, square natal Venus-Mars

There was an earth grand trine comprised of transiting Ate and Hybris activating the natal Venus-Mars conjunction Venus/Mars, and a wedge with the natal nodal axis. Lilith at 28 Aquarius formed a quincunx to natal Ate. Transiting Saturn was conjunct natal Sun and the transiting North Node was opposition the natal Sun. In addition, the transiting North Node was conjunct the progressed Moon.

Transiting Jupiter at 7 Aries was square the conjunction of Nemesis, Moon, and Jupiter, all present in the sign of Capricorn and in the third house (neighbor or nearby country).

Transiting Venus had previously contacted natal Hybris, with Venus as the ruler of the eighth and twelfth houses.

It is interesting to note that World War Two began with the invasion of Poland. With this act, Hitler violated the Treaty of Peace signed at Versailles in 1919, which established the conditions for peace after World War One.

Suicide, April 30, 1945

- Transiting Mercury, Venus, Nemesis, and Hybris (17-18 Aries) opposition natal Uranus and sextile natal Lilith
- Transiting Mars, 28 Pisces, square progressed Nemesis, 29 Sagittarius
- Transiting Lilith, 18 Libra, conjunction natal Uranus and trine natal Lilith
- Transiting Neptune, 4 Libra, square natal Nemesis (suicide)
- Transiting Venus, 17 Aries, opposition natal Uranus
- Transiting Ate, 5 Aquarius, trine progressed Pluto, opposition transiting Pluto, 7 Leo, and conjunction natal IC
- Transiting Saturn, 6 Cancer, conjunction natal Chiron and opposition natal Moon
- Progressed Moon square natal Mercury and natal Ascendant
- Progressed Mercury sextile natal Sun
- Progressed Mars trine natal Ascendant
- Progressed Jupiter conjunction natal Nemesis, 4 Capricorn
- Progressed Saturn square natal Venus-Mars
- Progressed Lilith, 25 Gemini, conjunction progressed Mars and trine natal Ascendant
- Progressed Nemesis, 29 Sagittarius, quincunx natal Ate

Suicide can be seen when analyzing the progressed planets: progressed Moon square natal Ascendant and natal Mercury, and Mars trine natal Ascendant.

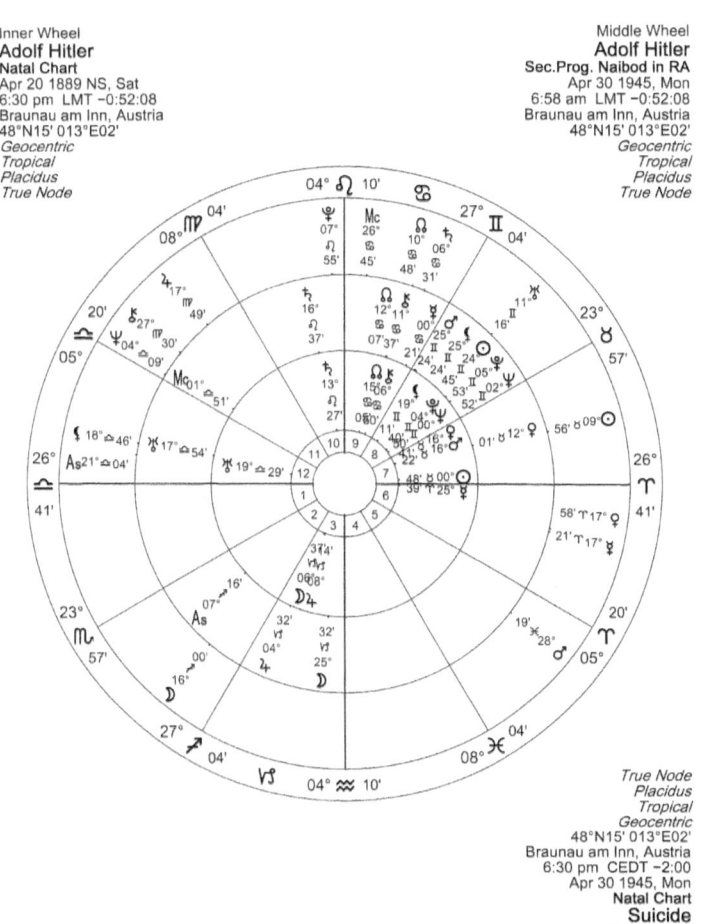

Progressed Lilith was conjunct progressed Mars in a tight orb, and both were trine the natal Ascendant.

When analyzing transits, note the configuration formed by the stellium of Mercury, Venus, Nemesis, and Hybris in opposition to transiting Lilith; this activated the natal Uranus-Lilith trine.

In addition, transiting Neptune (suicide) was square natal Nemesis, and transiting Saturn (fourth house ruler) aspected natal Chiron and was opposition natal Nemesis and the Moon.

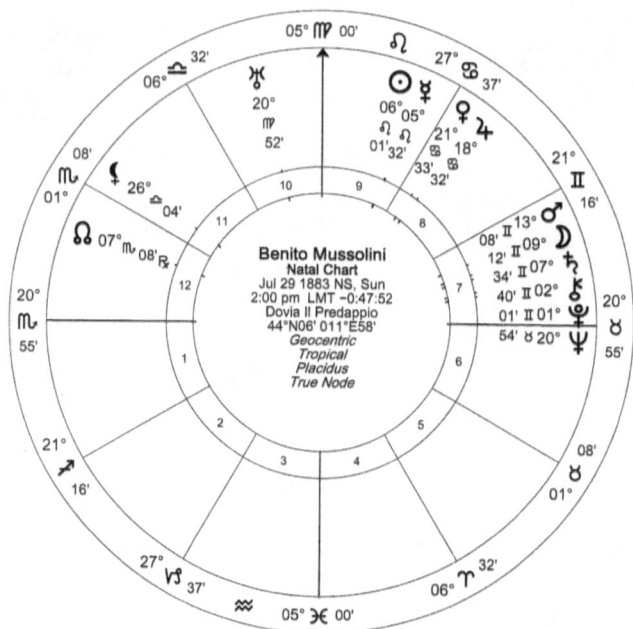

Ate, 12 Aries 55; Hybris, 1 Cancer 22; Nemesis, 18 Virgo 42

Benito Mussolini

Mussolini's Sun is in Leo conjunct Mercury, ruler of his Midheaven, in the ninth house, marking an orientation to foreign affairs and/or linked to politics, along with a Neptune-Pluto conjunction in seventh house. This aspect indicates a person who would interact with the major transformations and changes in the ideological and cultural context (because of its angularity), giving birth to a new historical epoch in the place where the person was born (Pluto rules his Ascendant).

The Moon is embraced by Mars and Saturn (symbolism of the "black shirts") in an angular house. This signifies a man who was born to cause structural changes in the society of his native country (Uranus in the tenth house).

Hybris, at 1 Cancer 22 in the eighth house, is the asteroid of excess and arrogance and here it is in the house of death and management of third-party resources and semisextile the modern ruler of his Ascendant. Cancer is the sign of nationalism—and Fascism, an ideological trend born to face the Socialists and Communists.

Ate in the fifth house forms a sextile to Mars (the other ruler of his Ascendant) and a square to Jupiter, which in turn is sextile the Nemesis-Uranus conjunction in the tenth house. Notice that Jupiter is co-ruler of his Ascendant, a combination that could signal the difficulties he experienced that led to such a complicated life.

Finally, it is important to note Nemesis conjunction Uranus in the tenth house (Uranus, ruler of his third house, with Aquarius intercepted); he was trying to communicate his revolutionary ideas to the people, the fate that the gods had prepared for him.

Creation of the Fasci Italliani di Combattimento, October 9, 1919

- Transiting Ate, 26 Scorpio, conjunction Ascendant
- Transiting Nemesis, 20 Virgo, sextile Ascendant
- Transiting Jupiter, 13 Leo, trine natal Ate, 12 Aries; both sextile natal Mars
- Transiting Hybris, 7 Sagittarius, opposition natal Saturn and square transiting Saturn, 7 Virgo
- Transiting Nemesis, 20 Virgo, sextile Ascendant
- Transiting Lilith, 28 Scorpio, square transiting Uranus, 28 Aquarius
- Progressed Hybris, 19 Cancer, conjunction natal Jupiter and trine Ascendant
- Progressed Nemesis, 1 Libra, sextile natal Chiron
- Progressed Ascendant quincunx natal Jupiter
- Progressed Midheaven at 13 Libra trine natal Mars

A transiting Venus-Saturn conjunction was present in the Midheaven, forming a T-square focal point with the transiting Hybris-natal Saturn opposition; this indicates the "black shirts."

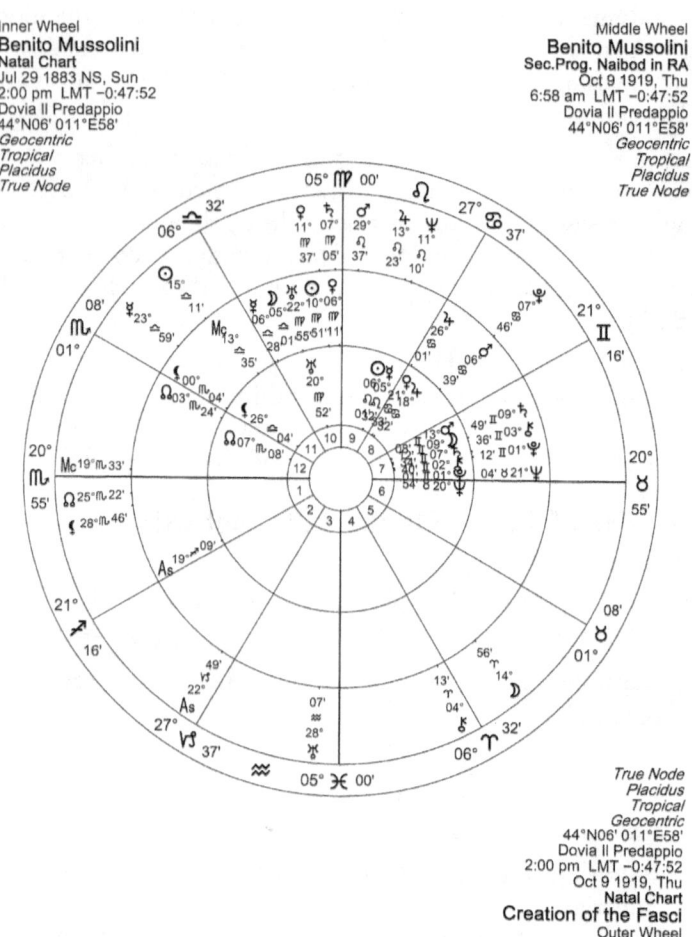

The Hybris seduction was activating the Venus symbolism.

Transiting Nemesis was conjunct natal Nemesis-Uranus, trine natal Neptune, and sextile the Ascendant. These factors contributed to the creation of armed groups.

Both transiting Jupiter and Neptune were trine natal Ate and sextile natal Mars. Finally, the progressed Ascendant and progressed Midheaven were aspecting natal Jupiter and Mars, respectively.

The symbolism of the asteroid Ate in the fifth house is emphasized because Mussolini armed squads of young people (fifth house) dressed in black shirts; their main traits were aggression and violence.

Below is a part of the speech (from Wikipedia, along with planetary notations by the authors) Mussolini gave on November 16, 1922, when he won the confidence vote with 316 in favor, 116 against and 7 abstentions. It was his first speech as president of the Council of Ministers (called "Discorso del bivacco").

> I have rejected the possibility of completely overcome, and I could. I put limits to me [Moon-Saturn]. I said to me, that the best wisdom is the one that is not abandoned after the victory [Ate-Aries]. With 300,000 fully armed youngsters [Ate in Aries in the fifth house] determined to everything and almost mystically [Neptune angle] ready to execute any order I give them, could be punished [Nemesis] to all who have defamed and tried to put mud on Fascism. I could make this dull and gray classroom a camp of soldiers: I could destroy with irons [Mars-Gemini] this Parliament and form a government exclusively of Fascists. I could, but I have not wanted to, at least at this early stage.

"Il Duce," Foundation of the Italian Socialist Republic, September 23, 1943

- Transiting Lilith sextile natal Mars and trine natal Ate, 12 Aries
- Transiting Hybris, 6 Sagittarius, trine natal Sun and opposition natal Saturn
- Transiting Nemesis, 12 Scorpio, in a yod with natal Mars and natal Ate, 12 Aries
- Transiting Mars conjunction natal Mars, activating yod
- Transiting Mercury square natal Hybris, 1 Cancer
- Transiting Chiron square natal Saturn

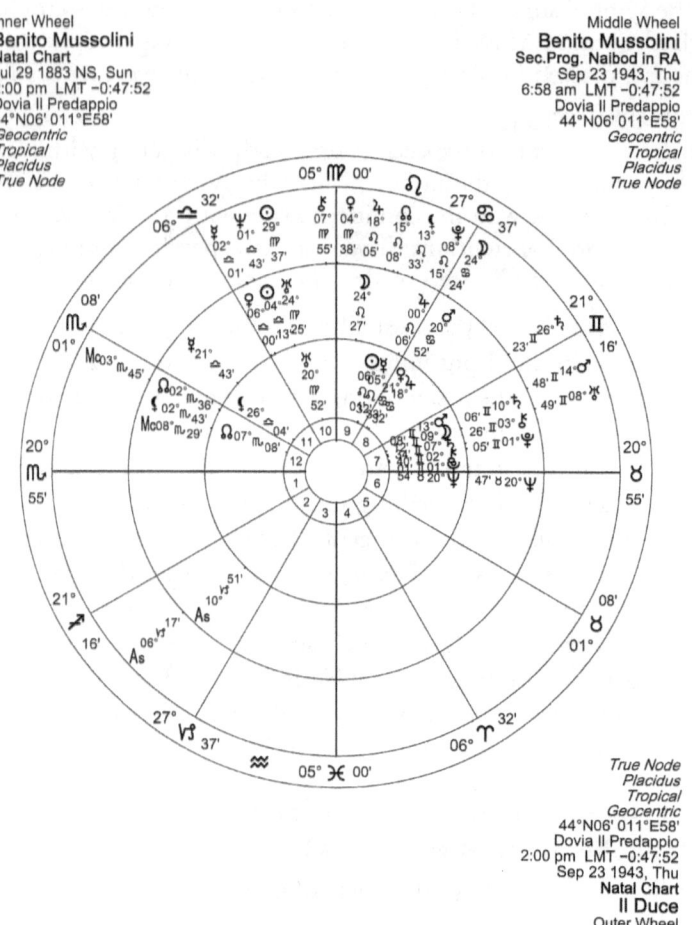

- Progressed Lilith quincunx natal Chiron
- Progressed Hybris, 0 Leo (sign of the king) sextile natal Pluto
- Progressed Nemesis, 10 Libra, trine natal Moon
- Progressed Ascendant quincunx natal Moon

The new republic was a puppet government of Germany's Third Reich, and the real power of Mussolini was located in German military authorities.

Transiting Hybris activated his natal Sun (ninth house: "Alien

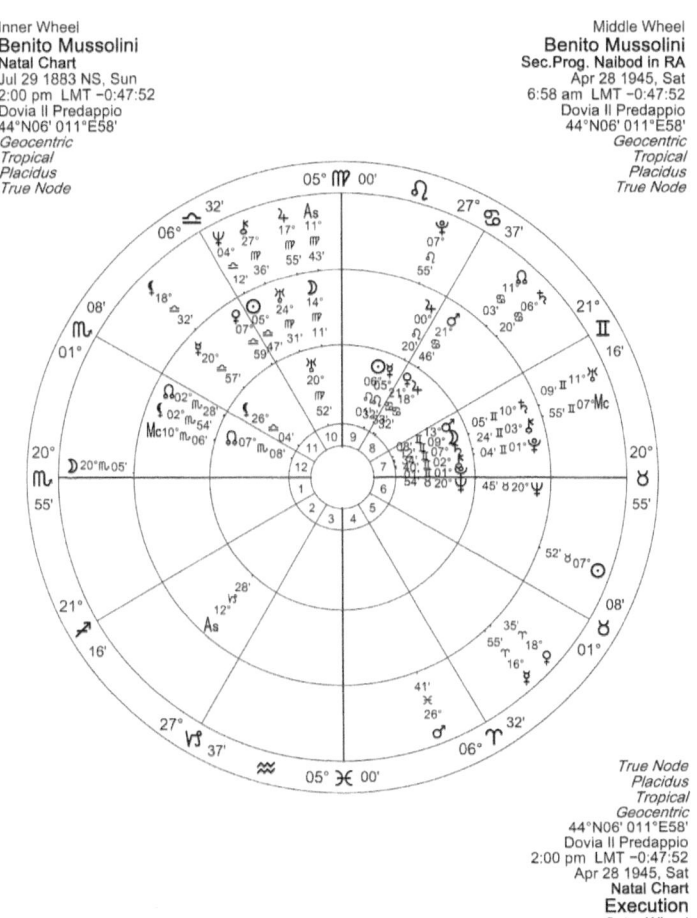

King") and opposed natal Saturn. Transiting Nemesis formed a yod with quincunxes to natal Ate and Mars.

Transiting Ate was square natal Mars, ruler of the Ascendant, while transiting Lilith was trine natal Ate.

Transiting Neptune at 1 Libra formed a square to natal Hybris and amplified the "unreality," while the transiting Moon was conjunct natal Jupiter and transiting Pluto aspected his natal Sun, pointing out that the real power was abroad.

Execution, April 28, 1945

- Transiting Jupiter conjunction natal Nemesis and quincunx transiting Nemesis, 17 Aries
- Transiting Mercury, Nemesis, Venus, and Hybris (16-19 Aries) square natal Jupiter, ruler of the fourth house, opposition transiting Lilith square Jupiter, forming a T-square
- Progressed Lilith trine natal Hybris

The execution of Mussolini was done by Communist partisans near the Lago di Commo. The stellium of transiting planets (Mercury, Nemesis, Venus, and Hybris) was quincunx natal Nemesis-Uranus in tenth house, with the latter two planets transited by Jupiter, ruler of the fourth house.

The symbolism of death is indicated by Mercury as ruler of the eighth house, referring to declared enemies (Venus as ruler of the seventh house) and justice (Nemesis) to the excess (Hybris) by adjusting the way of exercising power (Uranus-Nemesis in the natal tenth house).

Rafael Leonidas Trujillo

There is a stellium of four planets in the twelfth house (Mercury, Sun, Uranus, and Venus), while Pluto and Neptune make a tight conjunction in the seventh house.

Hybris in Capricorn in the second house can be interpreted as leading to thinking that is a "sweetening process" with the material world, perpetuation in government, and ambition.

Ate in the fourth house invites thinking about advice related to familiar topics and ancestors, and being eternally rooted in power. Trujillo resented his Haitian maternal ancestors, and such resentment was expressed when he made the decision to eliminate several Haitian natives in the Dominic Republic, an event known as the "Parsley Massacre." Moreover, Trujillo held conversations with General Franco of Spain to allow the immigration process of Spanish citizens in order to "whiten" the ethnicity of the Dominic Republic.

Nemesis, very close to the Midheaven and square the Ascen-

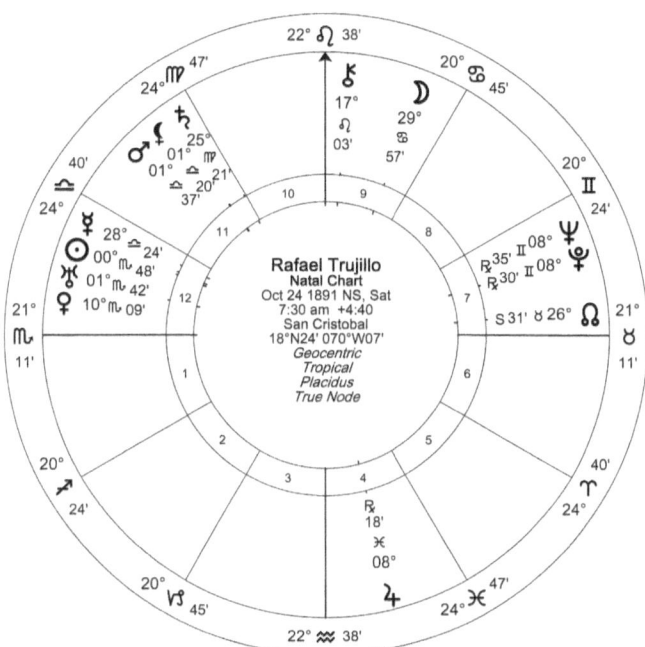

Nemesis, 21 Leo 19; Hybris, 12 Capricorn 48; Ate, 24 Aquarius 16

dant-Descendant indicates that law and order, when distributed, would have consequences in the exercise of his activities.

There is a conjunction of Mars, Lilith, and Saturn in the eleventh house, so the energy and ambition of his plans with groups may have had a free expression in this area. Of course the major stellium in the twelfth house invites thinking about secret enemies and their plans; Trujillo was unable to detect them.

Trujillo chart shows the Moon in Cancer in a critical degree and square Mercury, ruler of the eighth house.

First Presidential Inauguration, August 16, 1930
- Transiting Sun conjunction Midheaven
- Transiting Hybris, 15 Pisces, square transiting Nemesis, 17 Sagittarius
- Transiting Nemesis quincunx transiting Ate, 18 Cancer, and

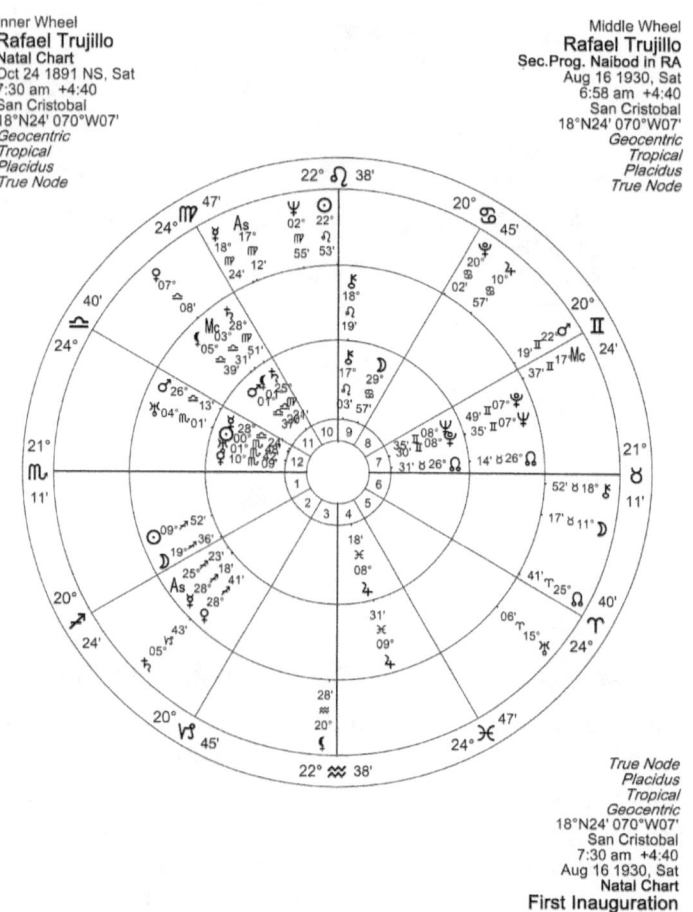

square transiting Mercury
- Transiting Nemesis, 17 Sagittarius, conjunction progressed Moon
- Transiting Lilith square Ascendant
- Transiting Mars sextile natal Nemesis, 21 Leo
- Transiting Ate, 18 Cancer, trine progressed Moon
- Progressed Ate, 0 Pisces, trine natal Sun and quincunx progressed Nemesis, 29 Leo

When the event chart of Trujillo's first presidential term is analyzed, it can be seen that the transiting Sun contacted natal Nemesis and transiting Mars was sextile natal Nemesis. Transiting Hybris formed an opposition to transiting Mercury that is part of a T-square with transiting Nemesis (Mercury, ruler of the eighth house).

Transiting Lilith was opposition natal Nemesis, as though the heavens provided him the responsibility to accept the distributive justice of Nemesis. But history would be written differently. Transiting Jupiter would form an opposition to natal Hybris, and thus Trujillo's belief systems were opposed to Hybris.

It is also important to note that there was a cosmic square between the transiting Sun and natal Nemesis in opposition to natal Ate, creating a square to the Ascendant-Descendant. This indicates an arid relationship with others, potential for distribution of justice but from rage as starting point, in a "Lilith's way" or a disguised one coming from progressed Ate (0 Pisces) trine natal Sun.

Million Parade, October 24, 1960

- Transiting Nemesis, 24 Virgo, trine progressed Ascendant and conjunction natal Saturn
- Transiting Sun, 0 Scorpio, sextile progressed nemesis, 0 Virgo
- Transiting Hybris, 11 Virgo, trine natal Hybris, 12 Capricorn, and transiting Saturn, 13 Capricorn
- Progressed Sun conjunction natal Hybris and sextile natal Venus and progressed Ate, 10 Pisces
- Progressed Uranus conjunction progressed Midheaven; both square progressed Hybris, 5 Aquarius
- Transiting Hybris, 11 Virgo, opposition progressed Ate, 10 Pisces
- Progressed Ate trine natal Venus

On October 24, 1960, Trujillo's collaborators organized an event called the "Million Parade." In this event, many hundreds of people of all social sectors were part of the show. The goal was

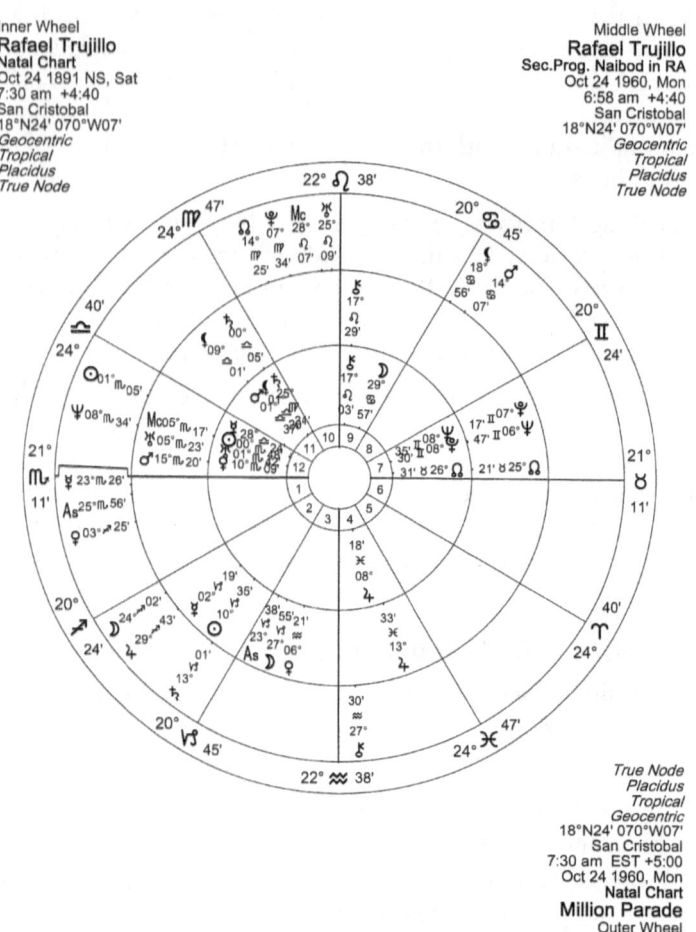

to reaffirm Trujillo's popularity and to solicit his candidacy for election in 1962.

That day, his sixty-ninth birthday, he celebrated on George Washington Avenue in Santo Domingo (at that time called Trujillo City) with a parade, at which he was asked to become the candidate.

Transiting Uranus was opposition natal Ate, indicating advice regarding innovation or a surprise or a massive presence. Transiting Saturn was contacting natal Hybris, and transiting Nemesis was contacting natal Saturn, indicating that this particular style to retain power would soon end with severity.

Transiting Nemesis was trine the progressed Ascendant: justice would govern his personality. Meanwhile, Trujillo continued with his narcissist celebration (transiting Hybris trine natal Hybris) without limits, but the action of Saturn in combination with Hybris and Nemesis suggests that the end of his government could happen in a short period of time.

Assassination, May 30, 1961
- Transiting Jupiter conjunction progressed Venus
- Transiting Sun conjunction natal Neptune
- Transiting Uranus conjunction natal Midheaven
- Transiting Nemesis conjunct natal Lilith-Mars
- Transiting Saturn conjunction progressed Ascendant and trine progressed Saturn
- Transiting Venus square progressed Ascendant-Descendant
- Transiting Pluto quincunx progressed Hybris, 5 Aquarius
- Transiting Neptune conjunction natal Venus
- Progressed Moon conjunction progressed Hybris, 5 Aquarius
- Progressed Sun conjunction natal Hybris, 12 Capricorn
- Progressed Mercury opposition transiting Mercury and square natal Lilith
- Progressed Nemesis conjunction progressed eighth house cusp, 28 Leo, and trine progressed Mercury

On the day of the assassination, transiting Saturn was opposition natal Moon, while transiting Hybris was sextile/trine the natal Ascendant-Descendant, along with a T-square between transiting Mercury and progressed Mercury (ruler of the eighth house), with everything pointing to natal Mars and Lilith, which were aspected by transiting Nemesis.

The transiting Sun was crossing natal Neptune and Pluto (Ascendant ruler). Transiting Uranus (fourth house ruler, end of

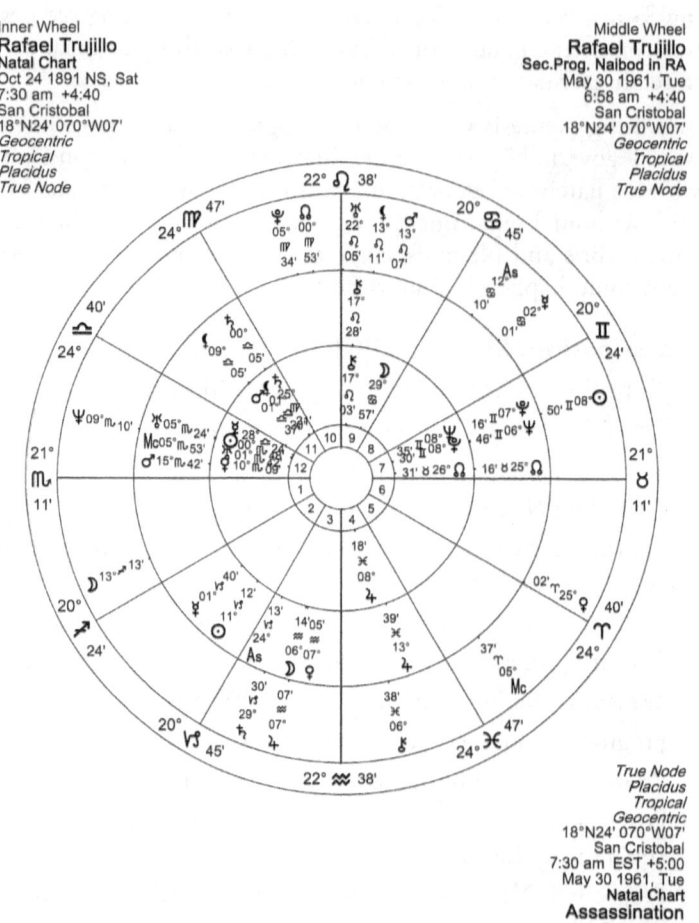

life) contacted natal Nemesis, while transiting Saturn crossed the progressed Ascendant. The progressed Moon was conjunct progressed Hybris and progressed Nemesis was conjunct the cusp of the progressed eighth house, revealing the strong interaction between asteroids and planets. Transiting Ate contacted natal and transiting planets on the date of the assassination.

In an ambush planned by various people in his circle, Trujillo's car was hit by more than sixty bullets, with seven of them hitting Trujillo.

Conclusions

The Hybris syndrome, understood as a psychological process, in correspondence with its astrological symbolism, responds well to historical facts. Charts show how planets and asteroids in the birth chart, in the progressed charts for the day of an event, as well as the transits, create hard aspects and dynamic configurations that highlight the event. In that sense, the mythological symbolism of Hybris, Ate, and Nemesis work well to illustrate the history of power from beginning to end, adding the performance of certain asteroids to make the event more prominent. It is generally perceived that there are harmonious aspects during the beginning of a term and the subtle participation of one or more asteroids; but when the power term is at its summit and, moreover, during the downfall, the asteroids and planets create configurations with hard aspects that reflect events. This can be seen in the interaction of transits with natal chart, as well with progressions.

The main traits of these leaders, with their particular personal and historical context, are:
- Perpetuation of power and their ideal.
- A sense of being god and the need of materialize this presence through icons and slogans to immortalize the name of the leader, as was so evident in the case of Trujillo ("Viva Trujillo," "God in Heaven, Trujillo on Earth," a mandatory slogan in the church), the use of the Svastic Cross by Hitler did, and nicknames such "Il Duce."
- Abuse of money and of the power, reaching the private life of the citizens, and in some cases, as with Ceausescu, a "celibacy tax."
- Double speech; in the name of Good, they do Evil.
- Creation of a sort of religion, worship to the leader, and selection of followers in a universal and unanimous way, and attacking those who are not tuned with the leader's ideas.
- In some cases leadership was colored by sentiments of racial discrimination.

It is possible that leaders who experience the Hybris syndrome come from a home that lacked economic resources and/or emotional support, but they can come from a family with strong familiar commandments, which is then reflected in the leadership style along with singular characteristics that facilitate the Hybris syndrome to be found in these leaders.

In some cases the leaders trespass boundaries in the name of "doing the universal good"; some of them had crossed the boundaries without taking into consideration the consequences or losing the perspective of their performance. For example, Trujillo and his personal worship ("God in Heaven, Trujillo on Earth"), Hitler and his "ethnic cleansing," Ceausescu and his birth regulation declaring the need to have a minimum of four children, Nixon and his Watergate scandal, Kennedy and his fight against communism that led the world close to a nuclear war, Mussolini with his Black Shirts, and Milosevic and his fervent nationalism.

All of these individuals studied have been seduced by Hybris, and in this confusion they lost perspective, making them blind and unable to recognize obstacles or boundaries, and even less to listen to healthy advice in order to avoid negative consequences.

In that sense, Nemesis is in charge of recalling mortality, especially with those people who feel they are gods on Earth, producing fatal consequences in the destiny of many nations.

References

All birth data from astrodatabank.com

http://www.elmundo.es/elmundosalud/2008/04/18/neurociencia/1208541838.html

http://es.wikipedia.org/wiki/Hibris

http://es.wikipedia.org/wiki/Ate_(mitologia)

http://es.wikipedia.org/wiki/Némesis

http://es.wikipedia.org/wiki/John_F._Kennedy

http://es.wikipedia.org/wiki/Crisis_de_los_misiles_en_Cuba

http://es.wikipedia.org/wiki/Richard_Nixon

http://es.wikipedia.org/wiki/Escándalo_Watergate
http://es.wikipedia.org/wiki/Benito_Mussolini
http://es.wikipedia.org/wiki/Slobodan_Milosevic
http://es.wikipedia.org/wiki/Discurso_de_Gazimestan
http://es.wikipedia.org/wiki/Nicolae_Ceausescu
http://historiasdelahistoria.com/2010/07/01/la-policia-menstrual-de-ceaucescu
http://es.wikipedia.org/wiki/Rafael_Leonidas_Trujillo
http://es.wikipedia.org/wiki/Masacre_del_Perejil

For more examples, visit the authors' Web site: http://hybrissindrome.wix.com/hybris-syndrome

Islamic Astrology: A History

By Joe Simon

ABSTRACT: Islamic astrology is the bridge between Hellenistic astral theology and pre and post enlightenment western astrologies. A historical survey of the development of astrology in the Golden Age of Islam, 800-1400 CE, is explored. Celestial observation ascertains the time for prayers and the orientation of the Qibla (the focus of the mosque, signpost of the direction to the Kabah in Mecca). Consequently, astronomical verities are central to the faith, and sophisticated mathematical techniques are employed in this enterprise. Hellenistic philosophies of numbers (Pythagorean, Platonic, and Neo-Platonic) assign magical properties to numbers, and the qualitative aspects of planetary and stellar influence becomes an area of study for the esoteric thinker. We will explore the evolution of this mystical stream from its beginnings in the Abbasid capital of Bagdad to its manifestations in the Persian east and the Iberian west during the Pax Islamica.

"If heaven will it, thou shalt know that Nature, alike in everything, is the same in every place."

The Golden Verses of Pythagoras

All ancient traditions recognize the great chain of being and seek the spirit animating material forms. A hierarchy of seven heavens is formulaic. Islam, the Vedas, Genesis all speak of the upper and the lower waters. The upper waters personify spirit, corresponding to different paradises; it is the sweet water. The salt water, of generation and decay, nourishes material form. Both are aspects of the Absolute.

The Vedas and Upanishads, the Pentateuch, the Psalms, Beatitudes and the Noble Qur'an are all revealed wisdom (sruti in Sanskrit). The Mahabarata, balance of Old Testament, Muslim astrologies and theology are among the inspired works of man (smirti in Sanskrit).[1] We look for a place between reason and revelation.

Muslim theologians need to develop a philosophy of religion after the revelation of the Noble Qur'an. These jurists opine that their book contains all the worldly wisdom. Beneath the Book are the three sister sciences of astrology, magic (talismans) and alchemy. Astrology shows the effect of spirit on spirit, magic the effect of spirit on matter, and alchemy the effect of matter on matter.[2] Expanding, could we say astrology shows the influence of the signs on the planets and the planets on the signs (both spiritual forces), magic, the influence of the signs and the planets on the houses, and alchemy, the effect of the signs and the planets in the houses on the native?

> "Rain is the brother of the widow and the father of the orphan."—Bedouin saying

One does not have the luxury of doubt in the desert. Things are black and white, unshaded, and the one certitude is divinity. The unrelenting Sun is an unfortunate entity for people and astrologers in the torrid zones[3], Islamic and Vedic alike. The desert itself is a manifestation of Saturn, the annihilator of matter, rising up and eclipsing man and his artifacts.

Arabs are children of the desert; they begin their unending migration from fertile Yemen and the life-giving oases throughout their peninsula. The various clans are constantly displaced by the more powerful and migrate to less and less fertile lands, by necessity becoming nomadic herders. They are as thin as twigs. Their search for fodder leads them out of the soft sand desert to the lava gravel deserts to the north, and they then turn west to Rume (the occident) or east to the paradise of the Euphrates.[4] They bring with them the revelation of Mohammed.

Islam's ascendancy is mercurial; within a century of its founding it controlled the area from Iberia to the Indus valley. (The Byzantine and the Sassanid Persian empires had exhausted themselves fighting one another.) Into this power vacuum leaped the acquisitive Arabs. The plunder completed, men of the sword began their transformation to men of the pen. Their Prophet had been born in 570 CE, the Year of the Elephant. An invasion by the Ethiopians and their king, the Nagus, had closed in on Mecca, bringing fearsome war elephants. Mecca was saved when crows attacked the elephants, dropping stones from their beaks and routing these Christians from Africa (perhaps it was the unfamiliar scent of the camels that thwarted the elephant's attack). Nonetheless, the Arabs were astonished by this act of God. A solar eclipse occurred before the birth of Mohammed, its path of totality extending from Iberia to Indonesia, the margins of the greatest extent of the Islamic empire.[5]

The body of Islamic astrology rests on the synthesis of earlier traditions with the Arab's own revelation, Allah's Qur'an. Hellenistic philosophy, the pre-Islamic Arab paganism, Jewish and Christian doctrine, and Persian and Vedic practice were subjugated to the admonitions of the Noble Qur'an (The Book of Signs), to create a cogent astrology.[6] Foremost in this project were Shi'ites (partisans of Ali, nephew of Mohammed), who had a more mystical bent than did their Sunni brothers in faith. (Sunni means following the exemplary life of The Prophet.) For the Shi'ite, the mystic outlook is based on a hidden message in The Book of Signs, while Muslim belief is that there is an outer (zahir) and an inner (batin) meaning in Allah's Book. Islam is a gnostic endeavor[7]; that is, knowledge is acquired through personal transformation. Al-Islam (surrender to God) is achieved through controlling the passions by the application of reason (aq'l). The reasonable theologian sees a rational cosmos and perceives unity in nature; thus, the motions in the heavens necessarily are reflected in the sublunary sphere.

> "The Sun revolves around the earth, according to the senses,"—Claudius Ptolemy, 150 CE

On the banks of the Euphrates, Islam created a new capital—Medina as-Salaam, the city of peace—close to an ancient Persian village known as Bagdad. When the Abbasid dynasty's first Caliph, al-Mansur decided to relocate his advisors, the Zoroastrian Naubakht, Persian Jew Mashallah ibn Athari and Arab Al-Farisi chose July 30, 762 CE as the propitious astrological date. The new city with the old name was destined to be the seat of imperial Islam. Al-Mansur, who was grandfather to al-Mamun (786-833), was confronted by a fair-haired, fair-eyed entity while dreaming.

He asked the Stygarite, "What is good?"

Aristotle responded: "What is good by nature and reason."

"What else?"

"What is good by religious law?"

"What else?"

"Nothing else."[8]

The Dream of al-Mamun became the impetus to establish "the Bayt al-Hikma" (House of Wisdom) in the round city (Bagdad is built in circular form). Al-Mamun sent emissaries to Constantinople to retrieve scholarly works. His delegation was led by the great translator Hunain ibn Ishaq (808-873 CE), known to the Latins as Yohanisius. Among the delegation was his son, Ishaq ibn-Hunain. The translator says of his boy, "I wanted to dissect him to find out why he is so stupid, but the caliph would not allow it."[9]

They were Nestorian Christians from Persia, the Nestorians having been expelled from the Byzantine lands by their Orthodox Christian overlords. They were followers of Nestor (5th CE Bishop) in Constantinople, who had a gnostic outlook regarding the Christ: one of a single, human nature. The Sasanians were happy to give shelter to Christians with beliefs different from their Byzantine rivals, and the erudite Nestorians came to dominate scholarship throughout the Middle East. They were the physicians, astrologers, magicians and scientists of their time who established centers of learning such as Jundishapur, deep in Iran. Brutality was the main impetus for the territorial growth of Islam, and Christian subjects were treated more justly by Muslim overlords, in part because they accepted their rule.[10] It is said that Muslim expansion was preceded by a sign in the heavens: an apparition shaped like a red sword moving north from Arabia was observed in Constantinople for a month.[11]

A different version gives supervision of the Bayt to a learned, Jew Yacov ben Tarik. The Jewish masters were well versed in Ptolemy's pure astrology, along with Neo-Platonic teachings. These wise Jews, under Tarik, combined their astrology with magic from the Talmud and mysticism from Kabbalah. Little of this magical tradition survived the Christian era.

Yacov al- Kindi (801-873 CE) is known as "the philosopher of the Arabs." Born to a distinguished family in Kufa (northeastern Iraq), he lived in Bagdad and flourished in the court of al-Mamun. He was a polymath and encyclopaediest, writing 250 books. At age 50 he devoted himself to phalsifa (philosophy) and kalam (theology). He established philasuf as a profession in Islam, and his perception was that phalsifa was a type of astrology. He wrote a commentary on Aristotle, "The Treatise on First Philosophy," based on "The Metaphysics." Aristotle stated that the eternal universe is set in motion by desire, and Al-Kindi argued against this. Accordingly, the universe is a creation of the one God and philosophical truth and the message of the Prophets are one and the same. Al-Kindi is often considered a Neo-Platonist, but there is no evidence that Proclus of Athens was interpreted into Arabic and Plotinus (Flutinus) is hardly mentioned. The primary influence seems to be Ptolemy, who stated that the first cause of the first movement (generation) was by an agent (deity), a cause and a creator; Ptolemy was almost entirely involved with judicial astrology (prediction).[12] Arabic practitioners employ two other systems, elections and interrogation (horary). These systems avoid the fatalism of prediction and are seen as valuable for medical purposes (medicine and magic were indistinguishable at the time).[13]

Al-Kindi gives pre-eminence to mathematical knowledge, arithmetic and geometry, being practical while harmonics and astronomy are theoretical constructs. In "On the Stellar Rays" the philosopher speaks of humanity as co-regent in this portion of God's creation, basing this authority on man's ability to speak, specifically by articulating the sacred sounds vocalized by the Arabic letters. Each of the sounds of the 28 Arabic letters is a manifestation of divinity, and he explains that the tongue is an agent of the angelic Hermes (Mercury) and that speaking power is a divine attribute.

Abu-Mashar (787-886 CE), a contemporary of al-Kindi, began his studies in astrology at the Bayt, beginning in his forty-seventh year. He wrote many books on mundane and natal astrology, including the Book on Religions and Dynasties (848 CE). This book, after being translated into Latin, introduced Aristotle's logic to Western Europe.

The Islamic empire, at the crossroads of civilization, reached out and drew from earlier traditions from all points on the compass. The first astronomical texts (there was no distinction between astronomy and astrology in this period), Indian and Persian, were translated into Arabic in the 8th century. The five astrology books attributed to the Persian prophet Zoroaster are among the earliest translated material. At the court of al-Mansur were two versions of the "Zij al Sindhind," astronomical handbooks with tables of planetary positions. Shortly thereafter, the "Zij al-Shah,"

Indian astronomy from Sasanid Persia, was translated. Ptolemy's Almagest and the Hellenistic "Small Astronomy Collection" were added to the corpus of instruction as well. There were four translations done of the Almagest; two are extant, from Hunain ibn Ishaq and Thabit ibn Qurra, the famous Harranian[14] who wrote forty books on astronomy; eight still exist and they show full understanding of Ptolomaic theory. The first original Arabic document is al-Kwarizmi's "Zij al Sindhind" (different from the aforementioned), which also contains tables for the luminaries and the five visible planets. Al- Kwarizmi also wrote the 'Kitab al-jebra wal muqulaba," the "Book of Hindu Reckoning" or the book of reductions. From this work the Arabs adopted Indian numerals that, when introduced to the West, were called Arabic numerals. The word "algebra" stems from this, indicating the mathematical discipline for finding the unknown quantity.[15]

The Harranian Jabir al-Battani wrote the "Sabaean Tables," circa 900 CE, a work of rigorous calculation that corrected the precession of the equinox to one degree in 66 years from the 100 years cited by Ptolemy. Al-Biruni (973-1048 CE) asked theoretical questions of Aristotle's "de Cielo" (on the Heavens), arguing for and proving that a vacuum in nature is logical. Ibn-Haytham (965-1039 CE) wrote his "al-shakuk ala Batlymus" (Doubts about Ptolemy) about the same time. These examples show that Arabic astrologers were revising the earlier teachings through their sophisticated mathematical techniques. These rational developments did not infringe on the Qur'anic world view. For example, al-Biruni says "Days of creation cannot be from the Sun, which like the Moon is created on the fourth day"[16]; the Qur'an's "in a day" is a measure of 50,000 years (surah 70:4). Thus we cannot measure epochs with our way of reckoning. Biruni considers time as generated by the Sun through zodiacal revolutions, bringing order out of chaos, days and nights, and historical periods.[17] In 12th century Andalusia (Iberia), astronomy focuses on planetary influence. Ibn-Bajja (Avempace), ibn-Jabirol, and ibn-Rushd (Averroes) try to reinstate Aristotle's concentric spheres, eliminating eccentrics and epicycles. This is a qualitative, philosophical approach. The Eastern schools focus on mathematical verities and observation. The height of this scientific enterprise in achieved at Maraga Observatory, 13th CE, under the supervision of Nasir al-Din al Tusi, mathematician and astrologer for the Mongol Khan Hulagu, destroyer of Bagdad.[18]

> The Rasa'il of the Ikwan al-Safa (the epistles of the brotherhood of purity). "Lubb," Arabic—"Seed" or "Core"—something in man which grows or blossoms.

Beneath the confluence of the Tigris and Euphrates, at the northern extreme of the Persian Gulf, lies the ancient city of Basra. It is here, in the 4th century after Hijra (10th CE), that the Ismaili sect of Shi'ism births the Ikwan al-Safa. They are esoteric thinkers who search for the hidden (Batin) meanings in the Noble Qur'an. They are known as "batiniyya," and write anonymously.[19] Their inspirations include a paraphrase of Plotinus' "Enneads" attributed to Aristotle and known as the "Theology of Aristotle." The Ikwan see numerical quality as the source of things: "the beings are according to the nature of the numbers."

Allah first created "from the light of His uniqueness" a simple substance called the active intellect (shown in the nativity by the lunar conditions). An Aristotelean term, it can be explained as the comprehension of the individual. Through its agency, man can rise to the highest level of insight and experience conjunction with divine revelation. This conjunction does not overcome the consciousness of separation from the Necessary Being and does not achieve "fana" (extinction of the ego), the ultimate goal of al-Islam (surrender to divinity).

The authors received wisdom from nature and revelation, and their instruction came from four books[20]:

1. Mathematical from the sages
2. Writings, such as the Torah, the gospels, and the Qur'an
3. Books of nature, such as the zodiac
4. Divine books from angelic entities and purified souls

They seem to have learned their astronomy from al-Fargani's (d 833 CE) "Compendium of the Science of the Stars."[21] They saw divinity articulated through a process of emanation, such as angelic and other intellectual agencies.

The Epistles consist of 52 chapters (rasa'il) divided into four topics, each of which contain astrological content. The first 14 chapters focus on mathematics and astronomy, the next seventeen on natural science and biology, ten on intellectual principles, and eleven on theological sciences- such as music and magic.[22/23]

In his observation of the heavens, the author counts 1,029 bodies, seven of which are in constant motion and revolve in concentric spheres, like the layers of an onion. The Sun occupies the middle position. There are two additional spheres above, that of the fixed stars, and that of the Prime Mover. Below are the atmosphere and the earth, making a total of eleven. Hell is the sublunary world of generation and decay, and paradise the lies above. Once the individual conquers the attachment to the physical, he abides above in everlasting bliss. This is the result of an inner struggle and an example of free will. (This doctrine is called "mutazillism" in Arabic and stands in contrast to our perception of Islam as totally fated.)

The luminaries carry the most importance, the Sun expresses the intellectual faculty and the Moon the speaking power. As the active intellect, the Moon acts as an intermediary between heaven and earth, or between reason and revelation. The moving planets correspond to the five physical senses. As the Moon receives light from the Sun, it disperses and casts down this illumination to the world below; that is, the speaking power receives intelligence and transmits through the sounds of the twenty-eight sacred letters in the Arabic alphabet, each of which is a divine revelation. This quality of sound is known as "Ilm al-Haruf," and another, "Ilm al- Jafir," is the science of letters based on their numerical value (similar to Kabbalistic and Vedic traditions). Additionally, there is a correspondence to the letters and the twenty-eight lunar mansions in Arabic cosmology.

The Ikwan practice astral theology during the auspicious heavenly placements. There are three ceremonies each month because the Muslim calendar is lunar. At the sighting of the crescent, a personal oratory is read; at the prevention (full Moon), a cosmic text is read while facing the pole star; and at the conjunction, a philosophical hymn, a prayer to Plato or Idriss (Hermes), is sung. Annually, at the Sun's ingress to the Ram, there is a remembrance to the Eid al-Fitr (acknowledging the end of Ramadan); at the Crab, the Eid al-Adha (the feast of the sacrifice, a remembrance of Ibrahim's offering of Ismael); and at al-Mizan (the balance), a celebration of the investiture of Ali at Gadir Khumm (a Shi'ite holiday when Ali ibn-Talib is given his inheritance as leader after Mohammed at the pool of Gadir). The winter solstice is a remembrance of "the seven sleepers in the cave," though not a celebration in the same vein as the above. (This event is also known in Christianity, and in both traditions the sleepers are Christians.)

Clearly, these Muslims follow Pythagorean and Hermetic doctrines (Haramisah, by which is meant followers of the antidiluvian Prophet, Idriss, or Ukhnukh, who they regard as the founder of the arts and sciences, as well as hikma, is wisdom and philosophy.[24]

> The Shayk al-Akbar (The Greatest Master) "It is the Law of God which has taken course aforetime. Thou will not find any change in the Law of God"—Surah 48:23

Abu-Abdullah Mohammed ibn Ali ibn Mohammed ibn 'Arabi is an Andalusian Arab born July 28, 1165 CE in Seville. He is known as Muhyiddinn ibn-'Arabi, meaning reviver of the religion, an honorific title given about every 100 years. In the Sufi circles he is called the Shayk al-Akbar, the greatest master. His birth was on the 17th of Ramadan, "the night of power." It was on this date that Mohammed was first confronted by the angel Jabri'al, and instructed "Ikra!" (recite). The Prophet deferred three times and each time he was embraced more tightly by the messenger until the words poured forth. This thrice denial is a shared response, by Abraham, Elijah, and Mary in the Jewish tradition. When the calling is accepted, each respond "Here I am."

Ibn-'Arabi was well-traveled, spending much time in the Ma'grib.[25] Here he encountered his first three spiritual teachers, all women, and the last an illiterate peasant. The Shayk told of meeting an advanced teacher on the coast whose young son peered into the sea and announced that a long-awaited ship would arrive in three days time. When this manifested, the boy explained that he saw the event through his father's eyes. He went on to the Fertile Crescent, where he met Rumi as a child. Rumi's father was an advanced teacher, and the Shayk proclaimed, "I have met a sea followed by an ocean." Ibn-'Arabi settled in Damascus, where he passed on in 1240 CE. He wrote prodigiously, more than three hundred books. He said each writing was prompted by divinity or commanded by the Prophet. His magnum opus was "al-Futuhat al-Makkiya," the Meccan Passages. His life was based on al-Islam, for when one's self is annihilated, what is left is divinity, and free will vanishes as an illusion. Ibn-'Arabi related that there are three steps to the threshold of truth: sincerity, insight, and patience. His tomb in Damascus remains one of the most visited sites in The Dar al-Islam.

During Mohammed's mission, he was persecuted by his tribesmen in Mecca. In his darkest hours he was transported by Jibra'il to Jerusalem on the back of the mythical beast, Baraka, with the head of a beautiful woman, the body of a beast, and the tail of a peacock, and set down on the site of the dome of the rock. There he ascended Jacob's ladder through the seven heavens. At each level, he met a Prophet who confirmed his mission, and he ascended to the highest heaven, "the Lote tree," where he received instruction from Allah. He descended, discoursing with the Prophets, chiefly Musa (Moses), and miraculously returned to Mecca. The Qur'an relates the event.

Ibn-'Arabi experienced his own "Night Journey" in which he was united with the planets and the Arabic letters. His insight was to create the correspondences between the twenty-eight Lunar mansions and the twenty-eight Arabic letters. He gave names to these houses, each of which is a name of Allah mentioned in the Qur'an. These names are known as "al-asma al-husna" (The Beautiful Names, of which there are ninety-nine). They signify divine attributes, and are manifest love (jamal) or majesty (jalal). Jamal expressed moral characteristics, such as the All-Merciful, the Forgiver, the Gentle, the Generous, the Compassionate, and the All-Loving. Jalal manifested metaphysical characteristics such as the Just, the Majestic, the Reckoner, the Victorious, the All-fashioner, and the creator. Life is lived amid the harmonies, the polarizations, and the tension between them. Adam, the first man, was taught all the names, and by virtue of this knowledge, man is superior to the angels.

Burkhardt provides some descriptions of the twenty-eight divisions:[26]

Al-Zuhal, Saturn, ar-rabb "the lord," from 8 Leo 34, aka al-Zubra, "the mane." This implies a reciprocal relationship; a being has no quality of leadership except to a servant. This relationship has a necessary and unalterable character.

- Al-Mustari, Jupiter, al-alim "the knower or the learned," from 21 Leo 25 aka al-Sarfah, "the changer." This reigns over the intellectual faculty.
- Al-Mirikh, Mars, al-qahir "the conqueror or the tamer," from 4 Virgo 17 aka al-awwa, "the barker." This reigns over the volative faculty.
- Ash-Shams, Sun, an-nur "the light," from 17 Virgo 8 aka al-Simak "the unarmed." This is the principle of truth, itself.
- Az-Zurah, Venus, al-musawwir" He who forms," from 0 Libra aka al-Ghafr "the cover." This is the artist in its feminine form; it is the imaginative faculty.

- Al-Utarid, Mercury, al-muhsi "He who counts," from 12 Libra 51 aka al-Jubana "the claws." This relates to number and distinct knowledge.
- Al-Qamar, Moon, al-mubin, "the apparent or the evident from 25 Libra 23, aka Iklil al-Jabhah "the crown." Manifestation, commentary, or proof.

This article is a short survey of some high points in Islamic astrology. Due to the authority of religious practice in all aspects of life in Islam, we cannot separate their theology from their astrology. We have seen the pervasive influence of the Persian/Indian doctrines along with the continuing evolution of Greek philosophy in Arabic sciences. When Ptolemy says we perceive the heavenly motions "according to the senses," he is expressing a subjective truth; from man's perspective, the cosmos is geocentric. This subjectivity is as valid as objective truth, from the perspective of the individual (when you look at the moon's reflection across a body of water, you are at its focal point, as is the person directly opposite on the water's further edge).

When the Caliph Al-Mamun traveled to Egypt, he explored the great pyramid of Cheops. His party broke down the outer door, finding a clay jar filled with gold coins inside. Investigating further, he entered the king's chamber and saw the remains of the king's body inside the sarcophagus. He then ended his quest so as not to desecrate the holy place.[27] Where in modernity can we find such reverence? Perhaps we can recover this sense of the sacred through 'ilm al-nujum, the science of the stars.

Endnotes
[1]Guénon, R. *Theosophy: History of a Pseudo-religion*. Sophia Perennis, 2004.
[2]Zoller, Robert. Workshop on Mundane Astrology. Vancouver, B.C., 2003.
[3]In the future of humanity, will "the warming" restore the dread attributes to the sun, will the moon regain pre-eminence with the scarcity of water?

⁴Lawrence, T. E. *Seven Pillars of Wisdom: a Triumph*. Random House LLC, 1926.
⁵Jayne, Charles Dell *Horoscope*. Dell Magazines, 1970.
⁶Lawrence, B. B. *The Qur'an: A Biography*. Atlantic Monthly Press, 2006.
⁷Nasr, S. H. *An Introduction to Islamic Cosmological Doctrines*. SUNY Press, 1993.
⁸Al-Khalili, J. *The House of Wisdom: How Arabic Science Saved Ancient Knowledge and Gave Us the Renaissance*. Penguin, 2011.
⁹Ibid.
¹⁰The parallels between Mohammed and the Byzantine emperor Heraclius are stunning, temporally and factually. They are contemporaries, both miraculously victorious against all odds, but Mohammed emerges ascendant while Heraclius is ultimately broken.
¹¹Wells, C. *Sailing from Byzantium: How a Lost Empire Shaped the World*. Random House LLC, 2007.
¹²*Tetrabiblos*, Book 2. (150 CE). Alexandria, Egypt.
¹³Saif, L. *The Arabic Theory of Astral Influences in Early Modern Medicine*. Renaissance Studies, 25(5), 609-626. 2011.
¹⁴The Harranians were star worshippers of Hellenistic persuasion who thrived in the city of Harran on the Syrian-Iraqi border. Harran, like Sana'a in Yemen, is known as "the Moon city," and its ruins contain seven temples or observatories.
¹⁵Algebra is considered a kind of magic in medieval Europe because of this feature.
¹⁶Kamiar, M. *A Bio-bibliography for Biruni: Abu Raihan Mohammad Ibn Ahmad* (973-1053 CE). Scarecrow Press, 2006.
¹⁷Saif, L. *The Arabic Theory of Astral Influences in Early Modern Medicine*. Renaissance Studies, 25(5), 609-626, 2011.
¹⁸Iraqi children today refer to soldiers as "Hulagu."
¹⁹Fakhry, M. *A History of Islamic Philosophy*. Columbia University Press, 2004.
²⁰Nasr, S. H. *An Introduction to Islamic Cosmological Doctrines*. SUNY Press, 1993.
²¹Fakhry, M. *A History of Islamic Philosophy*. Columbia University Press, 2004.
²²It is interesting to note that the Gnostic Nag-Hammadi manuscripts also contain 52 treatises.
²³El-Bizri, N. *Epistles of the Brethren of Purity: the Ikhwān al- afā' and*

Their Rasā'il: an Introduction, 2008.

[24]Nasr, S. H. *An Introduction to Islamic Cosmological Doctrines*. SUNY Press, 1993.

[25]The West, referring to North Africa, this word is the root of Morocco, westernmost after the Reconquista of Iberia in 1492.

[26]Burkhardt, Titus. *Mystical Astrology According to Ibn'Arabi*. Vol. 1. Granite Hill Publishers, 2001.

[27]Al-Khalili, J. *The House of Wisdom: How Arabic Science Saved Ancient Knowledge and Gave Us the Renaissance*. Penguin, 2011.

The Impact of Astrology on Carl Jung

By José L. Belmonte

ABSTRACT: This article is an introduction to the influence of astrology on the work of Carl Gustav Jung (1875-1961). Throughout his career he researched symbols and myths from fields heavily influenced by astrology, such as Mithraism, Gnosticism, Hermetism, and especially Alchemy. Far from examining all the archetypes defined by Jung, this article focuses on the Self, an archetype that symbolizes the center as well as integrity and wholeness. Having several astrological correspondences, the Self is usually depicted as a circle, a horoscope, the zodiac, a cross, a circle divided by a cross, a quaternity, the four elements, or as a human form personified by the figure of Christ or Buddha. While working on Aion (1951), Jung not only noticed that the historical Christ was symbolized by a fish right after the dawn of the age of Pisces, but also that the history of Christianity could have been predicted by the progression of the equinoctial point over the constellation of Pisces.

The Greek word *Aion*, which according to C. Lakeit means[1] "vital force," "life," "life span," "life destiny," "era or eternity," and "the cosmic spheres that by their rotation determine the epochs and the seasons" was the title for the English edition of one of Jung's late-works most influenced by astrology. Dedicated to the archetype of the Self and its symbols, the research for the book included astrologers such as Ptolemy, Julius Firmicus Maternus, Diodoros, Albumasar, Messahala, Cardan, Pierre d'Ailly, Nostradamus, John Dee, Kepler, Bouche-Leclerq, and German writers of astrology like Franz Boll. The ongoing presence of the fish symbol during the age of Pisces seemed to inspire Jung to prove statistically through astrology his principle of synchronicity (meaningful coincidence of two or more causally unrelated facts). Deirdre Bair expounded that Jung planned to use astrology to measure "an absolutely certain and indubitable fact . . . the marriage connection between two persons." To that purpose he set up a team of four women who had long been interested in astrology through the Tarot. One of them was Gret Baumann-Jung, his daughter and a teacher of astrology. They worked on the project for three years. Unfortunately, Jung was very ill at that time and could not evaluate himself thoroughly the results of the project.[2]

In a letter to Freud dated June 12, 1911, Jung wrote "my evenings are taken up largely with astrology" informing Freud about his making of "horoscopic calculations in order to find a clue to the core of psychological truth." Richard Noll wrote that by mid-1911, when Jung's ex-patient Antonia (Toni) Wolf became his assistant, she apparently introduced him to Eastern philosophies and astrology, most likely through Theosophical literature.[3]

The goal of Jung's analytical psychology was to achieve "individuation": to make the person whole through a lifelong process guided by the archetype of the Self, which contains our life's goal, the complete expression of that fateful combination we call individuality.[4] This archetype is related to the zodiac, the horoscope and the four elements. Jung envisioned the Self as the whole circumference which embraces both conscious and unconscious and is the center of this totality.[5] Jung's definition of the unconscious included "all the future things that are taking shape in me and will sometime come to consciousness."

As discussed in *Wandlungen und Symbole der Libido* (1911-12) (Symbols of Transformation, 1916)[6] Jung believed in a "god within" in the form of a blazing Sun or star. The concept, similar to the Indian atman as it appears in the Upanishads, is also shared by the gnostics: a little spark "to be found in thyself" (Elenchos VIII)[7]. Jung used lumen naturae (natural light) of Paracelsus to explain that "Man is a prophet of the natural light", which came primarily from the "astrum" or "sydus", the "star" in man.[8]

In *Aion,* Jung showed that the alchemist would place the Self, the "centre," not in the ego but outside it, "in us" yet not "in our mind," being located in that which we unconsciously are.[9] Paracelsus beheld the psyche, Jung wrote, as "a star-strewn night sky whose planets and fixed constellations represent the archetypes in all their luminosity and numinosity." Jung considered the vault of heaven as an open book of cosmic projection where the archetypes were reflected, forming a vision which joined astrology and alchemy: "the two classical functionaries of the collective unconscious."[10]

Springing from the unconscious, an archetype was an invisible source of psychic energy, a "magnetic field and energy center underlying the transformation of the psychic processes into images." The etymology of the word, wrote Jolande Jacobi, is self-explanatory: *arche* means "beginning, origin, cause, primal source and principle but also signifies position of a leader, supreme rule and government"; *type* means "blow and what is produced by a blow, the imprint of a coin . . , form, image, copy, prototype, model, order and norm."[11] Jung took the term from the Corpus Hermeticum, "Thou has seen in the Nous the archetypal form, the principle preceding the infinite beginning . . . " and from *On the Divine Names* by Dyonisius the Aeropagite.[12]

Within a horoscope, matching archetypes with astrological symbols is not straightforward. Being psychic energy invisible, the way to perceive an archetype is by its symbols: images loaded with energy, dreams, or visions. In *Aion*, referring to Pisces symbolized by Christ as a fish, Jung claimed that "the noncanonical fish symbol led us into this psychic matrix where the unknowable archetypes become living things, changing their name and guise in a never ending succession," and finally disclosing "their concealed nucleus." He considered the fish symbol "the bridge between the historical Christ and the psychic nature of man, where the archetype of the redeemer dwells."[13]

Yet in a chart the astrological symbols not only correspond to planets, zodiacal signs, and angles (Jung found symbols for north, south, east, and west), but also to the four elements. Jung saw the fire element as "passion, affects, desires, and the emotional driving-forces of human nature in general" and as everything understood by the term "libido."[14]

According to Jung, circular and spherical symbols were usually indicators of the Self. Since the *Timaeus* of Plato, Jung noted in *Aion*[15], the soul has been repeatedly defined as a sphere, arguing that "as the anima mundi, the soul revolves with the world wheel, whose hub is the Pole." He concluded that "the anima mundi is the motor of the heavens" noting that "the starry universe is reflected in the horoscope" which was called the "thema of birth." He then explained that the division of the heavens in twelve houses, calculated at the moment of birth and making the first house match the ascendant, makes the firmament "look like a wheel turning." Jung explained that Nigidius received the name Figulus ("potter") because "the wheel of heaven turn like a potter's wheel" and the "thema" is indeed a tropos ("wheel"). He then expounded that the horoscope gives a picture of the psychic and the physical constitution of the individual.[16]

Another indicator of the Self was a square, very popular according to Jung. In India today, as in Hellenistic and medieval times, horoscopes are still drawn within a square. The Self could be depicted by a quaternity or by quadratic figures divided into four or forming a cross, as the four angles in a astrological chart;

by four objects or, as in astrology, by the four elements. Jung regarded three as a relative totality: a quaternity missing an element (the unconscious element); and twelve as another variant symbolizing wholeness, like the zodiac or the year.

Besides the circle and the quaternity, other symbols suggesting containment of the ego in the greater dimensions of the Self were, according to Jung, a house, a castle, a vessel, a church, or even a city; another variant suggested was the wheel (*rota*), which emphasized the rotation "which also appeared as a ritual of circumambulation." This, Jung insisted, "leads easily enough to a relationship to the heavenly Pole and the starry bowl of heaven rotating around it", concluding that "a parallel would be the horoscope as the wheel of birth."[17]

Apart from the geometrical and arithmetical symbols, the human figure was the commonest symbol of the self, Jung explained. A god or god-like human figure transcending the ego personality, is the perfect example, like Jesus Christ, which Jung used extensively in Aion.[18]

For the stoics, the gods became natural forces. The older stoics had already called the Sun the "hegemonikon" of the cosmos. Posidonius of Apamea (c. 135 BCE-c. 51 BCE), astrologer who demonstrated the influence of the moon over the tides, most likely furthered the role of the Sun placing it at the center of the world, and equating it with the demiurge of Plato, insisted Hans Leisegang (1890-1959) in his paper "The mystery of the Serpent," written for the 1939 Eranos Lectures. Since Jung was an important participant in the organization of the Eranos conferences, Leisengang's paper, written earlier than Aion, was very likely a source of inspiration to Jung. Leisengang concluded that the Sun became the supreme cosmic force and the ultimate sphere encompassing the cosmos; the Sun was the *Agathodaimon*, the good spirit of light which measured the seasons and controlled the temporal destiny of the world, in other words: the Aeon (greek Aion). As Helios and Agathodaimon, wrote Leisengang, this Aeon "is represented in the religions and monuments of the period [beginning of our era] as the great serpent."[19]

As symbols heavily influenced by astrology, Jesus, the Aeon, Helios, Mithras, and the serpent played an important role not only in Jung´s work but also in the bible. Under the influence of the Hellenistic-Roman religions and mysteries (Mythras), the whole conception of the Aeon was present in the bible, argued Leisengang, claiming not only that in the gospel of John "Christ was the light of the world" but also that with him began the new Aeon and his birthday was set on the day of the Sol Invictus.[20]

Even though the symbol of the serpent was not common in early Christianity, Jung argued that comparing Christ with a serpent was more authentic than symbolizing him with a fish. Jung wrote that "Gnostics favoured because it was an old-established symbol for the 'good' genius loci, the Agathodaimon." Jung here clearly referred to the eleventh house of Hellenistic astrology: the good daimon.[21]

Certain old Gnostic sects, grouped by Hyppolytus under the name of Ophites (Naaseenes, Perates, and Sethites), developed the conception of Christ as a serpent, claimed Leisegang. Hyppolytus remarked that the symbol of the serpent in the system developed by the Sethites was derived from the ancient theologians; while the doctrine of the Naaseenes was ascribed to Greek Philosophers; and for the doctrine of the Perates, he imputed it to astrologers. Within Hellenistic circles, concluded Leisengang, these were the origins of the speculations Helios as Aeon and as Logos symbolized by the serpent.[22]

Saturn in antiquity was symbolized by a serpent. In the Orphic theogony attributed to Hieronymos, Chronos was described as a winged serpent with the heads of a lion and a bull and a third one in the middle representing a god. Snakes were also used to portray river-gods and hence were likewise chosen for the images of rivers as time. For Phylon of Biblos, Time was reflected in the figure of *Aion*.[23] The snake is the beast of Helios making it a fit symbol for the Aeon, concluded Leisegang adding the following quote from Phylon of Biblos: "the nature of the dragon and of the snakes was called godlike...this beast is the most pneumatic of all beasts and of a fiery nature. . . . It is the most long-lived of animals; not only can it cast off its age and rejuvenate himself, but in so doing actually adds to its growth."[24]

The uroboros or snake biting its tail and forming a circle was another symbol of wholeness, immortality, and integrity which, according to Jung, signified the cosmos itself. In the Timaeus, Plato presented a new conception of life after death called by Cumont "celestial immortality." Astrological doctrines in Hellenistic and Roman periods encouraged a sidereal eschatology promising the soul's ascension, after death, through the heavenly spheres to his true home in the stars.[25]

The Hermetic religion (a pre-gnostic and gnostic composite) had the concept, related to astrology, of the planetary equipment of the soul. Prior to embodiment, each of the seven planetary powers (spheres) made its contribution equipping the soul with gifts for his earthly existence, thus subjected to the influence of the stars and to heirmarmene (destiny). Gnosticism conceived the planetary constituents contracted during the descent of the soul through the cosmic spheres as corruptions of its original nature.[26]

> "As the souls descend, they draw with them the torpor of Saturn, the wrathfulness of Mars, the concupiscence of Venus, the greed for gain of Mercury, the lust of power of Jupiter; which things effect a confusion in the souls, so that they can no longer make use of their own power and their proper faculties." (Servius In AEN. VI. 714)

The epoch of Christian Gnosticism was also the age of Mithraism. Eine MithrasLiturgie (The Mithras Liturgy) by Albrecht Dieterich (1866-1908), described the liturgical mystery of ascent and presented the seven liturgical stages for the soul's journey.

Marvin Meyer described the book as "a syncretistic piety utilizing astrology and magic and emphasizing the ecstatic ascent of the individual soul."

To define the outcome of religion during the Hellenistic-roman culture, Leisegang quoted Paul Wendlan writing that "Astral religion . . . culminated in the cult of the Sun. . . . The history of ancient religion ends in a solar pantheism" concluding that the Chaldean solar and astral theology, very popular in the second century BCE with the advance of astronomical knowledge, was combined by Posidonius with the concept of unity between the soul and the stars, idea fed by the triumph of Mithraism from the fist century BCE.[27]

In the mysteries of Mithras, Saint Jerome listed seven initiatory grades, each associated with a planet: first grade (Mercury) is the Raven or corax, second (Venus) the Bridegroom or nymphus, third (Mars) the Soldier or miles, fourth (Jupiter) the Lion or leo, fifth (Moon) the Persians or perses, sixth (Sun) the Sun-runner or heliodromus, and seventh (Saturn) the Father or pater. In Wandlungen und Symbole der Libido (1912)—Psychology of the Unconscious (1916)—Jung used Franz Cumont´s Textes et Monuments (1899) to explain Mithraic inititations. Cumont believed the Osterburken relief represented "the ceremony of the initiation into the degree of Miles, in which a sword and a crown were conferred upon the mysthic." Jung wrote "Helios is, therefore, appointed the Miles of Mithra."[28]

In Rome, the frescoes of the Mithraeum beneath Saint Prisca show figures depicting the different grades, each one with a mantra (prayer) associated to a each of the seven planetary gods. The Mithraeum of Felicissimus at Ostia has a mosaic divided into seven panels, each panel showing devices for each of the seven grades. In a scene at Klagenfurt where Mithra mounts the chariot of Helios, Jung concluded "it is either for the ascension or the 'sea journey,'" treating the sea journey as a motive of the Sun myth. Jung wrote, "the primitive symbol, which designates that portion of the Zodiac in which the Sun, with the Winter Solstice, again enters upon the yearly course, is the goat, fish sign," concluding that "the Sun mounts like a goat to the highest mountain, and later goes into the water as a fish." For Jung the fish is a symbol for the renewal of the libido and "the entire Sun mythology is merely a psychologic projection to the heavens."[29]

According to Cumont, astronomy had led the old Chaldeans to belief that the sidereal gods were everlasting, arguing that this theological notion penetrated with astrology into Roman paganism. The epithet aeternus completed and explained that of invictus, both of them applying to the stars, and especially to the Sun, insisted Cumont.

Initiations leading to immortality were very present at certain points of Jung's career. In 1916, under the pseudonym of "Basilides of Alexandria", Jung wrote the "The Seven Sermons to the Dead": the first six sermons outlined a Gnostic cosmology and an exposition on Abraxas and the pleroma, the seventh revealed the key of inmortality[30]. Astrology can be seen behind Jung's immortality exposition. In "The mystery of the Serpent," Leisegang connected Abraxas with both the Sun and Mithras: "the magic word 'Abraxas,'" wrote Leisegang, "signifies the Aeon". It seems that the term Abraxas intended to express the numerical value 365 in one word, by computing the Greek letters that make up the word. Leisegang's source was a Latin excerpt by Saint Jerome, from which he translated "Basilides designated his almighty god by the magic word Abraxas. . ; this was the same god whom the heathen called Mithras." In some monuments of the cult of Mithras, Helios and the Aeon were associated with the winds, argued Leisegang, who claimed that "Mithras, as Sol Invictus, takes the form of a winged lion-headed god entwined in a snake," noting that "several Mithraic reliefs represent the four winds in their corners."[31]

Jung discussed on several occasions the association of wings and winged beings with the air element (pneuma). In 1925 Jung lectured about the mystery of deification explaining his own experience: "one gets a peculiar feeling from being put to such an initiation" claiming that "the animal face which I felt mine transformed into was the famous [Deus] Leontocephalus of the Mithraic mysteries," which the Mithras Liturgy described as the fire-breathing god Aion. In that lecture, Jung explained that the lion-headed god encoiled by the snake was Aion, the eternal being, which derived from the Persian deity "Zrwanakarana" meaning "the infinitely long duration." Jung interpreted that the lion was the young, hot, dry July Sun in culmination of light, the summer, while the serpent meant humidity, darkness, the earth: winter. Jung wrapped it up saying: "something divine happens when the pairs of opposites come together, begetting immortality." Finally, he wrote "wherever there is generation there is time, therefore Chronos is God of Time, Fire and Light."[32]

In Astrology and Religion among the Greeks and the Romans (1912), Cumont argued that infinity of Time was elevated to the dignity of Supreme Cause not only by individual thinkers, but by Oriental cults. The name Zervan Akarana, "Time Unlimited" was regarded by a sect of Persian Magi as the First Principle. This doctrine, Cumont wrote, was developed in Mesopotamia, adopted by the mysteries of Mithra, and passed with them into the West where this god was represented in the form of a monster with the head of a lion to indicate that he devours all things.[33]

The god Chronos (personified Time) appears in early Greek philosophers during the sixth and fifth centuries BCE. In Orphic Theogonies and cosmogonies the most characteristic epithet for Chronos was "unaging time." In his comparative material for Chronos, M. L. West included epithets corresponding to the Iranian god Zurvan and the Indian god Kala, and noted that Re in Egyptian cosmogony was called "the aged one who renewed his youth." Modern scholars understand Chronos as a reinterpretation of the former god Kronos, as it appeared in the Theogony of Hesiod. The later-on equation of Kronos with both Roman Saturnus and Time provided the basis for his role of "Father Time" and for the archetypal images of Time devouring his children. Jung defined the life of an archetype to be timeless and unlimited, and may be regarded as an organizer of representations, working from the unconscious.[34]

During his midlife, Posidonius settled in Rhodes, city which a few years earlier had been the hometown of Hypparchus (c. 190 BCE-c. 120 BCE), who has been credited with the discovery of the precession of the equinoxes. In his early life, Posidonius was a stoic. In The Origins of the Mithraic Mysteries (1989), David Ulansey suggested that the discovery of the precession of the equinoxes led stoics to hypothesize the existence of a new divinity of great power, capable of moving the structure of the entire cosmos. Jung did not know about Ulansey's hypothesis, which appeared two decades after his death, yet Jung saw something else in the precession of the equinoxes: the course of the history of occidental religion during the last Aeon could have been predicted by the transit of the vernal equinox over the constellation of Pisces.

But Christ was symbolized by a "single" fish, he wrote, arguing that Cumont believed that the fish cult of Atargatis, from Syria, was responsible for the appearance of the single fish image of Christian times, called Ichtys by the Greeks. Due to the double polarity of any archetype and being Pisces a double sign, Jung reasoned that if Christ was only one fish, the other fish of the symbol of Pisces would represent the Antichrist. Following his concept of enantiodromia (similar to restoring balance, the excess of any force inevitably produces its opposite), Jung researched Nostradamus, Pierre d'Ailly and Albumasar, focusing on their dates predicting the changing of Aeons and the appearance of Antichrist. Nostradamus, Jung wrote, gave the year 1792 as the appearance of Antichrist. According to Pierre d'Ailly, by using periods of ten revolutions of Saturn, Jung noted, "a Saturn period came to an end in 11 BCE," connected with the appearance of Christ; another period ended in 289 CE, this one connected with Manichaeism; then Jung wrote "the year 589 foretells Islam, and 1189 the significant reign of Pope innocent III; 1489 announces a schism of the Church, and 1789 signalizes—by inference—the coming of Antichrist."[35]

Jung also explored the actual astronomic shape of the constellation of Pisces and the spring point moving along it, writing about the transit over the northerly (or easterly) fish as marking the beginning of our era, and calculating different religious events when the spring point transited over "the so-called commissure" or the joint of the two fishes, and the transits over the southerly (or westerly) fish.[36]

The influence of astrology in Jung's work is vast and it would span a whole book. The influence of astrology in Hellenistic-Roman times was so pervading that it can be traced in our words, like consider, which comes from the Latin considerare meaning casting horoscopes. The god Aion, whose origins are entwined with astrological mythology, cosmology and astrological Aeons, played a significant role in the goal of Jung's psychology. His active-imagination technique and his very analytical psychology were inspired by myths closely related to astrology. By studying the gods, images, myths, religious rituals, and alchemical books of Hellenistic-Roman and medieval times, Jung was exposed indirectly to astrology. Through Dane Rudhyar, Liz Greene and others, that influence returned back to astrology enriching it with a new psychological approach still ongoing.

Endnotes

[1] Campbell, Joseph, ed. *The Mysteries: Papers from the Eranos Yearbooks*. Princeton: Princeton University Press. 1990, 215.

[2] Jung, Deirdre Bair. *A Biography*. New York: Back Bay Books, 2003, 549.

[3] Noll, Richard. *The Jung Cult: Origins of a Charismatic Movement*. Princeton: Princeton University Press, 1994, 191.

[4] Jung, Carl. *Collected Works Volume 4, Freud and Psychoanalysis*. Princeton: Princeton University Press, 1967, paragraph 404.

[5] Jung, Carl. *Memories, Dreams and Reflections*. New York: Vintage Books, 1989, 398.

[6]Noll, 240.
[7]Jung, Carl and Jung, Aion. *Researches into the Phenomenology of the Self, Collected Works, vol. 9, part 2.* Princeton: Princeton University Press, 1978, 222.
[8]Jung, Carl. *The Structure and Dynamics of the Psyche*, Collected Works vol. 8. Princeton: Princeton University Press, 1960, paragraphs 193-5.
[9]*Researches into the Phenomenology of the Self, Collected Works, vol. 9, part 2*, 169.
[10]Jung, Carl. *On the Nature of the Psyche*. Princeton: Princeton University Press, 1969, paragraphs 193-5.
[11]Jacobi, Jolande. *Complex, Archetype, Symbol in the Psychology of C. G. Jung*, 3rd ed. Princeton: Princeton University Press, 1974, 48-9.
[12]Ibid., 34.
[13]Aion, 182-3.
[14]Ibid., 132.
[15]Ibid., 136.
[16]Ibid.
[17]Ibid., 224.
[18]Ibid., 225.
[19]Campbell, 220.
[20]Ibid., 228.
[21]*Researches into the Phenomenology of the Self, Collected Works, vol. 9, part 2.*, 186.
[22]Campbell, 230-1.
[23]Ruiz, Carolina Lopez. *When the Gods Were Born: Greek Cosmogonies and the Near East*. Cambridge: Harvard University Press, 2010, 151-9.
[24]Campbell, 221.
[25]Ulansey, David. *The Origins of the Mithraic Mysteries*. Oxford: Oxford University Press, 1989, 86.
[26]Jonas, Hans. *The Gnostic Religion*. Boston: Beacon Press. 1963, 157.
[27]Campbell, 219.
[28]Jung, Carl. *Psychology of the Unconscious*. New York: Moffat, Yard and Company, 1917, 221.
[29]Ibid., 222-7.
[30]Noll, 242.
[31]Campbell, 222-4.
[32]Jung, Carl, William McGuire, R. F. C. Hull, and Sonu Shamdasani. *Introduction to Jungian Psychology: Notes of the Seminar on Analytical Psychology Given in 1925*. Princeton: Princeton University Press, 2011,

106-7.
³³Cumont, Franz. *Astrology and Religion among the Greeks and the Romans.* New York: Cosimo, 2006, 61.
³⁴Jacobi, 64.
³⁵*Researches into the Phenomenology of the Self, Collected Works, vol. 9, part 2,* 99.
³⁶Ibid., 93.

The Influence of the Tropical and Sidereal Zodiacs on Personal Transits

By Peter Meyer

ABSTRACT: The difference between the tropical and sidereal zodiacs is explained, as is their influence on personal planetary transits. This research shows that when using the tropical zodiac, personal transits occur earlier than when using the sidereal zodiac, and that for any given transit, the difference between the two zodiacs is larger for the outer planets and increases with a person's age.

From the point of view of an ideal observer at the center of the Earth, the sun traces out a complete circle against the background of the fixed stars during the course of a year, and it traces out the same circle every year. This circle (as seen from Earth) is called the *ecliptic* (for a reason having to do with eclipses) and it determines the *ecliptic plane*. (From the point of view of the sun, Earth revolves about the sun in the ecliptic plane.)

Each planet orbits the sun in its own orbital plane and (with the exception of Pluto) these orbital planes almost coincide with the ecliptic plane. Thus it is approximately true that all the planets move in the ecliptic plane, with slight movements above and below it (somewhat larger vertical movements in the case of Pluto), so at any given time the position of a planet is approximately specified by a longitude, called the *celestial longitude* (a.k.a. the *ecliptic longitude*). Astrologers usually ignore the angle of a planet above or below the ecliptic plane and consider only its celestial longitude.

Referencing Zero Degrees

Because there are 360 degrees in a circle, a longitude is a number from zero up to but not including 360 (so the maximum is 359 degrees 59 minutes and 59 seconds, abbreviated to 359° 59' 59"). But how to define the reference direction of zero degrees?

This is where Vedic (Indian) astrology differs from the Western astrology derived from Ptolemy (2nd century CE). For Vedic astrologers the reference direction is a line drawn from the center of the Earth through the center of the Sun to a point in the constellation Aries, and this reference direction is thus known as *zero degrees Aries*. For Western astrologers the reference direction is a line drawn from the center of the Earth through the center of the Sun at the exact moment of the vernal equinox (in the current year, or alternatively in some specified year, such as 2000 CE). At some time a few thousand years ago these two directions were the same, but due to the so-called *precession of the equinoxes* they have not remained the same.

Earth rotates once per day on its axis, but this axis of rotation wobbles (like a spinning top) over a period of about 25,700 years. An effect of this is that the position of Earth in its orbit around the sun at the exact moment of the vernal equinox changes very slightly from year to year, and thus the line drawn from Earth through the sun and onto the background of stars (the *celestial sphere*) does not remain pointing to the same place, but moves, and in the last 2,000 years it has moved from the constellation of Aries into the constellation of Pisces.

Western astronomers, however, continue to call this direction *zero degrees Aries* and to measure celestial longitude from it, so (in this tradition) at the vernal equinox the Sun always has longitude 0° 0' 0", and its longitude increases by approximately one degree per day during the course of a year.

Consequently, the longitudes of the Sun and the planets as calculated according to Vedic astrology are different from those calculated according to Western astrology. This difference is called the *ayanamsha*, and in 1960 CE its value was about 23° 18', increasing at about one degree in seventy-two years.

The zodiac is a system of designating planetary longitudes by reference to twelve so-called *signs*, which are formed by dividing the ecliptic into twelve equal parts of 30° each, starting from zero degrees Aries. The signs are named *Aries, Taurus, Gemini*, etc., in Western astrology, and these names are also currently used by Vedic astrologers. But since *zero degrees Aries* has a different meaning in Vedic astrology from its meaning in Western astrology, we thus have two different zodiacs: the *tropical zodiac* (Western astrology) and the *sidereal zodiac* (Vedic astrology). The longitude of any planet in one zodiac differs from the longitude of that planet in the other zodiac by the ayanamsha, which in 2010 was about 24° 0'. For example, on May 19, 2010, Mercury was located at 4° 59' in Taurus in the tropical zodiac, but at 10° 59' in Aries in the sidereal zodiac (10 + 24 - 30 = 4).

For Vedic astrologers it is obvious that the sidereal zodiac is superior, but this question is often debated among Western astrologers. Neither zodiac can be said to be "original" (unless both are) because at the time the zodiac first came into use (in Babylon) there was no difference between the two (the difference emerged only with the passage of time and the precession of the equinoxes). Ptolemy chose to adopt the tropical zodiac and this practice has been almost universally followed in the West since then.

How does the choice of zodiac affect aspects and transits? The short answer is that it does not, except in the case of personal transits. (A *personal* transit is the period during which a moving planet remains in a certain aspect to that same planet in a person's natal chart.) The presence or absence of an aspect between two moving planets depends on their angular separation, and at a given point in time this is the same whether the tropical zodiac or the sidereal zodiac is used. For example, on May 19, 2010, Pluto was located at 4 Capricorn 59 in the tropical zodiac, but at 10 Sagittarius 59 in the sidereal zodiac. It was thus in an exact trine to Mercury in both zodiacs. So, for world transits (that is, transits between moving planets) and natal charts the aspects are exactly the same regardless of which zodiac is used.

A difference does emerge, however, when considering personal transits. World transits and natal charts are concerned only with a single date, whereas personal transits depend on a comparison of planetary longitudes at one date—the birth date—with planetary longitudes at another (later) date.

When two planets form an aspect, their longitudinal difference may differ from the ideal value for that aspect by a few degrees (up to the value of the orb chosen for that aspect), and the difference is termed the *difference from exact aspect*. For example, if Venus has a longitude of 78° (18° Gemini) and Mars has a longitude of 165° (15° Virgo), then the difference in their longitudes is 87°, so they form a square aspect. But the exact value for a square aspect is 90°, so the difference from exact aspect in this case is 3°.

For a personal transit, if the second (later) date is about seventy years after the birth date and a transiting planet forms an aspect with a natal planet, then the difference from exact aspect will be about one degree different in the two zodiacs.

Consider, for example, a person born at noon GMT on January 1, 1900. At that time Saturn was at 5 Sagittarius 19 in the sidereal zodiac and at 27 Sagittarius 46 in the tropical zodiac. Now fast forward to 02:00 GMT on September 8, 1972. At that moment Jupiter was at 5 Sagittarius 19 in the sidereal zodiac and was at 28 Sagittarius 47 in the tropical zodiac. Thus according to the sidereal zodiac on September 8, 1972, transiting Jupiter was exactly (0° 0') conjunct the natal Saturn, but according to the tropical zodiac transiting Jupiter was conjunct natal Saturn but not exactly, differing from exact by 1° 1'. This is shown in the screenshots below (with color converted to black-and-white) from the *Planetary Aspects and Transits* software (sidereal is on the left, and tropical is on the right):

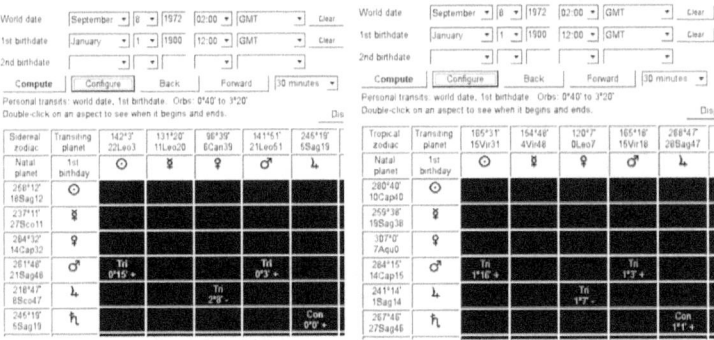

If we hold that for a transiting planet to be exactly conjunct a natal planet it is necessary for the transiting planet to occupy exactly the same position relative to the fixed stars as the natal planet did at the time of birth, then for calculating personal transits the sidereal zodiac is preferable.

Personal transits occur earlier with the tropical zodiac than with the sidereal zodiac, and the difference increases with a person's age.

Consider, for example, a person born at 9:00 GMT on March 4, 1900. Venus was at 0 Aries 02 in the sidereal zodiac and at 22 Aries 30 in the tropical zodiac (the ayanamsha in 1900 being approximately 22° 28'). At 05:00 GMT on October 18, 1973, Uranus was at 0 Libra 02 in the sidereal zodiac, and so was exactly opposite natal Venus, as shown in the screenshot below from the *Planetary Aspects and Transits* software:

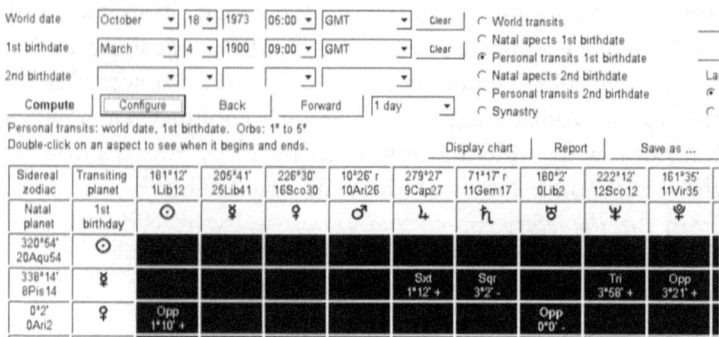

But with the tropical zodiac, transiting Uranus became exactly opposite to natal Venus at 22:00 GMT on October 1, 1973, as shown below.

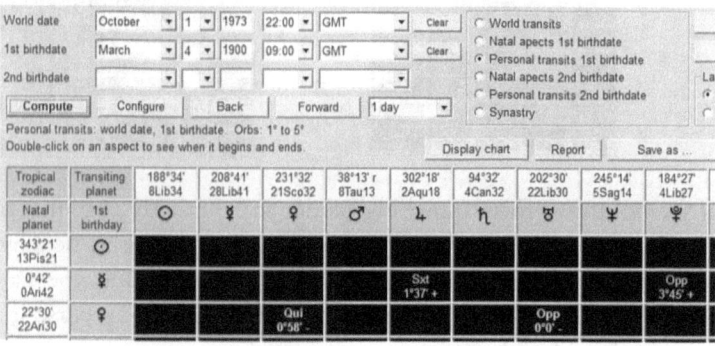

Thus transiting Uranus reached exact opposition to natal Venus about seventeen days earlier with the tropical zodiac than with the sidereal zodiac. This is shown graphically in the image on the next page. The bold line shows the difference from exact opposition of transiting Uranus to natal Venus in the tropical zodiac, and the non-bold line shows the same in the sidereal zodiac.

This can be explained as follows: In seventy-three years the direction which is called *zero degrees Aries* in the tropical zodiac moves backwards by 1° relative to the constellations. Thus in 1973 Uranus had a "head start" of 1° when traveling along the ecliptic to

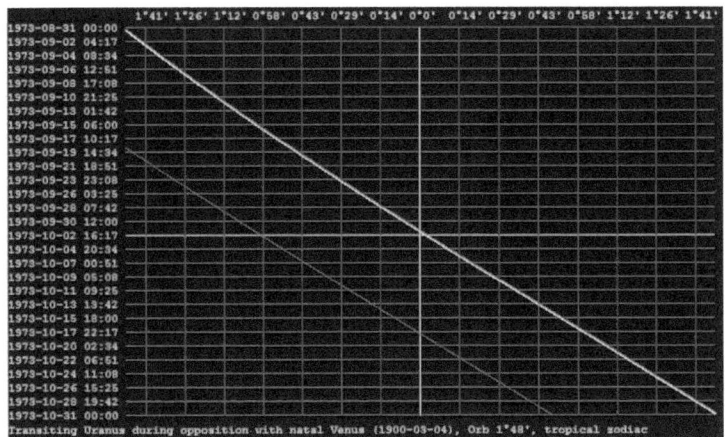

reach the position of 22 Libra 30 in the tropical zodiac (exactly opposite natal Venus), and so arrived earlier.

To illustrate the fact that the time difference between exact transits in the two zodiacs increases with a person's age consider again the person born at 09:00 GMT on March 4, 1900. Transiting Uranus reaches an exact square to natal Venus at 06:00 GMT on November 25, 1910, with the tropical zodiac, and with the sidereal zodiac reaches an exact square at 11:00 GMT on November 28, 1910, so the exact aspect occurs just three days earlier with the tropical zodiac rather than 17 days as in the case of the 1973 opposition considered above.

A similar phenomenon, of course, occurs with transiting planets other than Uranus. Since the inner planets move more quickly along the ecliptic than do the outer planets, we would expect that the time difference for the two zodiacs would be less for them since they take less time to traverse their "head start." Computation confirms this. Consider again the person born at 09:00 GMT on March 4, 1900. Transiting Mars reaches an exact trine to natal Neptune at 21:00 GMT on October 25, 1971, with the tropical zodiac, and with the sidereal zodiac reaches an exact trine at 23:00 GMT on October 27, 1971, so the exact aspect occurs 2 days earlier with the tropical zodiac rather than seventeen days as in the case of the 1973 opposition considered above.

Thus we may sum this up by saying that, when using the tropical zodiac, personal transits occur earlier than when using the sidereal zodiac, by up to two weeks or more, and that, for any given transit, the difference for the two zodiacs is larger for the outer planets and increases with a person's age. Thus when calculating personal transits the choice of zodiac does make a significant difference.

How Midpoints Feature in 2014 World Political Trials and Health Issues

By Pamela Rowe, LPMAFA, FMFAA

ABSTRACT: This study examines the impact of midpoints and the transiting Uranus-Pluto square in mundane charts and those of individuals as it relates to change. Also examined are degrees involved in a Grand Cross. Charts investigated include Australia, Australia's prime minister, Malaysian Airlines flights 370 and 17, Ukraine, and Robin Williams. An historical review of Pluto conjunction Saturn-Neptune midpoint is also examined.

Much has been written about the squares between Uranus and Pluto, extending from June 2012 to early 2016, which have coincided with many planned and unplanned life changes—changes of address, work and relationships, changes in outlook, procedure and leadership—changes that have unsettled many lives.

On April 23, 2014, Uranus in Aries and Pluto in Capricorn were joined by Jupiter in Cancer and retrograde Mars in Libra to form a Grand Cross across the zodiac at between 13 and 14 degrees of the cardinal signs. This had a powerful effect on anyone with

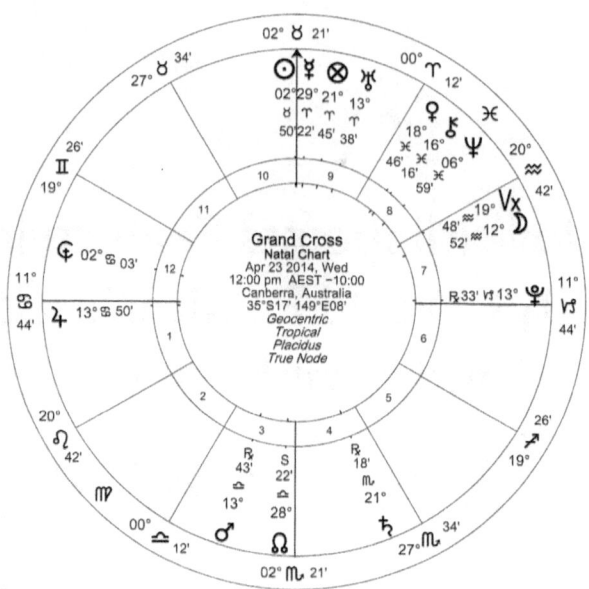

Grand Cross Wheel Above; Grand Cross Cosmobiology Dial Below

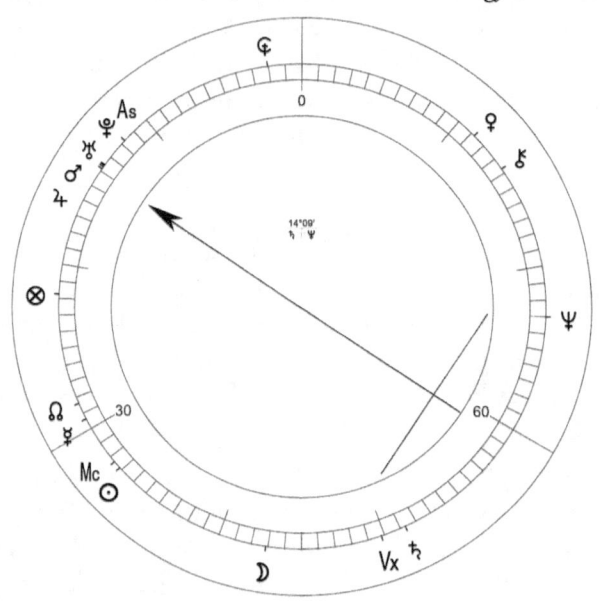

natal or progressed planets or points (particularly personal planets, the Ascendant, or Midheaven) at 13 to 14 degrees of Aries, Cancer, Libra or Capricorn. It also had a powerful impact on those with planets in 28 to 29 degrees of the fixed signs Taurus, Leo, Scorpio and Aquarius.

At the time of the Grand Cross, the Uranus, Mars, Jupiter and Pluto = Saturn/Neptune planetary picture was powerfully visual on the cosmobiology dial.

The Importance of the Grand Cross Degrees

The activation of these degrees in natal charts were of vital importance in the later months of 2014, when reactivated by other planets.

The Grand Cross had the potential to generate some amazing windfalls and indeed some extraordinary opportunities existed and were taken. But some found it to be a disaster, with financial or personal loss being the outcome. From a health perspective we need to look deeper to establish the most vulnerable health areas.

Saturn, Neptune, and Pluto are all slow-moving planets. As viewed from Earth they seem to move in a direct and retrograde motion. Astrologers take degrees of measurement, and in particular the planetary effects, very seriously. Because of the varying apparent direction changes, Pluto remained in close conjunction to the midpoint of Saturn and Neptune from late April until September 2014 as shown on the next page.

It can be seen that by September 23 the orb between Pluto and the Saturn/Neptune midpoint had increased to greater than the generally accepted level of 1½ degrees.

Because the conjunction represents an attempt to "blend" the energies together, the more incompatible the planetary interpretations, the easier it is for the pattern to work negatively. Hard work is required to get the best outcome from the Pluto con

Date	Pluto	Saturn/Neptune Midpoint
April 23, 2014.	13.33 Capricorn R	14.09 Capricorn (Saturn R, Neptune D)
May 23, 2014	13.14 Capricorn R	13.18 Capricorn (Saturn R, Neptune D)
June 23, 2014	12.34 Capricorn R	12.24 Capricorn (Saturn R, Neptune R)
July 23, 2014	11.49 Capricorn R	11.53 Capricorn (Saturn D, Neptune R)
August 23, 2014	11.13 Capricorn R	11.56 Capricorn (Saturn D, Neptune R)
September 23, 2014	10.59 Capricorn D	12.39 Capricorn (Saturn D. Neptune R)

junct Saturn/Neptune midpoint and 2014 has been a year of hardworking world leaders.

Saturn/Neptune is the midpoint of health and negativity, so if this transit is activated in your chart, new health conditions may have surfaced, or an existing condition may have flared up.

In addition I believe that those with natal planets or points on transiting Saturn during the April to September period (16 to 21 degrees of Scorpio) and those with natal planets or points on the transiting Neptune during this period (5½ to 7½ degrees of Pisces) would have felt the effect of this important energy configuration.

To some extent those with natal planets or points on 16 to 21 degrees of the other fixed signs (Taurus, Leo and Aquarius) and those with natal planets or points on 5½ to 7½ degrees of the other mutable signs (Gemini, Virgo and Sagittarius) have also been prone to action or reaction.

What type of illnesses have been widespread? In particular, immune and nervous systems have been sensitized, as have the liver, blood, and lungs. Muscles, accidents, and operative procedures dominated when Mars entered the picture. The outstanding feature of these illnesses is that many were highly unusual or completely unexpected.

In Australia we heard reports that double the incidence of influenza occurred during the southern latitude winter months.

In his book, *The Combination of Stellar Influences*, Reinhold Ebertin describes the Saturn/Neptune = Pluto midpoint as "A serious illness, heavy emotional depression."

It also involves severe and even toxic undermining of competitors, and also obsessional spirituality and sacrifices made on behalf of a cause or passion.

World health issues such as the ongoing Ebola epidemic in Africa have resurfaced, and the volatile, fragile relationship between Israel and the Gaza Strip has been a worldwide source of sorrow. The murder of innocents has enraged world powers and soldiers have been called to arms.

One passenger airplane has been lost and one shot out of the sky, intensifying pain and more loss of innocent victims.

However, during this Age of Aquarius let us not forget that with such extreme focus on the difficult expressions of this pattern, the extraordinary resourcefulness and spirit of humanity will direct the energy towards cures, medical breakthroughs, the resolution of toxic relationships and protection of victims—including victims of family abuse and violence.

The positive expressions should be cultivated in all children born between April and September 2014. Depending on other factors in their birth charts, they may have the capacity to be great doctors, researchers, and humanitarians.

Uranus-Pluto Squares

The squares recur on December 15, 2014 and March 17, 2015, with the final square within one degree of orb during January and February 2016. Although we have grown accustomed to this now familiar energy of change, those with natal or progressed planets and points aspecting the degrees of the approaching squares have yet to experience their personal revolution.

After the transiting Saturn/Neptune midpoint in Capricorn moves on from its conjunction to Pluto, it will form further squares to transiting Uranus on June 15 and September 25 in 2015. In early August 2016 the Saturn/Neptune midpoint will form its final square to Uranus (one degree of orb), before moving on. This pattern will heighten nervous energy and illnesses, and generate unrest and sudden reactions. The focus will be on nerve pain and brain and skin disorders.

Uranus rules all that is original and unusual, so we can expect some unexpected solutions or a surprising turn of events.

Australia's Chart

Australia's chart is calculated for January 1, 1901, the day that by royal decree Queen Victoria of England united all Australian States to form the Commonwealth of Australia. Because at that time Australia was closely tied to England, the Australian chart was calculated for January 1, 1901, 0 hours GMT, London England. This is the chart used in this article.

There is an alternative proclamation chart often used, which relates to the appointment of the first governor general in Sydney, Australia on January 1, 1901 at between 1:00 and 1:35 p.m. In her book, *Cosmobiology Beyond 2000*, Doris Greaves states that this proclamation chart "will cease to be significant if and when Australia becomes a Republic."

Australia's chart has the Sun in Capricorn conjunct Saturn, the Moon in Taurus, Ascendant in Libra, and Midheaven in Cancer. A heavily occupied third house with Venus, Uranus, Jupiter, Mercury, and Chiron in Sagittarius could describe Australia's Jupiterian reputation as "the lucky country." There is great focus on education, research, travel, and migration, as can also be seen by Neptune and Pluto in Gemini in the ninth house, opposing the Sagittarian cluster.

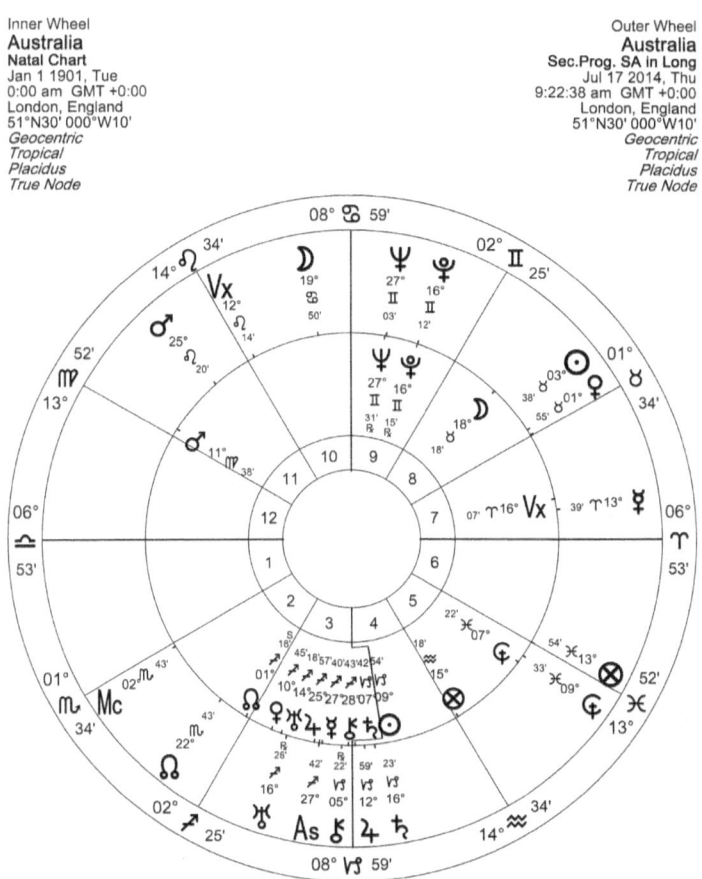

In recent years transiting Pluto in Capricorn conjunction Australia's natal Sun and Saturn, plus transiting Uranus in Aries square Australia's Cardinal points, has coincided with many disruptions to our leadership. For a short period we had our first female prime minister, Julia Gillard, followed by further power plays and reorganization. Although we have weathered the storm quite well, in September 2014, Australia's terror alert was lifted from Medium to High as Australia's involvement in overseas conflict increased. Australia's chart is progressed to the MH17 crash date.

Australian Prime Minister Tony Abbott

From a political viewpoint, Mr. Abbott has been caught in the thick of the difficult 2014 patterns. It is fortunate for him that with natal Mars rising in the first house, he is a healthy and fit individual or his energy may have been depleted. Mr. Abbott cycling in his stretch tights, running or swimming, is a common sight for Australians.

Due to retrograde Mars in Libra, Mr. Abbott experienced two Mars returns, in February and July, involving his first and twelfth houses, so the usual new incentive and plans associated with the Mars return were somewhat delayed.

No doubt he would have been more impatient than usual. "Too much too soon" seems to be the verdict of the people to his unpopular Australian budget, some of the most contentious measures of which have currently been blocked by opposition political parties.

Although the transiting Grand Cross appeared to be well placed in Mr. Abbott's chart, falling across the angles of his chart, with Jupiter culminating, Pluto on his IC in a direct midpoint to Saturn and Neptune was bound to attract toxic undermining and the threatening of his position and home environment. If his birth time is accurate, some major reaction to his way of life is possible.

As is sometimes seen, the major transformation patterns operating in the charts of our leaders can be projected onto the people at large.

During the transiting Pluto = Saturn/Neptune period, the outpouring of grief over the shooting down of Malaysian Airline Flight MH17 at Donetsk, Ukraine, plus the Middle East crisis, demanded action and policies from the Australian leader. Saturn moving through Mr. Abbott's Sun and Mercury signs of Scorpio no doubt increased his credibility, as he shouldered the additional responsibility.

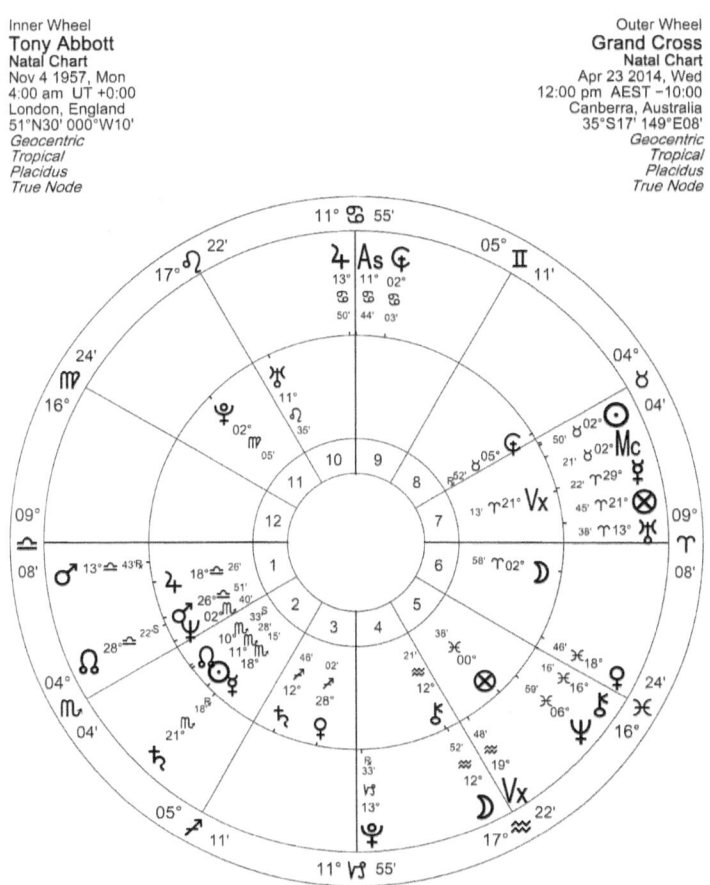

Australian Foreign Minister Julie Bishop led the Australian charge to retrieve, identify, and return the bodies of MH17 Australian victims to their loved ones. As this air crash occurred on Ms. Bishop's birthday, July 17 (1956), she would have felt personally involved in the rescue mission—and she indeed did Australia proud as, along with Mr. Abbott, she fronted world leaders with courage and conviction.

Loss of Malaysian Airlines Flights MH370 and MH17

The loss of both planes has had a major impact on Australians and their leaders. Flight MH370, was lost on March 8, 2014, supposedly at sea in the deep waters off the West Australian coast. Flight MH17, carrying thirty-six Australians, was shot down on July 17, 2014, near the border of Ukraine and Russia, killing all 298 passengers. Eighty of those killed were children and three were babies. The official verdict was that "MH17 was hit by a number of flying objects."

The departure or birth chart of a flight, like our personal birth charts, has the potential to assess the outcome of the flight. My interpretation of the disappearance of Flight MH370 appeared in the AFA *Today's Astrologer*, April 29, 2014.

Malaysian Airlines Flight MH17

In the departure chart the Ascendant marks the start of the journey and the IC the end of the journey. As in the Flight MH370 departure chart the Moon is opposition the Ascendant. In MH17, the Ascendant at 2 Libra 39 is opposition the Moon at 3 Aries 36.

Mars rising at 25 Libra 37 is conjunct/opposition the nodal axis, forming a T-square with the Sun in the tenth house. The Moon's South Node in the seventh house is three degrees from the eighth house cusp; Mars is the eighth house ruler.

In this chart the often underrated Hades is conjunct the Midheaven and Mercury and forming a T-square with the Moon and Ascendant. Venus, the chart ruler, is in the ninth house, five degrees from a conjunction to the Midheaven and Hades (bad news, vileness, mean tricks, destructive fire, disorder and unhygienic conditions).

Pluto in the fourth house aptly described the end of this journey. Pluto was only one minute of orb from its conjunction to the Saturn/Neptune midpoint. The explosive power and might of

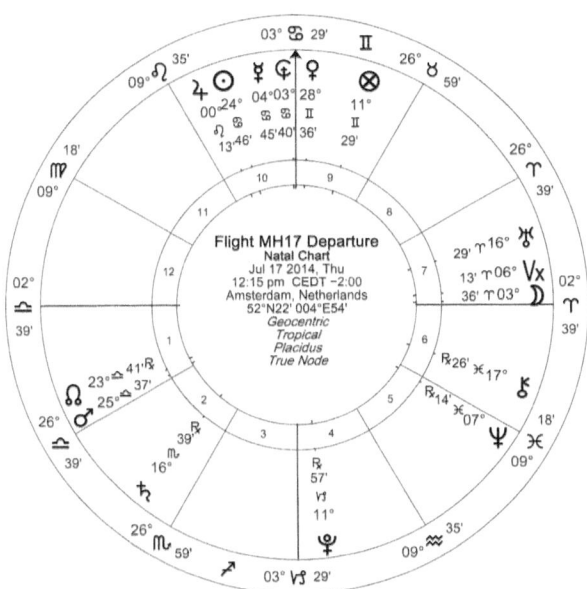

Flight MH 17 Departure Wheel Above; Cosmobiology Dial Below

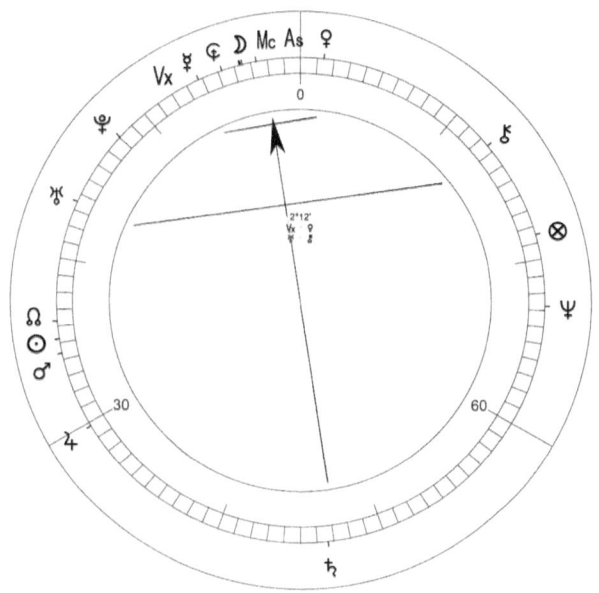

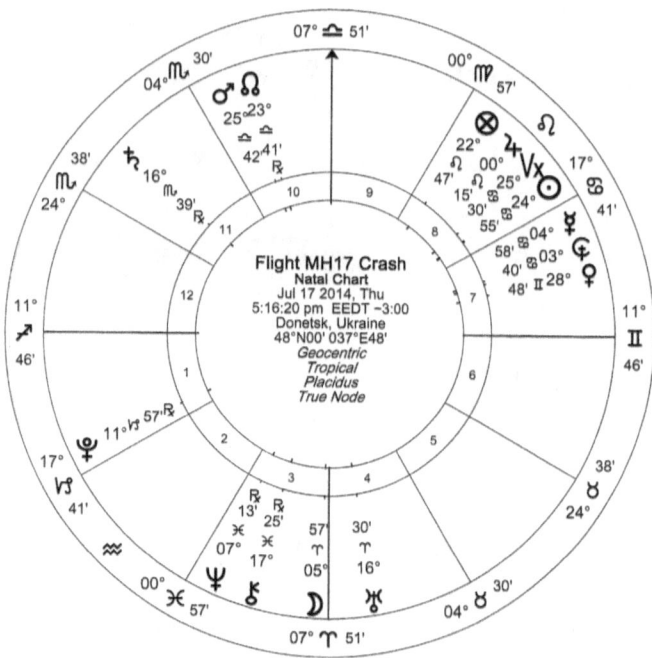

Pluto painted a different picture to the watery, mysterious Neptune end of Flight MH370.

The cosmobiology dial of the Flight MH17 Departure shows the intense syndrome pattern of Ascendant, Midheaven, Moon, Hades, Mercury, and Vertex aspecting Saturn, with the pattern in the midpoint of Uranus and Chiron.

Debris from the crash was scattered over a large area, but the crash chart has been located for Donetsk Ukraine, close to the Russian border. Sagittarius is on the Ascendant, with Pluto starting to rise in the first house and the Moon conjunction the IC. Chart ruler Jupiter had recently changed sign, entering Leo, and is placed in the eighth house, as was the Sun, conjunction the Vertex in its T-square to the Mars and lunar nodal axis.

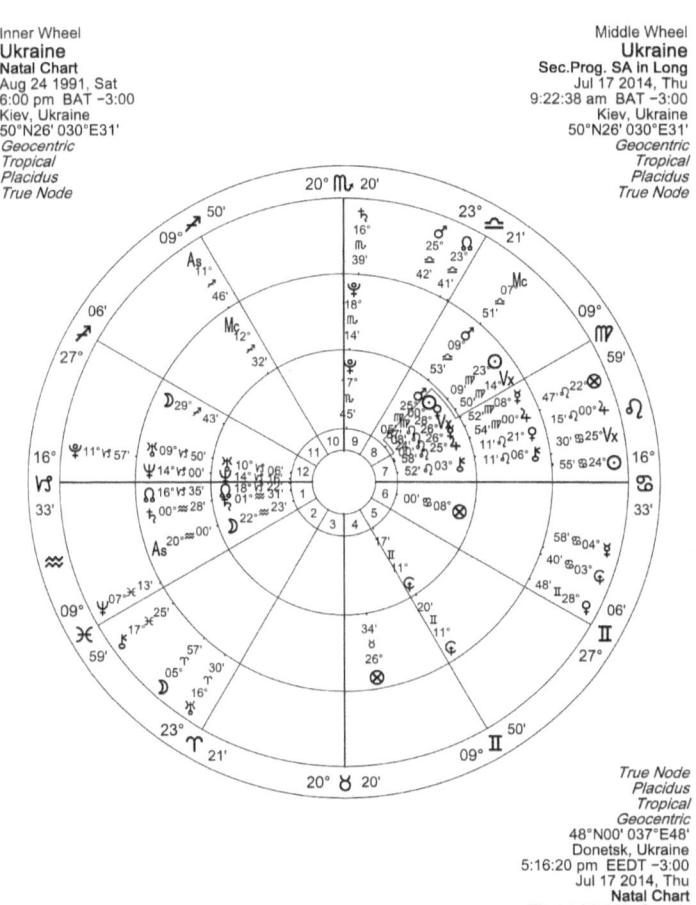

Ukraine

There are many indicators of the MH17 crash in Ukraine's chart (Rodden AA). Transiting Pluto = Saturn/Neptune fell into the Ukraine natal midpoint of Neptune and Uranus in the twelfth (undermining spiritual journeys, remaining at the mercy of external circumstances, hidden enemies).

The progressed chart shows Uranus joining Mars on the cosmobiology wheel (progressed Mars square natal and progressesd

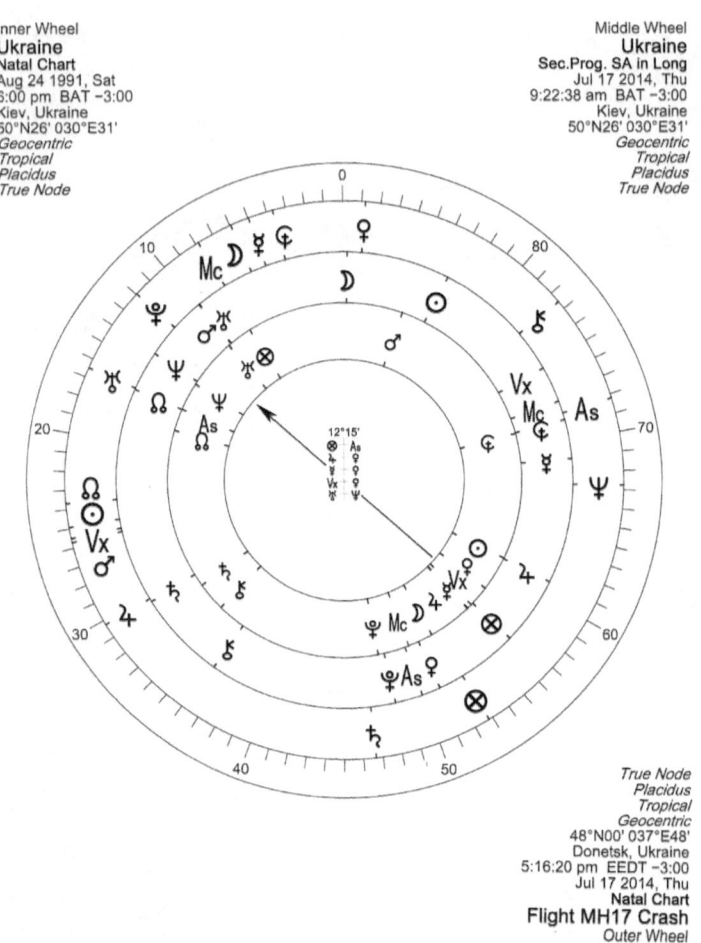

Uranus, conjunction transiting Midheaven). The transiting Ascendant was conjunct the progressed Midheaven opposition Hades. This is a classic accident pattern.

Progressed Jupiter was conjunct the natal Sun (three minute orb). This is a common pattern in such disasters, indicating overwhelming and magnified conditions, and legal, financial, and spiritual involvement. Reinhold Ebertin suggests that it brings "conflicts with the laws of the land."

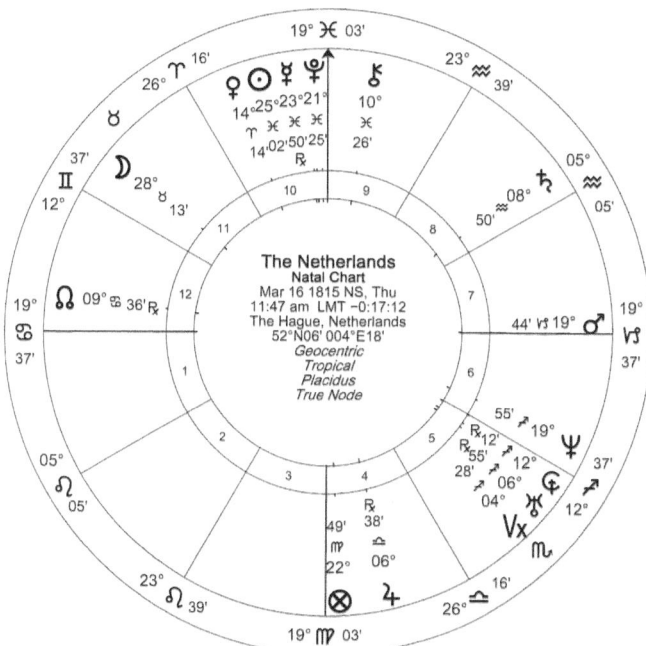

Transiting Saturn was applying to the conjunction to natal Pluto and the Midheaven, square the natal Moon and the progressed Ascendant, semisquare the progressed Moon, and sesquiquadrate transiting Venus = sacrifice, renunciation, loss of loved ones, murder.

Netherlands

By far the greatest loss of life from Flight MH17 was incurred by the people of Netherlands. In her book, Accurate World Horoscopes, Doris Chase Doane lists the birth chart of the Netherlands as March 16, 1815, 11:47 a.m. LMT, The Hague, with C. C. Zain as her reference.

With its watery geographic location it is not surprising that the Netherlands chart has a powerful water component. The Sun in Pisces is conjunct Mercury and Pluto in the tenth house and conjunct the Midheaven. The Ascendant at 19 Cancer 38 is in

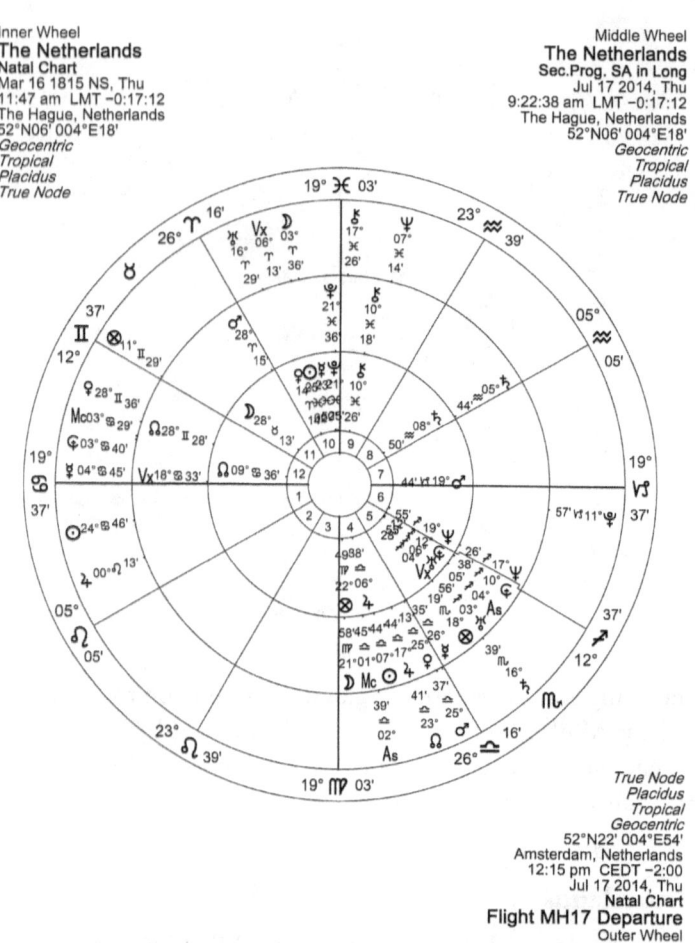

close opposition to Mars (seven minute orb). Mars is semisquare Uranus in the fifth house of creativity and children.

On the day of the crash the progressed chart for the Netherlands has the Ascendant at 4 Sagittarius 05 conjunct progressed Uranus at 3 Sagittarius 57 (eight minute orb) conjunct the natal Vertex in the fifth house (sudden, karmic events involving children and loved ones).

The progressed Moon at 21 Virgo 58 was opposition natal and

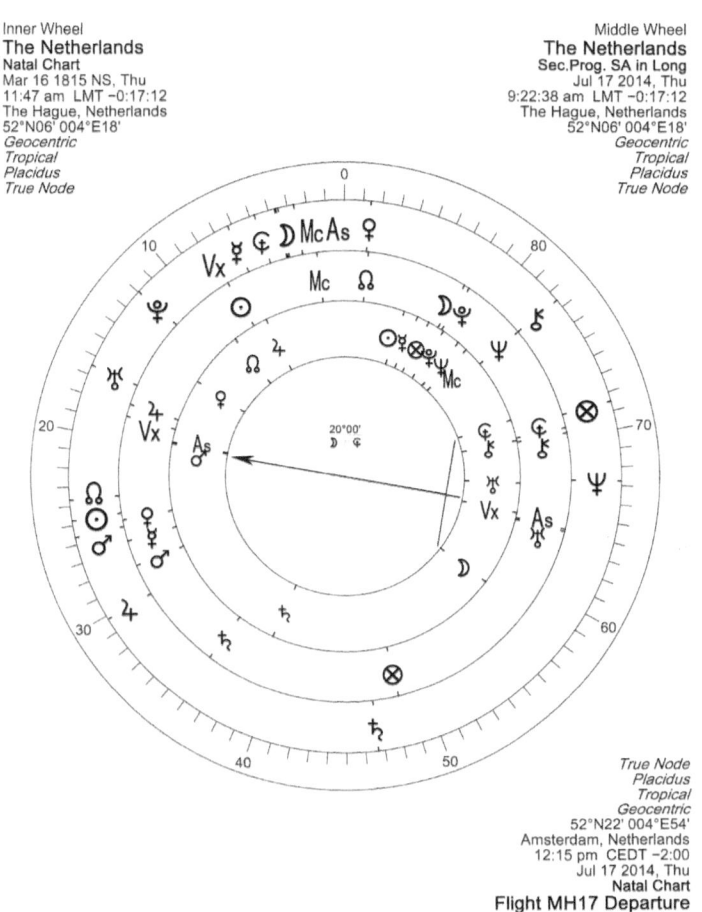

progressed Pluto. The progressed Moon was nearing the end of its progressed Balsamic phase to the progressed Sun. It has long been established by astrologers that this progression phase is one of the most vulnerable in the 29½ year secondary progressed lunation cycle. The Netherlands was and still is in a vulnerable phase.

Although the natal chart is nearly 200 years old, the fifty-year cycle of Chiron was activated in the ninth house of long distance travel. Natal Chiron was experiencing its fourth return and transiting Neptune was applying to a conjunction to natal Chiron (international mystery, loss, and wounds). Transiting Neptune was also square natal Uranus in the fifth house.

The combination aptly describes the intense soul-searching required by those left behind in order to reach understanding and acceptance.

The Netherlands cosmobiology tri-dial with natal, secondary progressed and transiting planets and points is also highly descriptive of the event.

Natal Mars, Ascendant, Vertex = progressed Uranus, Ascendant, Vertex, Jupiter = applying transiting Uranus = the accident, sudden shock of destiny.

Progressed Midheaven = transiting Saturn, Moon, Ascendant, Midheaven = separating force, loss, sadness, limitations.

Natal Pluto, Part of Fortune, Mercury/Neptune midpoint = progressed Moon, Pluto, Saturn = sacrifice, powerful emotions, torment, scandalous act.

In addition, the transiting Mars/Saturn midpoint (cutting of energy source) at 6 Scorpio 09 was square progressed Saturn (5 Aquarius 45), very close to the Netherlands' eighth house cusp.

As mentioned earlier, the transiting Pluto = Saturn/Neptune midpoint would activate the late degrees of the fixed signs and this can be clearly seen on the tri-dial. Transiting Pluto conjunction Saturn/Neptune is sesquiquadrate the Netherlands' natal Moon at 28 Taurus 14 in the natal eleventh house, describing fear, undermining of hopes and wishes, heartache, and emotional sickness.

The presence of Jupiter, lunar Nodes (natal) = Sun (progressed) = Vertex, Mercury (transiting), indicates a spiritual journey, far reaching loss, huge legal/financial implications, and helpful volunteers.

Historically—Pluto Conjunct Saturn/Neptune Midpoint

The orbit of Pluto means that the time frame for when Pluto is conjunct the Saturn/Neptune midpoint is inconsistent. The historic correlation of events to the pattern are still being researched. However, I have selected a few interesting dates. The first two periods in particular occurred around war times and already 2014 has produced several aggressive world situations.

Pluto was close to a conjunction with the Saturn/Neptune midpoint in Gemini in September 1912 and was in a conjunction in Gemini in late April 1913.

Pluto was close to a conjunction with Saturn/Neptune in Leo between late August and October 1942 and was in conjunction in Leo in April 1943.

Pluto was conjunction to Saturn/Neptune in Libra in early August 1976 and during February and March 1977.

There is also potential for research into the periods when Pluto was in other hard aspects to the Saturn/Neptune midpoint. I believe the "attempt to blend," as with the conjunction, interprets the pattern effectively.

Many of those born in the late 1800s had Neptune conjunct Pluto in Gemini, which meant that their Saturn/Neptune midpoint was very close to their Saturn/Pluto midpoint. In other words, they would be dealing with the total Saturn/Neptune/Pluto combination.

A couple of cases in point are World War II murderer Adolf Hitler, whose Saturn/Neptune midpoint at 7 Cancer 09 was conjunct Chiron and opposition his Moon. Hitler's Saturn/Pluto midpoint at 9 Cancer 04 was opposition Jupiter. These two midpoints were slightly wide at two degrees apart. However, combined with his Libran Ascendant, the total pattern suggests a wolf in sheep's clothing, who fooled many people for far too long.

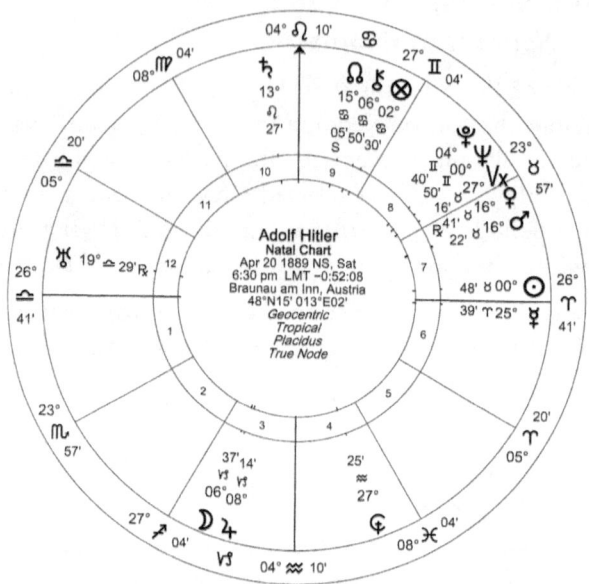

Adolf Hitler Wheel Above; Cosmobiology Dial Below

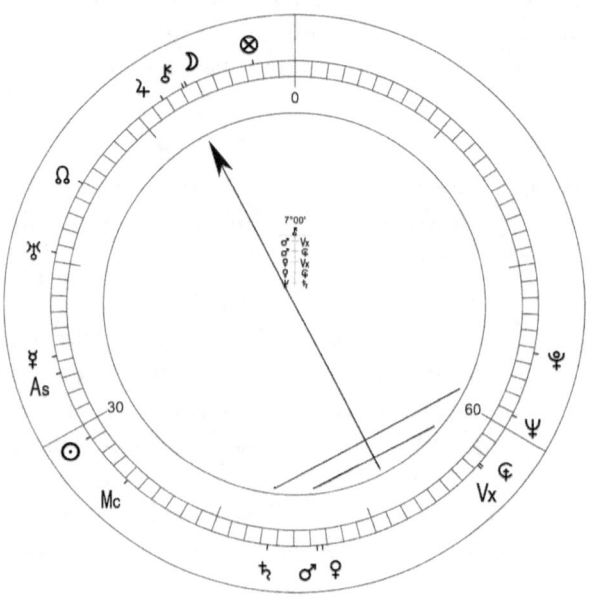

Midpoints in 2014 Political Trials and Health Issues

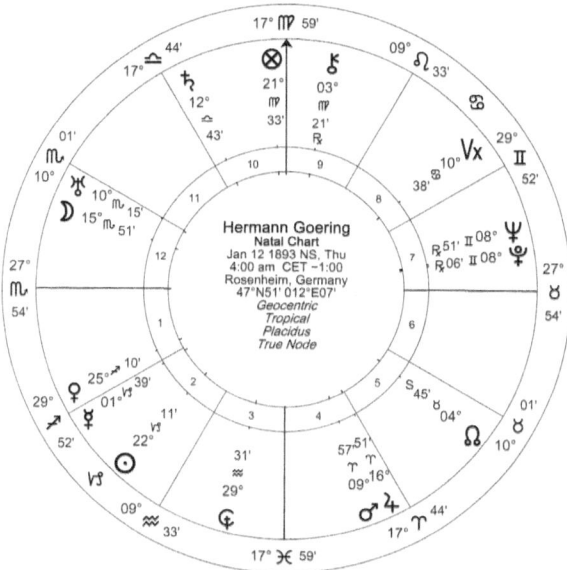

Hermann Goering, second in command in Nazi Germany, had a close conjunction between Neptune and Pluto. His Saturn/Neptune midpoint was 10 Leo 48 and his Saturn/Pluto midpoint was 10 Leo 25. On his cosmobiology wheel we can see that Venus and Uranus formed hard aspects to these midpoints.

Mars and Pluto, the rulers of his chart, are in a favorable aspect to each other. Mars in Aries is opposition Saturn, which could imply a fascination with death. However, Jupiter in Aries is also within orb of an opposition to Saturn, suggesting someone who had the ability to avoid the hand of justice until fate intervened.

Goering joined the Nazi Party in 1922, and his job was to set up concentration camps. The Venus and Uranus involvement in the negative Saturn/Neptune/Pluto pattern explains the sudden disruption and loss he created for so many families. In 1940, he became economic dictator of Germany. Six years later he was sentenced to death at Nuremberg at a war crimes trial. He committed suicide before his execution.

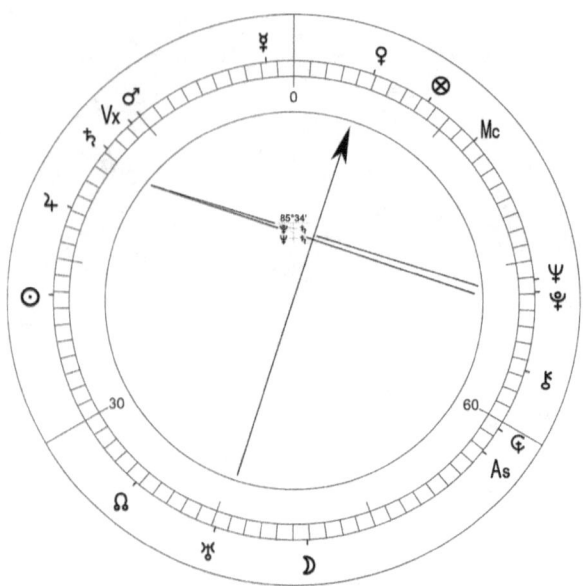

Hermann Goering Cosmobiology Dial

Not all those born in this era were murderers and villains. Neptune conjunct Pluto in Gemini can be seen in the charts of many fascinating communicators who chose to give rather than destroy. Two that spring to mind are Charlie Chaplin and Maurice Chevalier, both talented actors with musical gifts.

Both had the Neptune-Pluto conjunction, with approximately four degrees orb. Chevalier had Mercury and Venus in Libra trine the conjunction, plus Mars, Jupiter, and the Moon in Sagittarius in opposition to the conjunction. Despite hardships, he achieved great success.

However, Chaplin had Mercury semisquare and Uranus sesquiquadrate the conjunction, plus Mars square Saturn from the seventh to ninth houses. Although considered an artistic genius, Chaplin had a very hard life, including exile, which required great perseverance, and four marriages, in order to achieve the love and peace he sought.

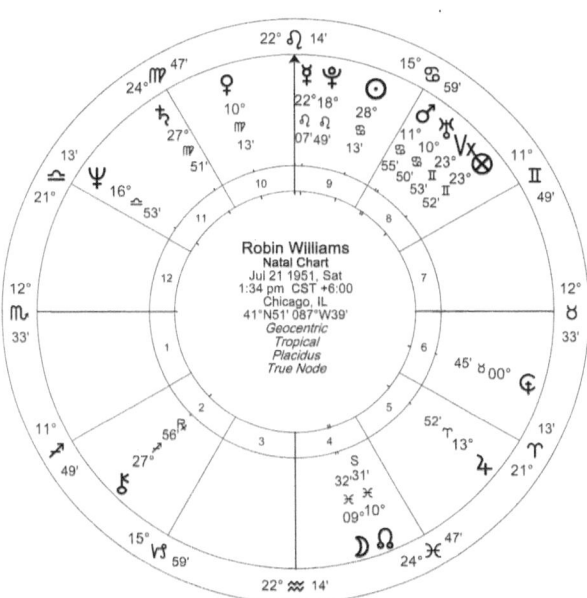

Robin Williams, The Sad Clown

To label Robin Williams a comic genius is a huge understatement. He was so loved worldwide that for many his death was felt as a personal loss.

The power and sharpness of his mind surpassed all borders worldwide (Pluto, ruler of his chart, conjunct Mercury and the Midheaven in Leo in the ninth house). Who can forget his movie portrayal of "Mrs. Doubtfire," the maternal and loving but sad father (Sun in the Pisces decanate of Cancer, quincunx Chiron).

An outstanding feature of Robin's chart is Mars conjunct Uranus in Cancer in the eighth house, which is semisquare Mercury (dynamic, explosive, machine gun responses and communications). The conjunction is also trine the Moon and North Node in Pisces in the fourth house and square Jupiter in Aries in the fifth (brilliant creative success).

However, the Mars-Uranus combination shows emotional aggression buried in the eighth house and kept private with his Scorpio Ascendant. It is not uncommon for suicide to be the result of anger and aggression directed at self, and Robin's chosen suicide method of hanging is consistent with his aggressive frustration.

If only he had discussed his feelings with a professional astrologer before taking action. At the time of his death on August 11, 2014, Robin's secondary progressed Sun at 29 Virgo 02 was opposition the fixed star Scheat (the drowning degree). It had passed his natal Saturn (27 Virgo 52) during the previous twelve months and was applying to his progressed Saturn, which is a limiting period for anyone—at any age.

Those born with Sun in fairly close proximity behind natal Saturn will experience the faster moving secondary progressed Sun conjunction to natal Saturn and the slow moving progressed Saturn, not necessarily in that order. Robin's natal Sun (in Cancer) was sextile his natal Saturn (in Virgo) at birth. His secondary progressed Sun was conjunct natal Saturn on June 1, 2013, but would not conjoin his progressed Saturn until February 28, 2021. Robin was already in this trough of "learning through hardship" a period that is renowned for health problems, especially if it occurs when people are older rather than younger.

At what age the conjunctions occur depends of course on the exact distance between the Sun and Saturn and also whether Saturn was retrograde at birth. Only a percentage of the population will experience this cycle in their lifetime.

Robin was not found until 11:55 a.m. on August 11, 2014, and had been dead for some time. From research done I have speculated the time of death as 5:55 a.m.

Robin's natal Ascendant in Scorpio is in a close semisquare to his natal Saturn and Chiron (the wounded healer). His secondary progressed Ascendant at 28 Sagittarius 37 had been conjunct his natal Chiron for many months and his progressed Moon at 25 Gemini 44 was applying to the opposition of this conjunction.

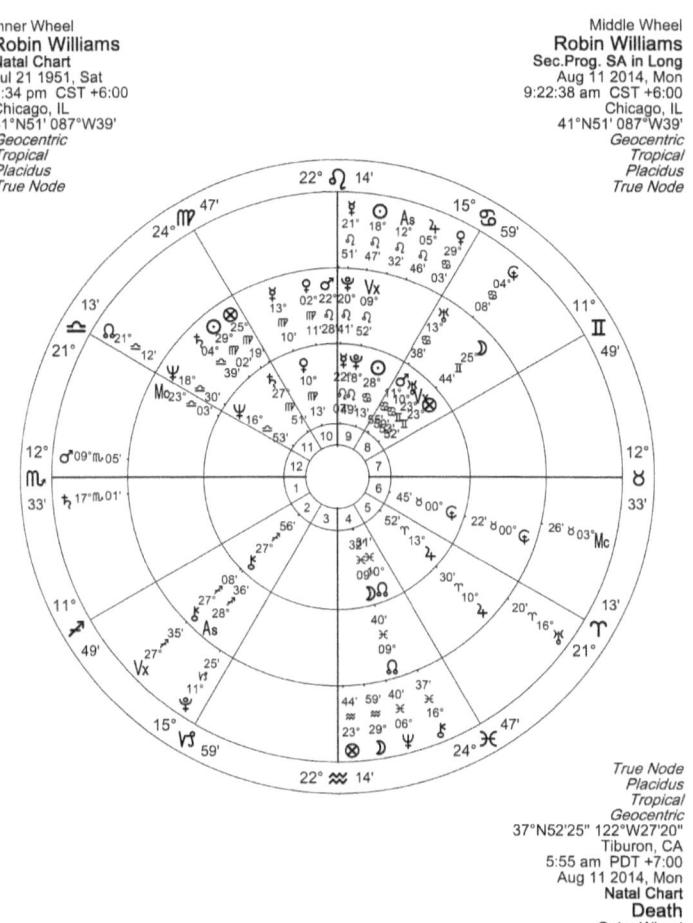

His progressed Sun and natal Saturn formed a T-square to this opposition.

Transiting Pluto conjunct the Saturn/Neptune midpoint was conjunct Robin's natal Mars in the eighth for the whole month of July 2014.

The Mars/Saturn midpoint can be interpreted as intense work, focus, cutting of ties, or the cutting of an energy source (death). Because of the involvement of Mars, it is naturally a much faster

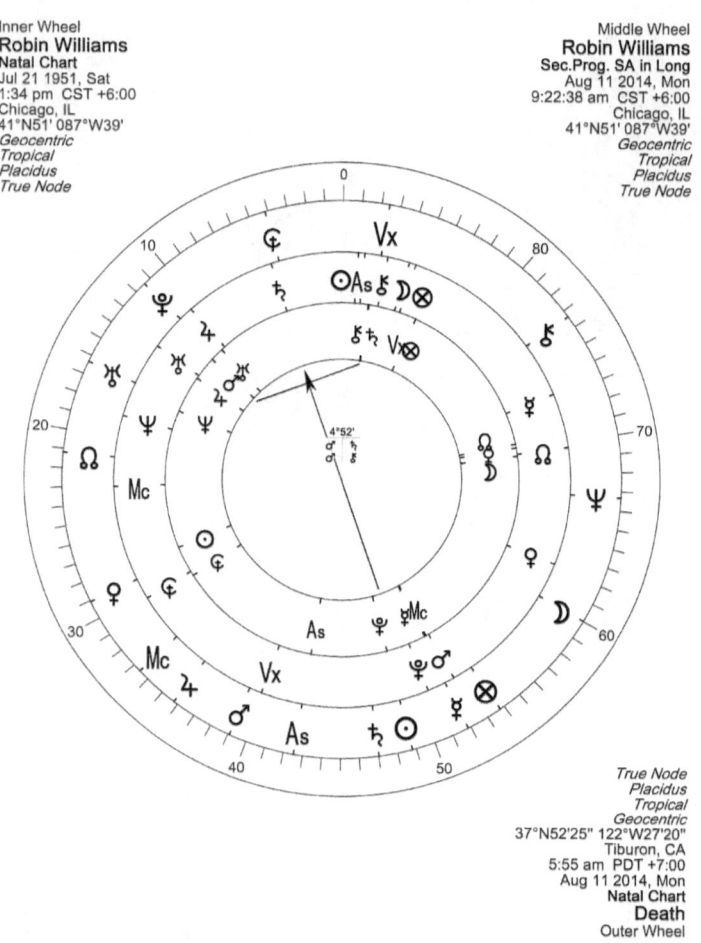

transiting midpoint than Saturn/Neptune. On August 11, 2014, the date of Robin's death, transiting Mars/Saturn was at 13 Scorpio 01 conjunct his natal Ascendant, which in turn aspected his natal Saturn and Chiron.

Reinhold Ebertin interprets Mars/Saturn = Ascendant as "A person whose advancement in life takes place with great difficulty only, obstacles or inhibitions caused by other people, illness, separation, mourning and bereavement."

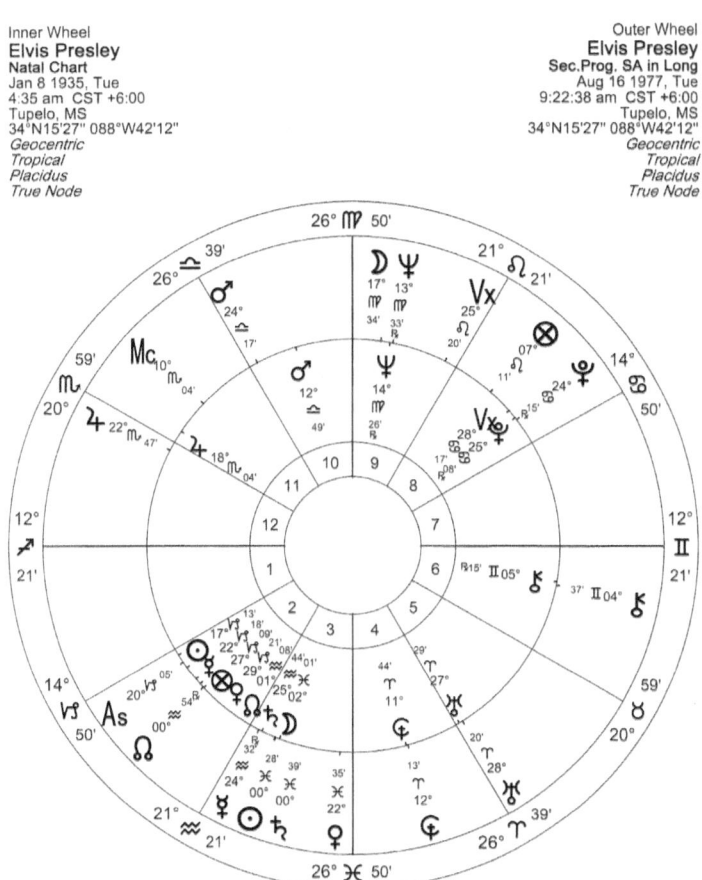

When examining Robin's chart in depth, his extraordinary suffering is apparent. Without confiding in others to gain an alternative perspective, it can be understood why he could not imagine another course of action at that time.

Elvis Presley and Secondary Progressions

Another interesting case in point is Elvis Presley, whose natal Sun at 17 Capricorn 44 was even closer behind his natal Saturn at 25 Aquarius 45. His progressed Sun was conjunct natal Saturn on December 12, 1972, which he weathered, but with declining health.

On the day of his sudden death, August 16, 1977, Elvis' progressed Sun had already changed sign to 0 Pisces 28 and his progressed Saturn was 0 Pisces 40, only twelve minutes of orb from the exact conjunction, which occurred after his death on November 4, 1977.

After such brilliantly successful careers, both Robin Williams and Elvis Presley in their own way, had chosen escapism as a way of dealing with the sense of rejection and limitation that this cycle brings. Robin chose suicide; Elvis made lifestyle choices which led to his demise.

A good discussion with a professional astrologer would have provided extra tools for both entertainers to deal with the circumstances in which they found themselves. Also some hope as to when the difficult patterns would improve, not necessarily to change their circumstances, but at least to feel better about this phase of their lives.

Data Source

All data from AsroDataBank, with the exception of speculative time of death for Robin Williams.

Astrology as a Ten-Dimensional Science

By Pamela J. Fernsler

ABSTRACT: Astrology has long been dismissed from the realm of science. Speculating on why this is so, there are a number of reasons why this most ancient of sciences has been orphaned. One primary perspective is that astrology has been used for non-scientific purposes, and relegated to mere fortune-telling, or astrolatry. Another is that astrology too heavily embraces effect to the exclusion of cause. Science by its own broad definition is the study of that which we know and which we strive to understand. In Latin it was defined as knowledge. Astrology is the father of astronomy, and now, with the reconnection of metaphysics with theoretical physics, an opportunity exists for it to be regarded anew in the recently derived field of noetics.

Two definitions are required before engaging upon a discussion of this paper's title. These are what astrology is, and what a dimension is. Also, there are no visuals; they are unnecessarily cumbersome, and one should be free of visual definitions to create one's own images. *You, the reader* must own them, not rent them from the presenter. Please feel free to take this paper and add your own images, according to your own inherent realizations.

There are various perceptions of astrology in our modern times, but they are not the definition. Astrology is currently meant as a study of the influence of the Sun, planets and their satellites upon the Earth. A corollary to this is the influence not only upon physical objects such as trees, metals, human bodies, plants, and animals but upon the unseen essence of each category. This influence is ultimately directed to humanity and can be studied mundanely and esoterically. To prefer mundane over esoteric or vice versa does not give as complete an understanding of these influences. Whether one allocates astrology to belief or truth, to fatalism or enlightened expression, the influences have been proven and evolved at least over three millennia throughout the entire world.[1] *Astrology is the study of relationships between moments of time* based on a unique point of view concerning how time works. Astrology's foundation is the knowledge of this concept of time. Time is dimensional—mundanely it is linear, but esoterically it is instant, there and yet not there, a participatory element.

Defining a Dimension

If we define a dimension as a fixed vibration of composite energies working synchronously to produce a set reality, then we can argue demonstrably that each realm, defined by such as the Para Vidya in the Mundak Upanishad, the Kabbala of the Hebrews, or *The Secret Doctrine* by H. P. Blavatsky, is a dimension acting upon our perceived reality. The trick is for us to recognize it and participate in it.

Given this, we can see astrology as a science of mathematical biology and dimensional entanglement.

Ancient sciences were part of a cultural whole, what we today teach in our schools as interdisciplinary studies—showing how one subject can be part of, or affect, another subject. It is not a far leap to see that the ancient sciences agreed on the existence of multi-dimensional realities.

A good basic reference for this is found in *The Tao of Physics* by Fritjof Capra. He writes: "The idea of participation instead of observation has been formulated in modern physics only recently, but it is an idea which is well-known to any student of mysticism. Mystical knowledge can never be obtained just by observation, but only by full participation with one's whole being."[2] The Upanishads say, "Where there is a duality, as it were, there one sees another; there one smells another; there one tastes another. . . . But where everything has become just one's own self, then whereby and whom would one see? Then whereby and whom would one smell? Then whereby and whom would one taste?"[3]

Modern physics does not go that far, but quantum theory has abolished the notion of basic objects that are separated and has come to see the universe as interconnected physically and mentally.

On a lower level we can observe animal behavior and call it instinct. They are all "hardwired" to behave in a specific manner, given specific situations. Some animals have shown that they can actually conceptualize and arrive at rudimentary (to our way of seeing intelligence) conclusions. I can tell my cat that it is hot outside and that opening the window is a bad idea. The cat insists on experiencing that for himself. He is not satisfied that the fact is all there is. In order to understand the heat, he wants to experience all the elements that not only comprise heat, but its influence on him. In that way, that mystical way, does he understand, through synthesizing all factors, that it is not a good idea to be influenced by such heat, and he turns away from the window. He will do this hours later in hopes that it is cooler and that I will either open the window for cooler air to enter or let him out. He knows that it can and does change, and is ready for the results that can come of it.

All animals know that participation and observation bring a complete understanding and *that it can change*. They do not ever compartmentalize. Given that humans are animalistic, it wonders me (Pennsylvania Dutch for "it puzzles me) why we deny such an integral part of our being in preference for not incorporating our own type of animalism, rather than accepting its elemental integration into our essence of what it means to be human.

An Integration of Influences

Astrology is an integration of influences. To interpret someone's birth influences is to integrate all the influences into one composite story. Sort of like using ingredients in baking to produce one object called a muffin, or pie, or cookie. To interpret someone's influences throughout life through the use of astrology is to comprehend the way the different dimensions act upon this person physically, emotionally, mentally, and spiritually.

A key phrase must be brought to light here: "act upon." We generally perceive ourselves as a solid form of matter; without the appropriate air and fluids, however, this solid form could not survive. "Act upon" implies we are receptors rather than initiators. Yet with all the vibratory influences that we adapt to each and every second, we are initiators in utilizing these ten dimensions we are born into. The second that we take that first breath after being born, is the second that the influence of the planets and sun, at that precise moment, enable us to move through these dimensions in a particular set of ways.

We know that the universe is comprised of vibrations. We have separated their vibrations into sensory categories: sound, color, heat, light, and so forth. We know what happens to the body when certain of these sensory vibrations is activated. The dimensions represented by each solar object in our solar system also are comprised by vibrations, often composite rather than singular. When we recognize these composite essences, we can *consciously* move *through* them as well as simultaneously reacting to their influence on us.

Astrology, in its most esoteric form, teaches us how to do that.

The astrologers who compartmentalize these influences do no service to the inquirer who is hoping and looking for results that can propel him or her forward toward their particular desires. Such readings leave the inquirer as only an observer, when it is also participation and application of these readings that will satisfy—proper and full entanglement.

The astrologer who knows how to synthesize the individual, is the one you want, the true scientist of quantum dimensions. A certain empathy for each individual, a certain experience of the individual on what is currently known as a psychic plane is a must for this kind of astrologer. It involves reaching into that unknown and integrating with what he or she sees in this individual's chart. It involves, to oversimplify, dimensional integration.

A Brief History

Before we go on to the exploration of the dimensions, a brief history of astrology might be in order. There were not always twelve signs of the zodiac in Western astrology, or twenty-eight houses in Arabic astrology, and so on. Before that, there was a mathematical system of eights. There were eight directions, eight planets or lights, and eight houses, and much of math was based on a system of eight. Dr. Patrice Guinard, Ph.D., cites various ancient astrologers such as Marcus Manilius, Seraphion of Antioch, Thrasyllos and Antiochos, plus the Brihat-Samhita. Nonetheless she tells us in her "Dominion" paper that "it is possible that the model of eight houses was organized in relation with the system of elements and elemental values, in a relatively distant epoch, one that antedates the first hermetical astrological texts (ca. 250-200 B.C)[4]

Before that, only the Sun's, the Moon's and Venus' influence on plants, geophysical elements and such were regarded, and not even applied to humanity because of the concept of free will. Humanity at that very ancient time considered itself not applicable to these influences, but as we suspect yet can't prove, they experienced these dimensions on a daily basis within themselves, using only the influences on the earth and plants, minerals, and such to determine the uses of lesser material vibrations. They regarded the astrology from other planets as too complicated to pursue.

When eight planets were finally considered to have an influence on the human body, mathematics got a lot more detailed. From Ptolemy's *Almagest,* these eight "planets" were regarded as the Moon, Mercury, Venus, Mars, Jupiter, Saturn, and fixed stars such as Sirius and the Pleiades. As each body of the solar system was observed, certain qualities of influence came to light, and thus these bodies were personified as gods or goddesses and given names, a kind of short-hand to let people know what to expect. Was Mars a pie, a cake, a muffin, or strawberry parfait? A brilliant fictional example of interdimensional movement can be found in *The HitchHiker's Guide to the Galaxy,* in the Tea Drive of the ship. Another example of consciously moving through a dimensional gateway is from the TV show and movie, *Star Gate.*

How Planets Affect Us

The question now begged is: how *do* the planets affect us? We all now know how light through the eyes can affect various parts of the brain, given a certain angle of beaming; we know how sound affects our bodies in the lowest ranges. Our astronauts experience how gravity increases as we travel at great speeds to escape Earth, and how magnetism works, and what certain types of radiation do to the body. So we know our bodies are affected by these planetary qualities.

But what about those qualities from other planets? Are they "third party"? Is their effect on us subliminal and hardly worth considering? Perhaps in a physical sense, no. That is, if we limit ourselves to a three-dimensional model. But this paper is considering ten dimensions as represented by the esoteric essences of each planet or celestial object in our solar system. These essences are in turn, represented by one primary principle, e.g. Mars as the Principle of Dynamic Energy.[5]

Most living organisms either live in water or are composed mainly of water. Water is the best conduit for dimensional access. A solid is not an amenable conduit (at least on this planet) for dimensional access, and air is too dissipated, especially the greater the altitude. Dimensional access does depend on gravitational pull, electromagnetic waves, weak and strong nuclear fields. Take Jupiter as an access to a particular "dimension." The air/gas composition is influenced by a powerful spin creating a powerful gravitational field, along with its nuclear fields, comprise a stable access to the Jovian dimension.

The clearest metaphysical circuitry produced on this world is the kabbala. It has ten dimensions and twenty-two pathways. Our physical solar system has a total of ten major bodies that we use, excluding Earth: the Sun, Earth's Moon, and the eight other worlds, regardless of how they are categorized. We currently use twelve zodiacal signs, and combining them with those ten solar objects we have twenty-two major pathways influencing us. Each of these objects is a quantum gateway to a specific composite quality, and this is what influences we humans, and to some extent, our animal cousins.

I mentioned mathematical biology at the beginning of this paper. In *The Book of Knowledge: The Keys of Enoch,* section 2-0-6 states that "The Torah Or is the celestial song of the Kaballah, the Eternal science of the many universes … [It] is the complete computer code from Alpha to Omega, for all sacred sciences extending the biophysical to the astrophysical… [and] cannot be limited to the first five books of the Bible, because the building of the foundation stone, the Great Pyramid, is mathematically given in the Book of Isaiah, and the Energy Vehicle of Becoming, numbered with the stars, is given in Daniel and other prophetic sections."[6] This may throw some light on why a computer picked out prophecies mathematically, and were written in volumes called *The Bible Code*.[7]

"The Torah is the mathematics separating the sacred chemistry from the secular chemistry," the book further states. "It is the coding which connects spiritual universes to physical ones."[8] Enoch explained to J. J. Hurtak,[9] the writer of *The Keys of Enoch*, that the Sanskrit and Tibetan languages were the vertical alignments of all the biological languages working on A-line vertical movement throughout the human body. Accordingly, the pictographic Egyptian and Chinese languages were the horizontal alignments of the biochemical languages working on B-line horizontal movement. The Hebrew "Language of Light" was chosen to synthesize the cosmology of this present cycle of creation."[10]

The Keys of Enoch is also full of esoteric and metaphysical writings, along with the future science. This book is not written for beginners in basic science. Section 2-1-1 might be the best introduction to this future science which corroborates the ten-dimensional aspect of astrology.

Ten-dimensional Access

But how are we, our bodies, open to ten-dimensional access? What is *our* conduit? Here is where astrology and the kaballah entangle. Our ductless glands are these doorknobs, if you will.

The primary ductless glands are, starting from the crown of the head descending, the pineal, the pituitary, thyroid, thymus, spleen and the two adrenals. All of these work together. Max Heindel, in a small book titled *The Mystery of the Ductless Glands* writes this: "The pituitary body is ruled by Uranus which is the octave of Venus, the ruler of the solar plexus where the seed atom of the vital body is located. Thus Venus keeps the gate of the vital fluid coming direct from the Sun through the spleen, and Uranus is the warder of the gate where enters the physical food, and it is the blending of these two streams which produces the latent power stored up in our vital body until converted to dynamic energy by the martial desire nature."[11] They are gates, they are doorknobs to dimensions represented by Venus and Uranus.

Briefly, the pineal is ruled by Neptune, the pituitary by Uranus, the thyroid by Mercury, the thymus by Venus, the spleen by the sun, and the adrenals by Jupiter. The dimensions represented by these solar objects are the physical world (adrenals) by Jupiter, the etheric region (spleen) by the Sun; the desire realm (thymus) by Venus; the world of thought dimension by Mercury (thyroid); the world or dimension of life spirit by Uranus (pituitary) and the world of divine spirit by Neptune (pineal). You may notice that Mars, the Moon, Saturn, and Pluto were not assigned ductless glands. They are assigned to organs such as stomach, mind, and heart and to various fluids of the body. They are doorknobs to more abstract concepts.

Among humanity are those of us having a little-known psychic ability known as transentience and it is paired with something more familiarly known as prescience, also thought of as a time sense. *Dr. Who*, a time-traveler from a world of time masters on a beloved British show of the same name, represents those people. But I assure you, we do not have two hearts like our favorite Gallifreyan. *Dr. Who* shows us on a concrete level, better than anything else, how time and space are not separated, how all is interconnected. Can transentients take their physical bodies through space? The composite vibrations of the physical body are limited, but they are not as restricted as we think. Every day, every hour we move through dozens of realities—ours as well as those with whom we interact.

Other than the glands being our doorknobs we have evolved several finer vehicles, if you will, to enable us to move through dimensional realities. Esoteric clairvoyants and sensitives have written these down over the centuries, and continue to write about it and teach it in long-standing mystery schools. In addition to the physical body, we have finer bodies that each of these mystery schools teaches from a different perspective. Again, from the Rosicrucian Fellowship teachings presented by Max Heindel, these are named emotional body, vital body, physical body, and mind.[12] If glands are the doorknobs, these are the gates. And transentients like myself practice this kind of travel through time and space using the ductless glands and the finer human vehicles.

The question begs: how can this be done on a material plane? It can't. This simple answer does one of two things, like the proverbial flow chart. It says "then it isn't real." Or it adds a second question, where can it be done? As you have heard earlier, in quantum physics, one can't measure without also participating in the measurement. The mind is where it happens. The two ductless glands, pituitary and pineal, are both the triggers of such activity. The larger they are, the more disciplined in hermetic sciences the person can be. Such discipline is hard to develop, and so you have people who can see and hear and even smell as through some kind of long distance tube or microscopic lens, but have no participation, and feel helpless about their condition, even resenting it or fearing it. The discipline necessary to USE these abilities comes through training not only the body but the mind—both working together. The only academies currently available for such discipline are the various mystery schools. You will not get a Ph.D. in psychic accomplishment at any university I am aware of, here in the West. You may get one in parapsychology, but knowledge without both able application and comprehension is like a musician having mastered technique but not interpretation, the union of which sets him or her apart as a master.

Some are born with these two glands already enlarged beyond what is considered usual. These individuals must then acquire understanding and technique, to use their native talent. Like the artistic painter who captures the essence of what is seen, it still requires hand-eye coordination, muscle memory, and an understanding of the times in which he/she lives. The clockwise or counter-clockwise movement of those seven major centers of the body determines whether one is at the mercy of so-named psychic energy or can direct willingly this energy. When the energy of each center is moving clockwise this mastery is attainable. Then these two glands can work together to glean insight into that which most of the world calls immaterial. They are the translators between etheric and material dimensions.

Traveling to Other Realms

How does one travel in mind to the solar planets, moons and suns? Desire/construction/action = result. The astrology chart also shows if you can, and if so, how you can. Everyone's astrology chart is the way their inner kabbalah has evolved. Each planet has a sign and a house. Sometimes there is more than one planet to a house or a sign. Not every sign and house need be occupied. Each planet has a progressive or retrograde direction at birth. And depending on the latitude, there may a house of more than thirty degrees that starts at the end of one sign, enfolds an entire thirty-degree sign, and begins a new house in the sign after that.

Think of your trip to the other realms as you being the spaceship. You have in your mind the dashboard containing the essential aids to get there: ignition, lights, acceleration, deceleration, temperature control, and so on. The astrology chart as a whole is you. The signs, houses, directions are the ignition, the option of motions, and the navigation system. They tell you what vibrational ranges are required to get to your destination, or what prevents you from getting there. Not all people are meant to be put in the driver's seat at first—there may be a waiting period, or it may not be applicable in this life.

Some psychics—you can think of them really as dimensional accessors—have more than one ability, though they may not all be at full power. For the uninformed, there are seven categories of dimensional accessors. Some of these terms you are already familiar with: telepath, empathy (medical talents, animal communicators), telekinetic, clairsentient, psychometer (dowsers, earth sensitives), transentient, time sentient. Within these, there are subcategories. Transentient and chronosentient are usually paired together, like the pituitary and pineal glands. Each of these has a modicum of the others as well. Most people think of clairvoyants, they who see. There are also clairaudients, they who hear, and then there are those who can smell. Most people think of telepaths as those who can read minds. Believe me when I say that most people broadcast their thoughts so loudly that even someone who is just intuitive can pick up somehow what someone else is thinking—or feeling.

Separately, the first five abilities don't get you to the other dimensions, to the dimension represented by each world and solar light. In combination with transentience and chronosentience, they do, and add to the experience. Respectively speaking, the five lower centers of the body are responsible for harmonization, so that the pituitary and pineal glands can have that green light for go, on whatever level is accessible.

Neptune and Uranus, the higher octaves of Mercury and Venus, are your MindGates. They affect your pineal and pituitary glands. Look where your Neptune and Uranus are placed, plus what mathematical aspects they form with others, if any, at birth. Some may attain psychic ability later in life, as well. If Neptune is in the ninth house of time-space sensitivity, and Uranus is in the third house of telepathy, opposite each other, the opportunity for equilibrium in direction between the two is open, with training; but if no training, one has a person who can travel to places he or she doesn't understand and "hear" what's being thought. If Uranus is in Scorpio, there is no distance too great to comprehend what may be occurring, and possibly participating in it. Your chart is your vehicle; it can be an ultra-glider or a helicopter.

There are intelligent beings on every world and in the sun, in our solar system. It is not always necessary to have a material layer to exist on a material world. Intelligent beings may vibrate normally at much higher rates than will allow for the lower, crasser rates of solidification on a material plane. This has been written about for thousands of years, the works changing to adapt to the changing perspectives of the human race.

It is written by those who can see these worlds and beings; but their interpretations are not always clear, and are subject to the way their chart allows them to see things. It is as was said at the beginning of this paper—all things interface, entanglement. To believe in just one way of perceiving something is sadly very one-dimensional. When one synthesizes what is presented, like a puzzle, when gets a greater understanding than simply choosing one segment and announcing it is the entirety. We all know in this day and age how silly that is, and yet there are those who persist in this preference.

To find out what each chart contains for psychic and intuitive ability, I use the Rosicrucian Fellowship software. This delineates plainly what the abilities are, among other things. The software does not give the interpretation. That is up to the astrologer or those who can read their own chart.

Time and Space

Let me return to the stretching of the mind into time and space. We have seen that we can travel to other worlds and see what's there, even communicate, if the skill is there. What about travel through time? Quantum physics has given us a confusing look at the nature of time. Material time appears linear. Mental time, such as memory, is immediate. Prayer and meditation are residual at various levels of time perception. How does one travel in time?

There have been many fun stories about physically doing it, but our bodies have not yet become refined enough to do that for now. We must do it mentally, or with the assistance of another being who can alter vibrations for us so that we can temporarily move through time as well as through materials. We can take our vital life force, desire body and mind along for the ride, but not yet physically. The closest any writer has really come to it is H. G. Wells' time machine, based on vibrational speed in one place, rather than motion through space, like Dr. Who. This was Western humanity's first attempt to reintegrate metaphysics with material science, since the European Renaissance. The time after World War II was one great clash of material scientists who segregated and compartmentalized knowledge without the essence of life that enlivens knowledge.

Some say there is no future to see because we haven't created it yet. Some say there are many futures, like parallel universes, to handle everyone's thoughts. There is a way to travel to the future and get a glimpse, if you do it in connection with all the persons you are, were, and expect to be. Harmonizing with that will attract you to that period of time where there is a reality. Again, time is fluid and elastic, and does not depend on linear measurement. Time is something in which to participate and experience. It is not meant to be measured.

In making a case for astrology to take its place among the sciences, this inquiry reveals several salient points in its favor.

Fluidity, gravity, electro-magnetism, and strong and weak nuclear fields are each world's composite vibrations, like a particular key for a particular lock, which demonstrates what one must vibrate to, in order to access that world. Each world has its own keynote and rhythm, its own principle.

Astrology must be perceived as mathematical biology and dimensional entanglement, designed for traveling through time and space relative to any individual at any desired time. Time is three-fold: linear, immediate, and residual. Time and space are participatory, a synthesis of experience, not a separation nor compartmentalization.

In order to experience the dimensions emanated by the sun and solar objects, one must harmonize with, or think of being, the essence of the celestial object. The water energies are the best to allow the greatest range of harmonization. Using our immaterial body layers we can access immaterial layers of other objects—Sun, Moon, planets, their satellites.

Attunement of the five lower energy centers, ductless glands, of the body, activate the pituitary and pineal together to go forth. Working with the pineal and pituitary glands, and direction from Neptune and Uranus, we find how much we can or can't do. Each person's astrology chart will indicate this.

By combining the physical and the metaphysical, the sciences of astrology and astronomy may find its partnership in the new science of noetics. Its practice will open new insights onto our solar system and our own expansion and evolution as humanity.

Endnotes

[1] Cf. Guinard, Patrice, Ph.D. *Dominion or the System of 8 Houses*. part 2/2, Chap. 4: Origin of Dominion and History of the Eight Houses, Dec. 1999. http://cura.free.fr/11domi2e.html.
[2] Cf. Capra, Fritjof. *The Tao of Physics*, 5th ed., chap. 10, 41.
[3] Cf. Hume, Robert Ernst, M.A., Ph.D. *The 13 Principal Upanishads*, 46.
[4] Op.Cit., Guinard (ref. to 1.).
[5] Cf. Bacher, Elman. *Studies in Astrology*, table of contents for vols 1 and 2.
[6] Op.cit. Hurtak, J.J. *The Keys of Enoch*. 227.
[7] Cf. "The Bible Code," *Theomatics*, www.biblecode.com/whatis.html
[8] Op.cit. *The Keys of Enoch*. 228.
[9] J.J. Hurtak regards himself not as an author, but as a messenger and conduit for the Enochian transference of higher science (or future science). The book used for reference is the 4th edition 1996. Higher math and formulae are used in this text.
[10] Op.cit. *The Keys of Enoch*, 230.
[11] Cf. Heindel, Max (with A Student). *The Mystery of the Ductless Glands*, chap. 8, 82.
[12] Cf. Heindel, Max, *The Occult Principles of Health and Healing*, 11.

The Astrology Code

By Michael Bergen

ABSTRACT: This article is a summary of my book, *The Astrology Code*, which is the result of twenty-one years of meditation and research on the nature of astrology and its techniques. The research was done in a manner similar to the Gauquelin studies by collecting large numbers of birth charts for multiple categories of people and then testing an astrological technique. The Gauquelins studied one technique using twelve categories of people, whereas my study involved twenty techniques using eighty categories of people. Most of the findings confirm our common understanding of the zodiac signs and planets. However, as with the Gauquelin study, which showed that planets are stronger after, rather than before, passing the diurnal axis points, some of my findings contradict conventional understanding. For instance, Virgo is shown to be a most unvirginly sign and Neptune is revealed to have a materialistic rather than spiritual influence.

In my recent book, *The Astrology Code*, I display the results of seven years of research testing almost every Western astrology technique currently in use by astrologers. To do this, I used 12,566 human birth charts, which were collected by Lois Rodden. I organized the birth charts into eighty different study groups ranging in size from sixty-nine to 1,240 people.

The groups vary widely in nature, providing a great source of comparison within the study itself. Almost every group showed a distinct pattern emphasizing particular zodiac signs and planets. Groups that are similar in nature often had the same sign or planet dominant across the spectrum of techniques studied.

For instance, the following groups were all dominant in Saturn: AIDS, birth defect, infant mortality, near-death experiencers, sex abuse victims, and stroke victims. Also, Scorpio was dominant for astrologers, mystics, psychiatrists, and spiritual teachers.

Statistical Analysis Methods

The statistical analysis for this project was done in two ways. The first method was to compile the raw data for each technique studied, then calculate the positions on a Normal Curve without regard for planetary cycles or population trends. This was done by comparing the actual results to the same expected value for every planetary position in a study group. If the result for a finding was in the upper or lower five percent, it was considered significant.

For instance, there are 216 people in the Military study group. The average number of people with the Moon in each zodiac sign is eighteen (216 divided by 12). In this case, twenty-five people with the Moon in any sign would be in the upper five percent of the Normal Curve. In the Military study group, twenty-nine people have their Moon in the sign of Capricorn and it is therefore considered a significant finding.

This method is used to show the dominant trends for each study group since it best reflects the way astrology works. Astrologers only consider whether people with a certain factor have a particular trait. Astrological interpretations are not altered if a planet spends a disproportionate amount of time in a particular sign position or if more of the population is born at a particular time or season. A person with the Sun in Leo will be just as much a Leo regardless of the proportion of the population with the Sun in Leo. In turn, a group of people dominant in Leo, such as models, will demonstrate attention-seeking qualities, regardless of the group's comparative population.

The second method was to compare the raw data for each technique studied with control groups that are best suited to the data. The sum of each planetary position and aspect for every study group is compared to its expected value, which is based on the amount of time planets spend in each position or aspect as well as the population density for the study group. This method was used to calculate all numerical probabilities of each event occurring. In the book, there are over sixty-five findings with odds above one in 1,000, which is equivalent to tossing a coin on its head ten times in a row.

In the first chapter of the book I attempt to show how the universe is organized and how the planets and zodiac reflect this pattern in our solar system. The urge to exist in many forms and experiences caused our self to initiate the first duality: existing as undifferentiated inward awareness vs. individualized conscious expression, symbolized by the Moon and Sun. This duality gave rise to the other three dualities: self vs. other, symbolized by Mars and Venus; self vs. group, symbolized by Jupiter and Saturn; and self vs. whole, symbolized by Neptune and Uranus.

These four dualities are also expressed in the zodiac's four quadrants (see illustration on the next page). The first quadrant symbolizes the duality of individual expression, which is experienced most intensely during childhood as the struggle between the need for inner security and outward development. The second quadrant symbolizes the duality of relations, which is experienced most intensely during youth as the struggle between being competitive with and communing with others. The third quadrant symbolizes the duality of group involvement, which is experienced most intensely during adulthood as the struggle between being independent and conforming to groups. The fourth quadrant symbolizes the duality of universal purpose, which is

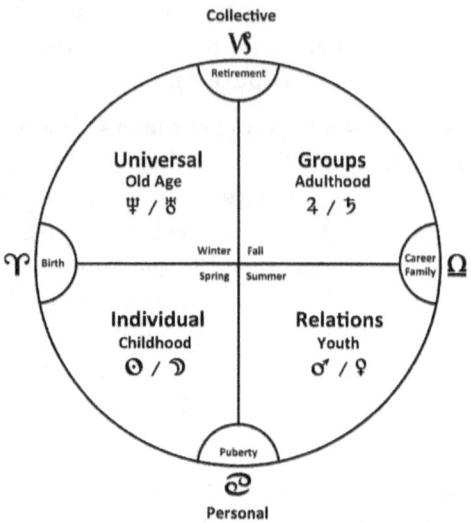

Four Dualities in the Four Quadrants

experienced most intensely during old age as the struggle between being focused on personal dreams or collective needs.

Every feature of the zodiac is analyzed statistically in the tropical zodiac, which uses the Sun's position at the spring equinox as its starting point for Aries. I studied the quadrants, the four elements, the three modes, the six pairs of opposite signs, and the twelve signs.

In the study on the zodiac signs, I analyzed the 1st harmonic, the 9th harmonic, and the 108 1/9th portions of the signs. Outer planets were not used (Uranus, Neptune, Pluto, and Chiron) since they move so slowly that all the study groups were strong in just a few signs in the 1st harmonic. In the book, full statistical results and descriptions are shown for the individual seven planets as well as their sum total in each sign. Most results are consistent with traditional meanings for the signs.

In following chapters, the results of the studies on planetary aspects and planets on the four axis points are shown (Ascendant, Descendant, Midheaven, and Imum Coeli). For aspects, I used the 36th harmonic, which is the first division of the zodiac containing all of the major traditional aspects as well as the nonile, 1/9th aspect. This study shows that two planets have a meaningful relationship when in any of the thirty-six points spaced every ten degrees from each other around the zodiac.

In the course of studying the many planetary cycles, I noticed that the annual, daily, lunar and aspect cycles all follow the same pattern. There is a trough, where reflection and planning occur, then birth, where plans are initiated. Then there is a climax at the peak of the cycle, where goals are accomplished, and a conclusion, when goals are finalized and released.

These four moments represent the critical points of any cycle and each initiates its own phase or stage of existence. Birth initiates the individual stage of existence, where we take action on our motivations. The climax initiates the relations stage of existence, where we fulfill our goals and interact with others. The conclusion represents the end of a personal focus and initiates the group stage of existence, where we make use of our efforts for the collective well being of our family and community. The trough of the cycle initiates the universal stage of existence, where we resolve the past and look forward to the future.

	Birth	Climax	Conclusion	Trough
Annual Cycle:	Spring Equinox	Summer Solstice	Fall Equinox	Winter Solstice
Diurnal Cycle:	Ascendant	Midheaven	Descendant	Imum Coeli
Lunar Cycle:	1st Q Moon	Full Moon	3rd Q Moon	New Moon
Aspect Cycle:	1st Square	Opposition	2nd Square	Conjunction

Following this are a few examples of how to apply the findings in the book to birth chart readings. Included are the charts of some famous sports figures, a comparison of Bill Gates and Steve Jobs, and studies of O. J. Simpson and Adolf Hitler.

In the final section, each group's findings are shown in detail and include a summary of the major findings. Each group's section has a summary table listing all relevant findings. Most have a noticeable theme, which strongly validates the study.

For example, actors are strong in Aquarius in both the 1st and 9th harmonics, have frequent Venus aspects, have Venus frequent on the four axis points, and are strong in the fixed mode and fixed sector. (The fixed mode represents love and stability.)

The appendices include studies on a number of topics such as the rising sign, houses, planetary rulership of signs, the sidereal zodiac, retrograde planets, midpoints, parallels, lunar phases, and the Moon's nodes. Many of these techniques are shown to have validity, but others were contradictory to astrological theory.

The following is a summary highlighting the findings:

Zodiac Quadrants

In the study of the zodiac's quadrants, people with largely personal goals are strong in quadrants one and two. Sports showed up strongly in quadrant one, verifying the idea that this quadrant is about personal ambition and asserting one's will. Quadrants two and three contain many affliction groups, which were strongest in the signs Virgo and Scorpio (these are the quadrants where the Sun is diminishing in strength for the majority of the population). Most of the groups strong in quadrant four demonstrate mental skills and seek to affect the way we understand the world, thus having a broad and lasting influence on society.

Zodiac Elements

The study on the four elements did not reveal too much about the nature of fire and air because almost no groups were statistically strong in these elements. Instead, most of the groups that were strong by element were in earth and water. The groups strong in earth were largely performers, which is not apparently highly consistent with the element's conservative, practical nature. The groups strong in water were largely contemplative types, which is consistent with this element's private, sensitive nature.

Zodiac Modes

The groups strong in cardinal signs are full of initiative, leadership skills, and power. The groups strong in fixed signs represent love in its many positive and negative expressions. From this study, the fixed mode can be clearly seen to have been underestimated as merely representing such qualities as steadfastness and stubbornness (which are true of Taurus and Scorpio, but not as much of Aquarius and Leo). The groups strong in mutable signs mostly represent qualities of intelligence and mental activity.

Zodiac Signs

Most of the signs revealed themselves to have strength in the type of groups that astrological theory would have predicted. For instance, Aries was strong for salespeople. Taurus was strong for the groups same job ten-plus years, life long eighty-plus years, and marriage fifteen-plus years. Gemini was strong for twins. Cancer was strong for teachers K-12, child prodigy, and infant mortality. Leo was strong for models. Virgo was strong for medical practitioners. Scorpio was strong for sex symbols, mystics, psychiatrists, criminals, and the wealthy. Sagittarius was strong for scientists. Capricorn was strong for military and technical professions. Pisces was strong for artists.

However, some of the signs showed surprising results. For instance, Virgo was strong for sex abuse victims, sex offenders, sex symbols, and sex workers. Virgo also seemed to be a dumping ground for bad experiences with groups like AIDS, alcoholics, cancer, drug abuse, and obesity all being especially strong. The opposite sign, Pisces, had mostly positive groups, including life long eighty-plus years, and was weak for afflicted groups.

In addition, Aquarius was strong for groups of attractive people with relationship success such as actors, comedians, sex symbols, and marriage fifteen-plus years. This led to the conclusion that this sign actually behaves in the manner traditionally used for Libra and that planets in Libra have Aquarian traits such as rebelliousness.

Top Findings

1. Out of Body/NDE	Virgo	1 in 11,393
2. Artists	Pisces	6,766
3. Scientists	Capricorn	3,759
4. Comedians	Aquarius	3,532
5. Politicians	Pisces	2,195
6. Sex Workers	Virgo	1,237
7. Fighters	Capricorn	1,132
8. Composers	Capricorn	1,013
9. Technical	Capricorn	793
10. Children 4+	Aries	709
11. Life Long 80+ years	Pisces	523
12. Sex Abuse Victims	Virgo	467
13. Sex Symbols	Virgo	456
14. Children 4+	Taurus	441
15. Stroke	Gemini	432
16. Marriage 15+ Years	Aquarius	387
17. Sex Offenders	Virgo	350
18. Math/Physics	Capricorn	323
19. Royalty	Scorpio	312
20. Lawyers	Leo	289
21. Models	Leo	265
22. Astrologers	Leo	259
23. Inheritance	Capricorn	257
24. Singers	Taurus	202
25. Activists	Scorpio	194

Odds are by probability of being an accident, which were calculated by comparing the sum of the seven visible planets in each sign, Moon to Saturn, with expected values from control groups.

Planetary Aspects

Most of the planets revealed themselves to have strength in the type of groups that astrological theory would have predicted. The Moon is strong for those with culinary careers. Mercury is strong for brilliant-minded people and engineers. Venus is strong for child performers. Mars is strong for short-lived people and weak with long-lived people. Jupiter is strong for sex symbols. Saturn is strong for scientists, mathematicians, and physicists, as well as people in the birth defect and infant mortality groups. Uranus is strong for engineers. Neptune is strong for homicide victims. Pluto is strong for AIDS victims. Chiron is strong for medical professionals (the healers) and military staff (the wounders).

The Sun and Pluto were found to have a stronger influence when unaspected by other planets. The groups with an unaspected Sun are strong in leadership qualities: politicians, priests, professors, and salespeople. The groups with an unaspected Pluto are very powerful: fighters, sports, and royalty.

The major exception to astrological theory is the results found for Neptune. The groups corporate tycoons, criminals, business owners, military, and lawyers are all strong in Neptune. Current theory holds that Neptune represents idealism, dreams, and spirituality as well as confusion, deception, and loss. It seems that Neptune's actual influence is very personal and materialistic. The transcendence of problems such as poverty and violence is Neptune's greatest concern.

Top Findings

1. Obesity	Jupiter	1 in 1,048
2. Engineers	Mercury	442
3. Life Short 29- years	Mars	413
4. Homicide Victims	Neptune	335
5. AIDS	Pluto	304
6. Child Performers	Venus	279
7. Sex Symbols	Jupiter	167
8. Lawyers	Pluto	156

Odds are by probability of being an accident, which were calculated by comparing the sum of the 36th harmonic aspects for each planet with expected values from control groups.

The Four Major Axis Points

In the study of the planets on the four axis points, most categories fit with the traditional meanings for the planets. The Moon, representing femininity, is strong for models. The Sun, representing outer success, is strong for the wealthy and for those who lived long lives of eighty or more years. Mercury, representing facility with the hands and voice, is strong for musicians, including singers and instrumentalists.

Venus, representing the arts, pleasure, and money is strong for those with culinary careers, fashion designers, royalty, and transvestites. On the IC, Venus is strong for contemplatives such as composers and poets because these people love the privacy of their homes. Mars, representing industry and conflict, is strong for people with math and physics careers and victims of child abuse. Jupiter, representing positivity, exploration, and excess is strong for people married more than fifteen years, members of royalty, and those with careers involving criminal activity.

Uranus, representing awakening, is especially strong on the Midheaven-IC axis for insightful thinkers. Pluto, representing the hidden and taboo, is strong for sex workers such as prostitutes and porn actors. Chiron, representing wounds, is strong for murderers. Chiron is also strong on the Descendant for thinking types, showing its analytical nature.

Top Findings

1. Culinary	Venus	1 in 25,472
2. Sex Workers	Pluto	3,196
3. Royalty	Jupiter	1,099
4. Murderers	Chiron	1,080
5. Criminal Careers	Jupiter	836
6. Twins	Saturn	648

Odds are by probability of being an accident, which were calculated by comparing the sum each planet on all four Axis points with expected values from control groups

The 9th Harmonic of the Zodiac

Like the 1st harmonic study, most of the findings are consistent with what astrological theory would have predicted. For instance, Aries is strong for sex workers. Taurus is strong for alcoholics. Cancer is strong for people working in the culinary field, as well as child prodigies. Scorpio is strong for fighters, murderers, and psychiatrists. Sagittarius is strong for scientists. Capricorn is strong for military staff. Aquarius is strong for actors and people married fifteen or more years. Pisces is strong for priests. Nineteen groups were strong in the same sign(s) in both the 1st and 9th harmonics.

Signs Strong in 1st and 9th Harmonics

Actors	Aquarius
AIDS	Virgo
Alcoholics	Virgo
Business Owners	Gemini
Child Performers	Virgo and Scorpio
Child Prodigy	Cancer
Composers	Capricorn
Corporate Tycoons	Cancer
Culinary	Cancer
Homosexuals	Scorpio and Capricorn
Marriage 15+ years	Aquarius
Marriage late/never	Virgo
Mental Illness	Scorpio
Military	Virgo & Capricorn
Only Child	Aquarius
Out of Body/NDE	Virgo
Psychiatrists	Scorpio
Salespeople	Aquarius
Scientists	Sagittarius

The Rising Sign

It appears to me that the rising sign's importance is questionable. Here is the reason: The rising sign, which is taken to have great influence in how people outwardly express themselves, displays an increasingly uneven distribution the further north or south of the equator people are born. Eighty percent of the people born at a latitude of 60N (such as Alaska, Scandinavia, and Moscow) have their rising sign in half of the signs, the signs where the declination of the Sun is decreasing (Cancer through Sagittarius). It simply is not realistic that the personality traits of human beings could be so heavily skewed.

In the study the results were consistent with astrological theory for Aries, Taurus, Cancer, Virgo and Scorpio, but weak for Gemini, Leo, Libra, Sagittarius, Capricorn, Aquarius, and Pisces.

The Houses

I have five causes for concern over the current use of houses: 1) their order is opposite from the path of planets during the diurnal motion of the Earth; 2) the Gauquelin studies show the spaces after the angles to be strongest (not the angular houses); 3) the signs are not necessarily connected to the angles or house cusps; 4) the assigned planetary rulerships of signs are probably not accurate; 5) the Ascendant-Descendant axis is often inaccurate for determining whether a planet is above or below the horizon.

In studying the houses, I used both the Placidus and Whole Sign house systems. The findings were mostly random and inconsistent with defined house meanings. The Placidus results were accurate for houses four, six, and eight, but inaccurate for all other houses. The Whole Sign results were accurate for houses five, six, and eight, but inaccurate for all others.

The Horizon

Planets above the horizon are thought to have a much stronger effect than when below the horizon. I used each planet's altitude for this study instead of the Ascendant-Descendant axis because it accurately measures a planet's location relative to the horizon. A planet could be above the Ascendant-Descendant axis but below the horizon and vice-versa.

The results are somewhat significant, especially for Mars, Saturn, Neptune, Pluto, and Chiron. Neptune is strong with many of the same groups as the study on planetary aspects. The imaginative groups of people usually associated with Neptune are also strong.

The Sidereal Zodiac

The construction of the sidereal zodiac, with twelve equal thirty-degree signs, appears to have been based on the calendar system, which is based on the annual cycle of seasons—the source of the tropical zodiac. Therefore, it appears that the tropical zodiac's reality was the basis for the equal sign sidereal zodiac and itself has no substantial realty.

In the study on the sidereal zodiac, of which there are many different versions, I found much less evidence for its accuracy than the tropical zodiac. The findings are much more random and not very well fitted to the signs. The 9th harmonic findings also do not match the 1st harmonic findings.

In the tropical zodiac study, there are twenty-two cases of a group being strong in the same sign in both harmonics. In the sidereal zodiac study, this only occurred six times in the Fagan-Bradley zodiac and two times in the Lahiri zodiac. (The expected number of times for eighty randomly generated groups to do this is 2.4.)

Planetary Rulership of Signs

I observed which signs were the strongest and weakest for each planet. This was determined by observing the signs where each planet has the most groups expressing their positive or negative natures in both the 1st and 9th harmonics.

Out of twenty-eight total positions, only five are the same as traditional rulerships, with seven being the opposite. Venus is the most consistent with traditional theory, being both strong in Taurus and weak in Virgo. Mercury is the least consistent, being both strong in Pisces and weak in Virgo.

The Sun is strongest in Aquarius, its traditional detriment, in both the 1st and 9th harmonics. Mars is strongest in Leo in both the 1st and 9th harmonics. Leo is the most benevolent sign, being strong for three planets in the 9th harmonic. Virgo is the most problematic sign, being weak for every planet except Saturn. Saturn is best in the two signs where the other planets are weakest, Virgo and Scorpio, since it has the effect of restricting their deleterious effects.

	Planetary Strength		Planetary Weakness	
	1st Harmonic	9th Harmonic	1st Harmonic	9th Harmonic
Moon	Libra	Leo	Aries	Virgo/Scorpio
Sun	Aquarius	Aquarius	Virgo	
Mercury	Pisces	Libra/Aquarius	Scorpio	Virgo
Venus	Taurus	Cancer	Virgo	Sagittarius
Mars	Leo	Leo	Virgo	Cancer/Scorpio
Jupiter	Sagittarius	Leo	Cancer/Virgo	
Saturn	Scorpio	Taurus/Virgo	Sagittarius	Capricorn

Retrograde Planets

Of all the planets, Mercury and Venus show the most notable effects from being direct or retrograde in motion. Mercury shows the expected result of the retrograde effect of repressing the qualities of the planet. The groups with the most Mercury retrograde have serious problems with their minds. The groups with the least Mercury retrograde are mostly great thinkers and communicators.

For Venus, the very opposite situation occurs. The groups most representative of the positive Venus qualities are strongly retrograde, while the more negative side of Venus is most apparent for groups with Venus least retrograde. Unlike Mercury, which prefers direct communication, Venus prefers to act in an indirect manner, always considering the desires of others.

Midpoints

The study on midpoints showed promising results. The following groups were strong for two or more planetary combinations: The Moon for married late/never and fiction writers; Mercury for brilliant minds, politicians, and priests; Venus for artists; Mars for corporate tycoons, priests, and wealthy; and Uranus for mystics.

The Moon's Nodes

I did studies on the sign placements and aspects of the True North Node of the Moon. Overall, the results are moderate in the 1st harmonic, but strong in the 9th harmonic. There are also some positive indications such as the life long and priest groups being strong in Pisces in the 1st and 9th harmonics, which corresponds with the rest of the study. Corporate tycoons are strong in Capricorn in both the 1st and 9th harmonics, which is the opposite of the main study. But this indicates that the South Node is the main influence for this group.

I also looked at the Mean Node and found that most of the significant results disappeared. For example, the groups where the 1st and 9th harmonics were strong in the same sign, such as life long and priests in Pisces and corporate tycoons in Capricorn, were no longer strong in the 9th harmonic, where one to two degrees makes a big difference.

For aspects, conjunctions within three degrees of orb were used. There are many findings that correspond with astrological theory, which states that a planet's positive qualities are emphasized and sought after on the North Node and its negative qualities are emphasized and struggled with on the South Node. One interesting result was to see that so many of the groups with afflictions were strong for Chiron on the North Node.

Lunar Phases

To study the effect of the lunar phases, I observed the New, Full, and Quarter Moons, which translate as a conjunction, opposition, and square between the Sun and Moon. I used a fifteen-degree orb, since astrologers consider each phase in effect under a wide orb. There were no meaningful results for the Quarter Moon phases. However, there were strong results for New and Full Moon phases.

The New Moon and Full Moon were strongest for groups associated with childhood and reflective thinking. The New Moon is stronger with childhood groups and the Full Moon is stronger with contemplative types, as well as people who experienced difficulty in childhood. This makes sense since the New Moon joins the nurturing influence of the Moon with the Sun's life energy, while the Full Moon separates the nurturing influence of the Moon from the Sun's life energy but allows us to reflect upon the nature of life since it is the phase with the most separation between the Sun (outer) and Moon (inner).

The most statistically relevant finding was that adopted children are strong in both lunar phases. The likelihood of this finding being a random accident is 1 in 2,285.

Outer Planet Conjunctions

There have only been three outer planet conjunctions in the last

150 years. The first was Neptune-Pluto in 1891, in Gemini. The second was Uranus-Pluto in 1965, in Virgo. The third was Uranus-Neptune in 1993, in Capricorn, which was too recent to study.

The 1891 conjunction was in the sign of Gemini and produced a whole generation of great thinkers and writers, as is typical of Gemini. The 1965 conjunction was in Virgo and led to a generation of very troubled people, which we witnessed in the 1980s. This is highly consistent with the findings for Virgo in the rest of the study.

Neptune-Pluto (Gemini)	Uranus-Pluto (Virgo)
Activists	Adopted
Astrologers	Birth Defect
Composers	Criminal Careers
Fiction Writers	Drug Abuse
Life Long 80+ years	Fighters
Math Physics	Life Short 29- years
Military	Mentally Handicapped
Mystics	Mental Illness
Poets	Models
Presidents	Same Job 10+ years
Professors	Sex Offenders
Spiritual Teachers	Sex Workers
Technical	Sports
Writers	

Conclusion

My book presents the results of my statistical research project in terms that any student of astrology can understand and apply. It reveals statistical findings as well as a model of the nature of the planets and the structure of the zodiac. To my knowledge, this is the first project of its kind. Its contents are original and can enhance the way people view astrology. It can also improve the knowledge and accuracy of astrologers, giving them a solid basis for their interpretations. My hope is that my book will stir enthusiasm in many others to do similar research into astrology's effects on human and planetary existence and the many ways that it can be used to better our lives.

Tidy Vesta Can Warn Us of Messy Disasters

By Sue Kientz

ABSTRACT: When governing figures such as mayors, governors, and presidents are faced with a massive disaster, could Vesta signal the onset of crisis? Jean Shinoda Bolen (*Goddesses in Everywoman*) and Demetra George (*Asteroid Goddesses*) proposed that mythic Vesta displays strong associations with work and "restoring order"; in that light, this paper argues that asteroid Vesta might form some significant aspect in the charts of civic leaders faced with a catastrophe that requires extensive cleanup or other recovery work. Huge calamities put pressure on the political leader in charge, adding to their workload, and this could be reflected in Vesta's placement. An examination of the birth charts of officials in charge during famous disasters of the 20th and 21st centuries confirmed that Vesta forms close angular aspects with personal planets in such officials' progressed charts, as well as in transit.

Astrologers need to find a way to provide sufficient warning of terrible events with relatively pointed accuracy. But how can this be done? We all know the transiting planets are out there dancing for everyone, and when they arrange into grand crosses or malignant T-squares including, for instance, Saturn, Pluto, and Mars, they manifest in people's lives in such a wide spectrum of ways. One person's divorce is another's mother dying suddenly, and another's home swallowed by a sinkhole. When such a menacing-looking configuration begins to form, how could we possibly pinpoint the place, as in the country, much less the state, city, or town that might find itself somehow involved in a natural or politically-inspired catastrophe?

You might argue that we do not have the wide range of statistics necessary to predict at that scale. No one wishes a government to manipulate its population data in Big-Brother fashion, but if we had everyone's birth info in a data bank and could calculate *en masse* the progressions and transits of such large groups, only then could one see when a section of a state or large city had persons whose progressions/transits suggest they are up for a significant trial. That has to be the case, correct? If a plane goes down, at the least, the loved ones of all aboard were set for some nasty squares, oppositions, and/or conjunctions relating to their chart. The wider community is affected, as even eye witnesses to a disaster can be traumatized, so wouldn't processing all those birthdates show us a trend towards some disturbing event?

To be honest, such Orwellian methods may not be needed. There's perhaps an easier way to figure out where natural or man-made disaster is imminent or threatening. You might simply need the birth info of the top politicians of the place that is ripe for trouble. Why? Because they are going to be in the thick of the proverbial maelstrom.

Certainly this theory should be easy to test by examining (in) famous calamities of the past. If disaster hadn't hit in those now-historic situations, the mayors and governors involved would likely have almost disappeared in the public record, leaving their name but rarely a birthdate for our perusal. But if the big earthquake hits, the flood overtakes the city, or the tallest buildings ring down to the ground, those city and state leaders will certainly have their birthday in Wikipedia.

Vesta and Work

What would you look for specifically that might presage catastrophic conditions? Surprisingly, what many would dismiss as just a minor planetary body could be a useful bellwether of trouble: dwarf planet Vesta, fourth largest object in the Asteroid Belt. This little workhorse has a message for us: if I'm in your secondary progressed chart angularly challenging your Sun, Mercury, and/or Mars, you are going to be working your tail off and burning that midnight oil.

Why would Vesta play such a role? Jean Shinoda Bolen in *Goddesses in Everywoman* theorized in 1984 that the archetype of Hestia (the Greek Vesta) "puts… her house in order."[1] This focus on work, especially in a "home" environment, was elaborated on by Demetra George in *Asteroid Goddesses,*[2] cementing an association of work with asteroid Vesta. It therefore makes sense that Vesta might crop up when a massive cleanup or drive to "put things right" might be required. Huge calamities like earthquakes, tsunamis, floods, terrorist attacks, or sudden acts of war put pressure on the central political leader in charge, so naturally that individual would be "burning the midnight oil" and working on overdrive. A telltale major Vesta contact in progression to Sun or Mercury could aid in predicting where a major storm or terror attack might strike, by checking the charts of the governing personages whose sphere of responsibility is in a storm's path or where terrorist acts are being threatened. Even lacking the time of birth, this technique can still be used because Vesta is slow and doesn't move much in 24 hours. So this industrious little dwarf's relationship to the Sun or personal planets in transit or progression can be pinpointed quite accurately, unlike a predictive strategy that might depend on the Moon's location or house positions.

This study researched some of the most famous catastrophes of the 20th and 21st centuries, and found that Vesta indeed appears in leaders' progressed charts, in some form of culminating aspect, usually with progressed Sun. Analysis also revealed that the event charts of man-made catastrophes showed Vesta prominent in transit, many times with Mars, indicative that the accident or attack (Mars) entails a considerable cleanup effort (Vesta). Even enterprise charts like when Japan's Fukushima Reactor No. 1 first went online, and the founding chart of Japan from 660 BCE, when progressed to the 2011 Earthquake/Tsunami, display Mars/Vesta warnings.

Let's jump right into some examples to see all this happening in fact:

Mayors on Point

Rudy Giuliani (May 28, 1944, 2:30 p.m., Brooklyn, New York[3]), mayor of New York City on September 11, 2001, when the two World Trade Center towers were hit; Giuliani's progressed Sun (1 Leo 58) was conjunct progressed Vesta (4 Leo 52).

The applying conjunction foretells a long transit of progressed Sun-progressed Vesta, corresponding to the protracted cleanup of lower Manhattan. Giuliani's stint as mayor did not last through that period, as he reached the end of term limits early the next year. Nevertheless, he continued to be associated with the after-effects of the attack. Giuliani ran for president in many ways based on this reputation as the tough mayor who led New York City through that horrific time. So whether due to political expediency, genuine concern, or a mixture of both, Giuliani remained connected with 9-11 relief efforts as his progressed Sun-Vesta conjunction perfected and separated.

Ray Nagin (June 11, 1956, New Orleans, Los Angeles[4]; 7:00 a.m. used), mayor of New Orleans during the onslaught of Hurricane Katrina (August 29, 2005, "early morning" landfall; 7:40 a.m. first damage reported[5]): Nagin faced this widespread disaster with his progressed Sun (7 Leo 31) square progressed Vesta (7 Scorpio 47).

Richard Riordan (May 1, 1930, Flushing, New York[6]; 7:00 a.m.

used), mayor of Los Angeles during the Northridge Earthquake (January 17, 1994, 4:30:55 a.m.[7]), as his progressed Mercury (28 Gemini 59) was sextile progressed Vesta (0 Virgo 32).

Riordan was stupefied to find that most city government agencies were woefully unprepared for this crisis, and used his many contacts (Mercury) to get private corporations to help (Vesta) in the days after the quake hit.[8] Riordan went on to create the Department of Emergency Management to handle future disaster management.

Mike Rawlings (August 24, 1954, Dallas[9]; 7:00 a.m. used), mayor of Dallas during the Ebola crisis (September 30, 2014, to November 7, 2014[10]; earliest date used), as his progressed Sun (0 Scorpio 41) was trine progressed Vesta (1 Cancer 59).

The panic about a possible spread of the virus subsided in a few weeks—fortunate for Rawlings and his constituents, which is perhaps reflected in the auspicious trine aspect.

State/City Leaders Tackle California's Worst Disaster

Each of these civic leaders had Vesta semisquare personal planets in progression when the Great San Francisco Quake of 1906 hit.

Eugene Schmitz (August 22, 1864, San Francisco[11]; 7:00 a.m. used), mayor of San Francisco during the 1906 Earthquake, sprang into action with his progressed Sun (10 Libra 18) semisquare progressed Vesta (25 Leo 32), immediately forming a committee of 50 prominent politicians, businessmen, and other city leaders to address the crisis.

Frank K. Mott (January 21, 1866, San Francisco[12]; 7:00 a.m. used), mayor of Oakland during the 1906 Earthquake, as his progressed Sun (12 Pisces 05)-Venus (13 Pisces 26)-Mercury (13 Pisces 25) applied to a semisquare with progressed Vesta (0 Aquarius 50). Oakland was affected by the quake because of an influx of about 150,000 refugees from damaged and fire-stricken San Francisco.[13]

George Cooper Pardee (July 25, 1857, San Francisco[14]; 7:00 a.m. used), governor of California during the 1906 Earthquake. With his progressed Mercury (15 Libra 04) applying to a semisquare of progressed Vesta (3 Virgo 53), Pardee traveled to the affected region and set up a command center in Mott's Oakland office. He reportedly worked twenty-hour days, managing all the necessary details to aid not just San Francisco but all affected cities.

The Top Job Feels the Heat

These presidents and prime ministers experienced difficult square or semisquare aspects between Sun (or Mars) and Vesta during their respective crises:

Franklin D. Roosevelt (January 30, 1882, 8:45 p.m., Hyde Park, New York[15]), U.S. president at the time of the attack on Pearl Harbor (Dec. 7, 1941[16]), as his progressed Sun (11 Aries 05) was semisquare progressed Vesta (26 Taurus 52).

Jimmy Carter (October 1, 1924, 7:00 a.m., Plains, Georgia[17]), U.S. president during the Three Mile Island Accident (March 28, 1979[18]). At the time, Carter's progressed Sun (2 Sagittarius 29) was square progressed Vesta (29 Aquarius 36).

Rajiv Gandhi (August 20, 1944, 6:34 a.m., Bombay, India[19]), prime minister of India during the Bhopal Disaster (Dec. 3, 1984[20]), as his progressed Mars (20 Libra 27) was semisquare progressed Vesta (5 Virgo 03). Cleanup, victim compensation, and legal resolution of the incident dragged on for years.[21]

Naoto Kan (October 10, 1946, Ube, Japan[22]; 7:00 a.m. used), prime minister of Japan during the 2011 Tōhoku Earthquake/Tsunami (March 11, 2011[23]), as his progressed Sun (20 Sagittarius 25)-Mars (26 Sagittarius 40) were square progressed Vesta (26 Pisces 31).

Yoshihiko Noda (May 10, 1957, Funabashi, Japan[24]; 7:00 a.m. used), prime minister of Japan after the resignation of Prime Minister Kan. Noda became responsible for the earthquake/

tsunami disaster response after September 2, 2011,[25] as his progressed Sun (20 Cancer 31) was square progressed Vesta (16 Aries 31), and progressed Mars (13 Leo 36) was trine progressed Vesta (16 Aries 31).

Noda's progressed Mars trine Vesta bodes unusually well, which seems counter to first estimates that Japan would need years to recover economically from the tsunami's effects.[26] However, in December 2011, Prime Minister Noda declared the Fukushima Daiichi facility stable after shutdown of its reactors was completed.[27] By early 2012, reports surfaced that industry had recovered to pre-earthquake levels of production.[28]

Intriguingly, the event chart for the *Fukushima Daiichi No. 1* plant going online (March 26, 1971, Fukushima, Japan[29]; 8:00 a.m. used), progressed to the 2011 Tōhoku Earthquake/Tsunami, has the same revealing indicator as the politicians: progressed Mars (0 Aquarius 32) conjunct progressed Vesta (1 Aquarius 45).

Even the traditional founding of Japan chart (February 19, 660 BCE, 8:00 a.m., Yamato, Japan[30]), progresses a whopping 2,671 years to the 2011 Tōhoku Earthquake/Tsunami to reveal progressed Mars (3 Gemini 53) semisquare progressed Vesta (17 Aries 11). The date may be only legendary, yet it works.

Disasters Mean Jobs Jobs Jobs

The event charts of the following catastrophes, many referred to above, show Sun or inner planets in sextile aspect with Vesta. Certainly the cleanup jobs were far from easy. However, in each case, aid organizations (local, national, and in some cases international) were able to mobilize and assist the affected areas. In other words, aid and cleanup workers (Vesta) supported (sextile) the return of normal life (Sun). You might even venture that such occurrences attract participation of those predisposed to work: those who like to work, need work, and/or excel at work.

Bhopal Disaster (December 3, 1984, Bhopal, India, "early morning hours"[31]; 2:00 a.m. used), Sun (10 Sagittarius 51) sextile Vesta (9 Libra 57) and Mars (12 Aquarius 54) trine Vesta (9 Libra 57).

Chernobyl Disaster (April 26, 1986, 1:23 a.m., Chernobyl, Ukraine, USSR[32]), Mars (13 Capricorn 08) sextile Vesta (15 Pisces 43).

Hurricane Katrina (August 29, 2005, "early morning" landfall, New Orleans; 7:40 a.m. first damage reported[33]), Sun (6 Virgo 16) sextile Vesta (5 Cancer 50).

1906 San Francisco Earthquake (April 18, 1906, 5:12 a.m., San Francisco[34]), Sun (27 Aries 34) sextile Vesta (29 Aquarius 12).

1994 Northridge Earthquake (January 17, 1994, 4:30:55 a.m., Northridge, California[35]), Sun (27 Capricorn 10)-Mars (21 Capricorn 44) sextile Vesta (23 Pisces 20).

2011 Tōhoku Earthquake/Tsunami (March 11, 2011, 2:46 p.m., Tokyo, Japan[36]), Sun (20 Pisces 18) sextile Vesta (20 Capricorn 14).

Difficult Recoveries

Some incidents make cleanup difficult, whether due to the threat of radiation poisoning, pre-existing poverty, or other extraordinarily dangerous conditions at the disaster site. Inhospitable Mars conjunctions or hard aspects to Vesta are frequently found on such occasions.

Three Mile Island Accident (March 28, 1979, 3:00 a.m., Middletown, Pennsylvania[37]), Mars (22 Pisces 26) conjunct Vesta (21 Pisces 12).

Hiroshima Atomic Bombing (August 6, 1945, 8:16 a.m., Hiroshima, Japan[38]), Mars (9 Gemini 12) sesquiquadrate Vesta (27 Libra 19).

The surprise of the attack and ongoing war with the rest of the world precluded any outside humanitarian aid being offered to

Japan after Hiroshima was bombed. Years passed before more organized efforts inside Japan and outside assistance were mobilized.[39]

Nagasaki Atomic Bombing (August 9, 1945, 11:02 a.m., Nagasaki, Japan[40]), Mars (11 Gemini 16) sesquiquadrate Vesta (28 Libra 35).

Even after the Hiroshima bomb devastated that city, Japanese leaders refused to act, either to surrender or to prepare for more bombings, due to disbelief that the Americans had indeed perfected atomic weaponry.[41]

2010 Haiti Earthquake (January 12, 2010, 4:53:10 p.m., Port-au-Prince, Haiti[42]), Sun (22 Capricorn 35)-Venus (22 Capricorn 50) sesquiquadrate Vesta (6 Virgo 21).

Even after an international relief effort was mobilized to help and various sources donated nearly $1 billion to the cause,[43] widespread poverty already present before the quake made satisfactory "restoration" of order difficult. By 2012, more than a half-million people still lived in tents in the capital.[44]

Malaysian Airlines 370 Lost (last transmission March 8, 2014, 1:19 a.m.[45]; Kuala Lumpur, Malaysia), Sun (17 Pisces 03) sesquiquadrate Vesta (29 Libra 51) and Mars (27 Libra 18) conjunct Vesta (29 Libra 51).

An international search and recovery effort was unsuccessful due to the impossibly vast area of ocean where the aircraft might have crashed.

Malaysian Airlines 17 Shot Down (July 17, 2014, 4:20 p.m.,[46] Grabovo, Ukraine[47]), Sun (24 Cancer 53) square Mars (25 Libra 41)-Vesta (25 Libra 23).

The ongoing conflict between Ukraine and separatists fighting for union with Russia made inspection and recovery of the crash site a dangerous enterprise.

Hitler Milestone	When Hitler Reaches	Vesta Cues Some Big Trouble	What Happened
Born: April 20, 1889, 6:30 p.m., Braunau am Inn, Austria[48]	The Beer Hall Putsch, Nov. 8, 1923[49]	Progressed Sun (4 Gemini 12) conjunct progressed Vesta (4 Gemini 05)	Hitler miscalculated and the coup failed. He was convicted of treason and spent a year in prison.
Attempted Coup: Beer Hall Putsch, Nov. 8, 1923, 8:30 p.m., Munich, Germany[50]	Defeat at Stalingrad, Feb. 2, 1943[51]	Beer Hall Putsch event's progressed Sun (4 Sagittarius 46) conjunct progressed Vesta (4 Sagittarius 39)	850,000 Axis casualties (dead and injured),[52] plus Hitler must explain to the German people what went wrong, as earlier he claimed victory.
Named Chancellor of Germany: Jan. 30, 1933, 12 p.m., Berlin, Germany[53]	Berlin Besieged by Russians, April 30, 1945[54]	Chancellor of Germany events progressed Sun (22 Aquarius 32)- progressed Mercury (25 Aquarius 25) square progressed Vesta (25 Taurus 45)	Hitler commited suicide and let aides (Mercury) clean up the mess this time. He could not face the total ruin he created for Germany.

Hitler: Self-Creating Disaster

Vesta not only warns of coming chaos generated by nature or evil others. It's possible for anyone to be his or her own worst enemy and make a mess of things. If you're Adolf Hitler, for example, you have a rather stunning talent for eventually creating havoc whenever you launch any new enterprise, as in attempting a coup, or becoming chancellor of Germany, or even taking your first breath:

Managing Global Disarray

Winston Churchill (November 30, 1874, 1:30 a.m., Woodstock, England[55]), prime minister of England. When Germany invaded Poland on September 1, 1939, Churchill's progressed Mars (24 Scorpio 46) was within orb opposition progressed Vesta (29 Taurus 47).

Certainly this suggests the devastation wreaked on British cities by the German *Blitzkreig*, but the Mars-Vesta opposition did not reach exactitude until June 1952, hinting that the "disorder" that the Nazis began and about which Churchill was most concerned, was not confined to Britain. In fact, the implication is that the spread of Communism was the greater disaster that

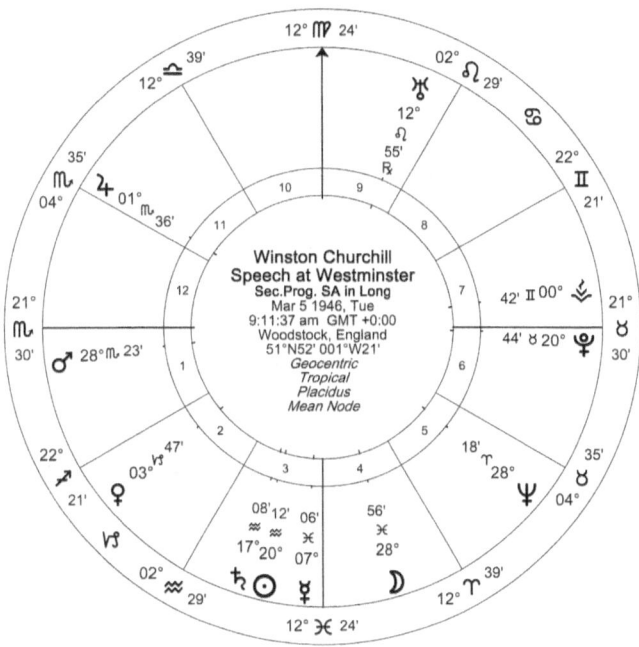

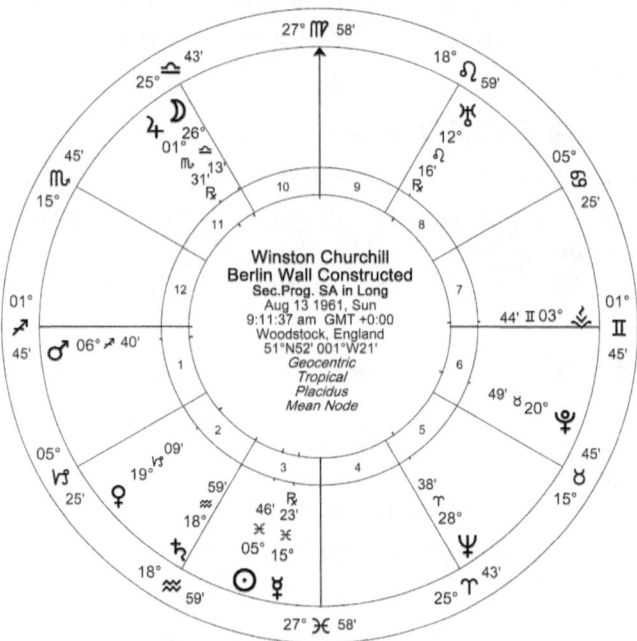

World War II inflicted on the world.

That Churchill himself intuited this threat and felt moved to challenge it is indicated by his progressed Moon (28 Pisces 57) becoming involved in the Mars-Vesta opposition, significantly trine Mars (28 Scorpio 23) when he spoke at Westminster College on March 5, 1946, warning "an Iron Curtain has descended on the Continent..."[56] (see chart on previous page).

At the time of this now-famous and prescient speech, Churchill's progressed Sun was moving to square progressed Vesta, a figure that would later pass exactitude at the erection of the Berlin Wall (initial barbed wire barrier erected August 13, 1961[57]), thus forming a progressed T-square with Vesta (see chart above). Churchill's fears were indeed realized. He would not live to see the fall of the infamous wall in 1989, signaling the end of Communism.

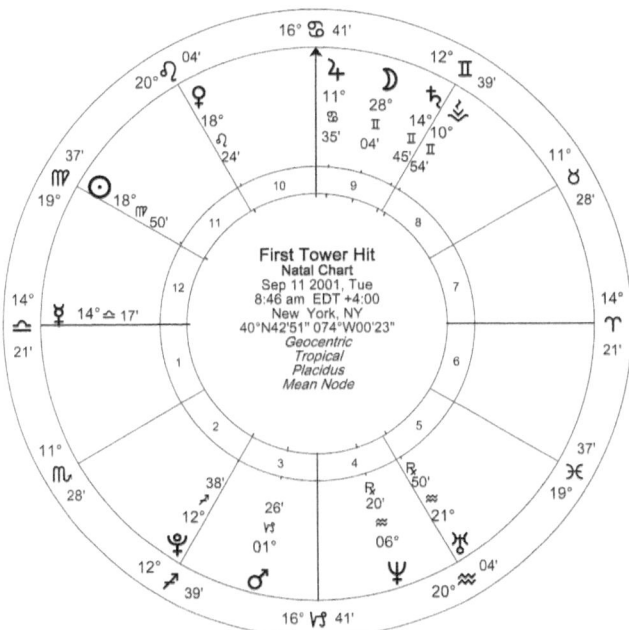

When Cleaning Up Isn't Enough

September 11, 2001, Terror Attacks (Sept. 11, 2001, first tower hit 8:46 a.m., New York[58]), Sun (18 Virgo 50) square Vesta (10 Gemini 54).

Perhaps the wide Sun-Vesta square seems a reach in our search for significance (see chart above). But maybe ever-efficient Vesta wasn't attempting a culmination with the Sun, but aiming toward a more determined, powerful partner to make things right.

Restoring order for many Americans necessitated that the main perpetrator of the September 11, 2001 attacks be brought to justice. That would not happen until nearly 10 years later on May 2, 2011, when Osama Bin Laden was killed by Navy Seals in Abbottabad, Pakistan.[59]

Interestingly, progressed Vesta again plays a role in such closure. Witness the chart of 9-11 itself, progressed to Bin Laden's death

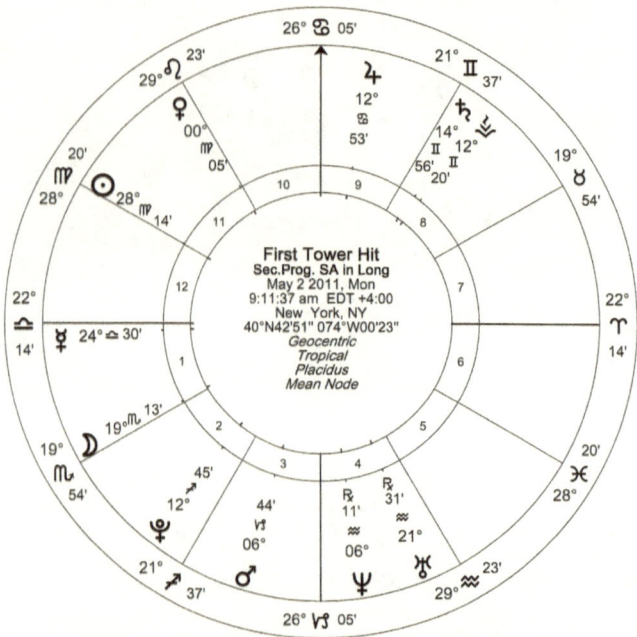

(see chart above), with its progressed Vesta (12 Gemini 20) completing opposition with progressed Pluto (12 Sagittarius 45). In this case, Vesta "put our house in order" at last, using Pluto's deadly force.

Conclusion

To sum up, dwarf planet Vesta can indeed indicate an imminent community crisis. An examination of civic leaders of major disasters revealed numerous instances of secondary progressed Vesta forming major aspect(s) to progressed personal planets. Each official's progressed Vesta figure persisted during the time of the intense work or involvement needed to restore order to their constituents' daily lives. Additionally, the event charts of those disasters showed Vesta in angular relationship to Sun and/or Mars, and the type of aspect well described the overall success or difficulty of the recovery effort. Related enterprise charts also showed progressed Vesta/Mars warnings timed to the onset of the emergency. Checking Vesta's condition proved so worthwhile that surprising reevaluations arose about what a tumultuous event's long-term effects actually were, or what the public needed for full closure besides resumption of basic services. Without question, Vesta indeed "works" as an invaluable predictive marker and could well serve politically-engaged astrologers or those in a position to advise government.

Endnotes
All URLs accessed in December 2014
[1] Bolen, Jean Shinoda. *Goddesses in Everywoman: A New Psychology of Women*. New York: Harper and Row, 1984, 111.
[2] George, Demetra. *Asteroid Goddesses*. San Diego, CA: ACS Publications, Inc., 1986, 130.
[3] http://www.astro.com/astro-databank/Giuliani,_Rudy
[4] http://www.notablebiographies.com/newsmakers2/2007-Li-Pr/Nagin-Ray.html
[5] http://en.wikipedia.org/wiki/Hurricane_Katrina
[6] http://www.encyclopedia.com/topic/Richard_J_Riordan.aspx
[7] http://earthquake.usgs.gov/earthquakes/states/events/1994_01_17.php
[8] http://www.dailynews.com/general-news/20140116/1994-northridge-earthquake-served-as-defining-moment-for-la-then-mayor-richard-riordan
[9] http://en.wikipedia.org/wiki/Mike_Rawlings
[10] http://dfw.cbslocal.com/2014/11/09/dallas-reaches-end-of-ebola-monitoring-period/
[11] http://www.sfmuseum.org/hist1/schmitz.html
[12] http://en.wikipedia.org/wiki/Frank_K._Mott
[13] Ibid.
[14] http://www.nga.org/cms/home/governors/past-governors-bios/page_california/col2-content/main-content-list/title_pardee_george.html
[15] http://www.astro.com/astro-databank/Roosevelt,_Franklin_D.
[16] http://www.history.navy.mil/faqs/faq66-1.htm
[17] http://www.astro.com/astro-databank/Carter,_Jimmy
[18] http://www.nrc.gov/reading-rm/doc-collections/fact-sheets/3mile-

isle.html
[19]http://www.astro.com/astro-databank/Gandhi,_Rajiv
[20]http://news.bbc.co.uk/onthisday/hi/dates/stories/december/3/newsid_2698000/2698709.stm
[21]http://en.wikipedia.org/wiki/Bhopal_disaster
[22]http://en.wikipedia.org/wiki/Naoto_Kan
[23]http://www.cnn.com/2013/07/17/world/asia/japan-earthquake-tsunami-fast-facts/
[24]http://en.wikipedia.org/wiki/Yoshihiko_Noda
[25]Ibid.
[26]http://www.theguardian.com/world/2011/may/11/japanese-tsunami-survivors-search-for-mementos
[27]http://www.britannica.com/EBchecked/topic/1761942/Japan-earthquake-and-tsunami-of-2011/299864/Northern-Japans-nuclear-emergency
[28]http://www.britannica.com/EBchecked/topic/1761942/Japan-earthquake-and-tsunami-of-2011/299865/Relief-and-rebuilding-efforts
[29]http://en.wikipedia.org/wiki/Fukushima_Daiichi_Nuclear_Power_Plant
[30]Griffis, William Elliot. *The Mikado's Empire, Book I: History of Japan from 660 B.C. to 1872 A.D.* New York and London: Harper & Brothers Publishers, 1903, 59
[31]http://news.bbc.co.uk/onthisday/hi/dates/stories/december/3/newsid_2698000/2698709.stm
[32]http://www.astro.com/astro-databank/Accident:_Chernobyl_Explosion
[33]http://en.wikipedia.org/wiki/Hurricane_Katrina
[34]http://earthquake.usgs.gov/regional/nca/1906/18april/index.php
[35]http://earthquake.usgs.gov/earthquakes/states/events/1994_01_17.php
[36]http://www.cnn.com/2013/07/17/world/asia/japan-earthquake--tsunami-fast-facts/
[37]http://www.nrc.gov/reading-rm/doc-collections/fact-sheets/3mileisle.html
[38]http://www.history.com/this-day-in-history/atomic-bomb-is-dropped-on-hiroshima
[39]http://www.atomicbombmuseum.org/4_ruins.shtml
[40]http://www.history.com/this-day-in-history/atomic-bomb-dropped-on-nagasaki

⁴¹http://www.hiroshima-remembered.com/history/nagasaki/page6.html
⁴²http://earthquake.usgs.gov/earthquakes/eqinthenews/2010/us-2010rja6/
⁴³http://www.cnn.com/2013/12/12/world/haiti-earthquake-fast-facts/
⁴⁴http://www.washingtonpost.com/world/clearing-earthquake-camps-in-haiti-is-not-pretty/2012/01/27/gIQAnxzNOR_story.html
⁴⁵http://www.cnbc.com/id/101501573#.
⁴⁶http://www.latimes.com/world/la-fg-malaysia-air-flight-17-ukraine-facts-20140718-htmlstory.html
⁴⁷http://www.spiegel.de/international/europe/a-trip-to-the-site-of-the-crash-of-flight-mh-17-a-983268.html
⁴⁸http://www.astro.com/astro-databank/Hitler,_Adolf
⁴⁹http://www.ushmm.org/wlc/en/article.php?ModuleId=10007884
⁵⁰Ibid.
⁵¹http://www.history.com/topics/world-war-ii/battle-of-stalingrad
⁵²Craig, William. *Enemy at the Gates: The Battle for Stalingrad.* New York: Penguin Books, 1973.
⁵³http://www.historyplace.com/worldwar2/riseofhitler/collapse.htm
⁵⁴http://www.history.com/this-day-in-history/adolf-hitler-commits-suicide-in-his-underground-bunker
⁵⁵http://www.astro.com/astro-databank/Churchill,_Winston
⁵⁶http://history1900s.about.com/od/churchillwinston/a/Iron-Curtain.htm
⁵⁷http://www.history.com/this-day-in-history/berlin-wall-built
⁵⁸http://www.history.com/topics/9-11-timeline
⁵⁹http://www.cnn.com/2013/09/09/world/death-of-osama-bin-laden-fast-facts/

Yods in Suicide and Homicide Charts

By Arlene DeAngelus

ABSTRACT: Family, friends and fans were stunned when Whitney Houston died in February 2012. This article examines her chart and others, including four members of the 27 Club (musicians who died at age twenty-seven), three people who died as a result of homicide, and three people whose deaths were questionable. Using yods and critical degrees in comparing the charts, this study questions whether there are similarities in these charts that are related to their habits or lifestyles.

I look for yod formations when interpreting charts for homicide, suicide, and other deaths. A yod, sometimes called the "finger of fate," is a configuration involving a sextile (60 degrees) and two inconjunct aspects (180 degrees) aspects. Many astrologers believe that the yod shows that the soul chose a special reason or purpose to accomplish, to fulfill, or to complete.

I also look for a critical degree. These are identified as:
- Cardinal (Aries, Cancer, Libra, Capricorn)—0, 13, 26
- Fixed (Taurus, Leo, Scorpio, Aquarius—9, 21
- Mutable (Gemini, Virgo, Sagittarius, Pisces)—4, 17

In *Simplified Horary Astrology*, Ivy Jacobson states that "The 29th degree shows some misfortune connected with the matter, the person or matter asked about is changing, at the end of his/her rope or patience, or desperate." The zero degree can be a new start, a new path, or a new beginning. Therefore, I also consider these two degrees to be sensitive ones.

Suicides

Whitney Houston

Was Whitney Houston offered an opportunity to begin a new life course and to free herself from addictive habits, which unfortunately she did not accept? The autopsy showed traces of cocaine, marijuana and several prescription medications in her system.

There were two interesting yods in Houston's chart at the time of her death:

Yod One: transiting Jupiter at 4 Taurus 03 in the second house, progressed Sun at 3 Libra 42 in the seventh house and transiting Chiron at the critical degree of 4 Pisces 19 in the twelfth house. The activation points of this yod were transiting Uranus at 2 Aries 15 and transiting Venus at 4 Aries 04. Both Uranus and Venus were in the first house of self, which indicated that Houston had a choice.

Jupiter in Houston's second house could indicate additional money, while the Sun in her seventh house in Libra could indicate a happy balance in personal relationships. Chiron at a critical degree in Pisces in the twelfth house also offered her healing from the Piscean vices of life or the potential for self-undoing.

Yod Two: transiting Venus at 4 Aries 04 in the first house, natal Uranus at the critical degree of 4 Virgo 27 in the sixth house and the progressed Midheaven at 5 Aquarius 23 in the twelfth house.

Love and harmony were important to Houston. Uranus in a critical degree rules unexpected and unpredictable circumstances

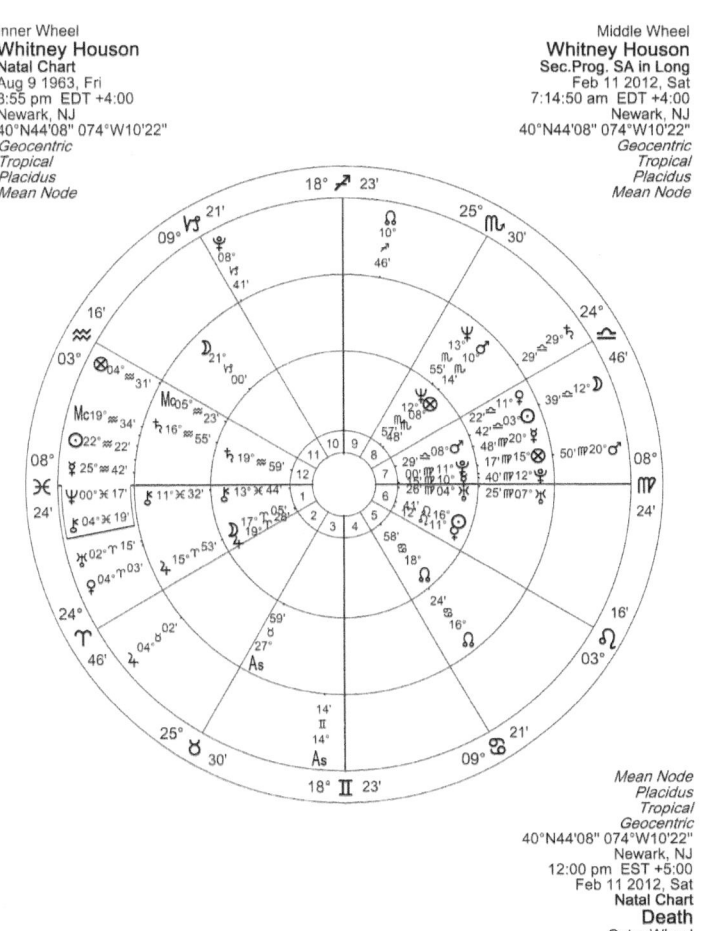

with one's health and work. The progressed Midheaven and aims in life in Aquarius in the twelfth house suggest the possibility of unexpected and self-undoing behavior.

The activation point of this yod is transiting Chiron at the critical degree of 4 Pisces 19, also in the twelfth house and ruling Houston's potential for healing or self-undoing.

Transiting retrograde Saturn at 29 Libra 30 was in Houston's eighth house of transformation. Transiting Neptune, ruler of

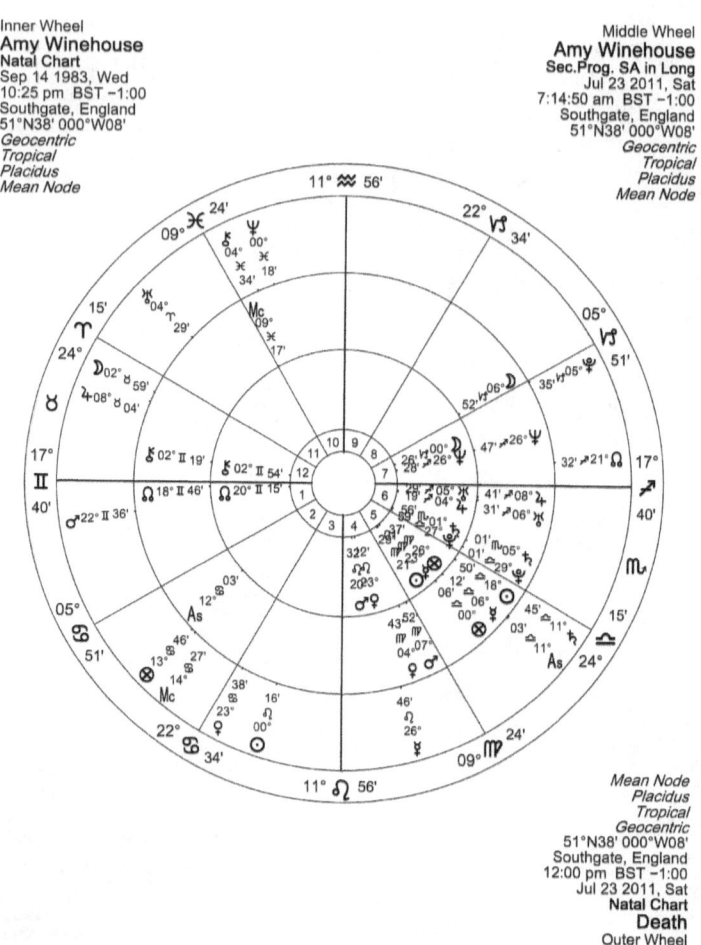

drugs and alcohol, was in her twelfth house of self-undoing at 0 Pisces 18, indicating a new path or a new beginning.

Amy Winehouse

Amy Winehouse struggled for years with drug and alcohol abuse. However, no illegal drugs were found in her system when she died on July 23, 2011 at age twenty-seven. The cause of death was accidental alcohol poisoning because of a blood-alcohol level that was more than five times the legal limit. The only drug found in her system was Librium, a sedative to help ease her symptoms of alcohol withdrawal. She died in her London flat.

Yod One: progressed Venus at the critical degree of 4 Virgo 43 in the fourth house; progressed Saturn at 5 Scorpio 01 in the sixth house; and transiting retrograde Uranus at 4 Aries 30 in the eleventh house.

Was Saturn suggesting that Winehouse learn to take better care of her health and that otherwise Uranus could bring unexpected circumstances concerning her life's direction?

Yod Two: natal Saturn at 1 Scorpio 57 in the sixth house; natal Moon at the critical degree of 0 Capricorn 26 in the seventh house; natal retrograde Chiron at 2 Gemini 55 in the twelfth house; and progressed retrograde Chiron at 2 Gemini 19 in the twelfth house.

Saturn intercepted in the sixth house required Winehouse's responsibility for her health and work, as did Chiron in the twelfth house.

Yod Three: transiting Sun at 0 Leo 16 in the third house, progressed Part of Fortune (Misfortune) at the critical degree of 0 Libra 06 in the fifth house; and progressed retrograde Neptune at 0 Pisces 18 in the tenth house.

This yod indicated a new start. Winehouse needed to balance her fun with responsibility. Progressed Neptune at 00 degrees could have offered her a new path away from drugs and alcohol.

Kurt Cobain

Kurt Cobain was an American singer and guitarist who performed with his group Nirvana. A copy of Cobain's death certificate lists the cause of death as suicide on April 5, 1994, as a result of a self-inflicted shotgun wound to the head. He died at his residence in Seattle, at age twenty-seven.

Twenty years after Cobain's death, the Seattle Police Department

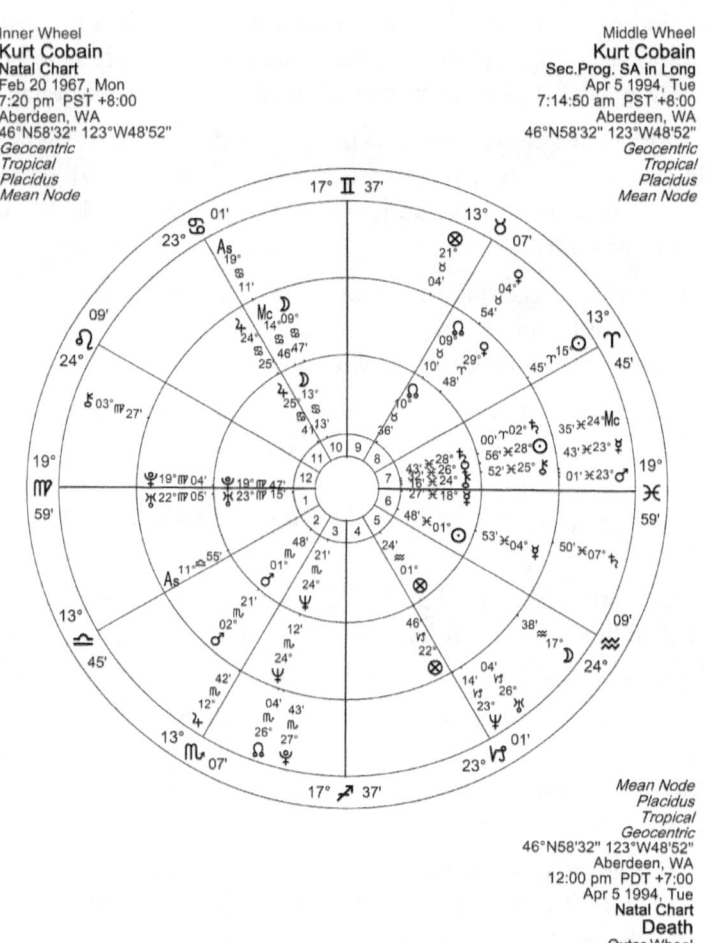

reexamined a point in the case. His death had been officially ruled a suicide; however, in the succeeding years some people have questioned whether it was murder or if his wife, Courtney Love, could have been involved. Police did not reopen the case.

Yod One: natal Mars at 1 Scorpio 48 in the second house; progressed retrograde Mars at 2 Scorpio 21 in the second house; progressed Saturn at 2 Aries 01 in the seventh house; and transiting retrograde Chiron at 3 Virgo 28 in the twelfth house.

Natal and progressed Mars conjunct in the second house suggest that Cobain may have been having disagreements over finances, perhaps with a seventh-house partner.

Yod Two: natal retrograde Uranus at 23 Virgo 15 in the first house; natal Neptune at 24 Scorpio 21 in the third house; progressed retrograde Neptune at 24 Scorpio 12 in the third house; transiting retrograde Pluto at 27 Scorpio 44 in the third house; and progressed Venus at 29 Aries 49 in the eighth house.

Natal Uranus in Virgo in the first house may indicate that Cobain was self-critical and that his personal communications were unexpectedly disagreeable. Progressed Venus at 29 Aries 49 in the eighth house could be of concern, possibly indicating death.

Jim Morrison

Jim Morrison died July 3, 1971 of an assumed overdose of heroin, possibly combined with the effects of alcohol; he was twenty-seven. Pamela Courson, his long-time girlfriend, said she found Morrison dead in the bathtub at their apartment in Paris.

There were several discrepancies as to where Morrison actually died. The official coroner's report listed the cause of death as heart failure, although no autopsy was performed. The circumstances surrounding Morrison's cause of death are still questioned.

Yod One: transiting Mars at the critical degree of 21 Aquarius 36 in the first house; progressed Part of Fortune (Misfortune) at 22 Cancer 11 in the sixth house; progressed Midheaven at 25 Sagittarius 02 in the eleventh house; natal retrograde Mars at 11 Gemini 40 in the fourth house; natal retrograde North Node at the critical degree of 9 Leo 25 in the sixth house; progressed Sun at the critical degree of 13 Capricorn 46 in the eleventh house; transiting Saturn at 1 Gemini 44 in the fourth house; natal Venus at 0 Scorpio 23 in the ninth house; and natal Mercury at the critical degree of 0 Capricorn 53 in the eleventh house.

The activation points of the above yod were transiting retrograde

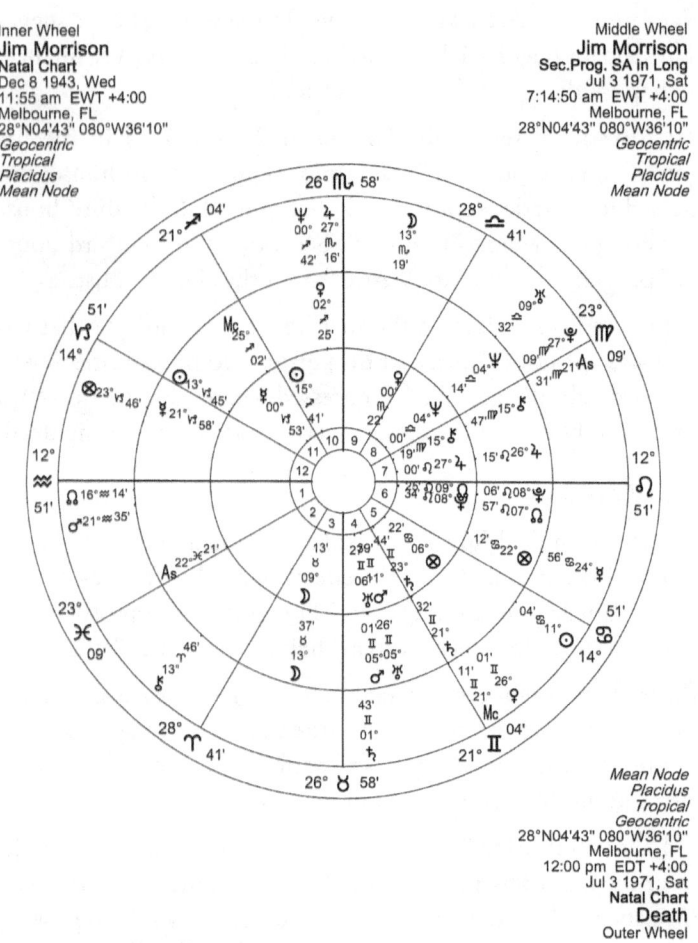

Neptune at 0 Sagittarius 42 and progressed Venus at 2 Sagittarius 25, both in the tenth house.

It was stated that Morrison had gone to a nightclub to purchase heroin for his girlfriend. A bouncer later noticed that Morrison was missing and subsequently went to the men's room, broke down the door to a locked stall, and discovered Morrison unresponsive. At that point, two drug dealers supposedly carried Morrison home and put him in the tub where he was later found.

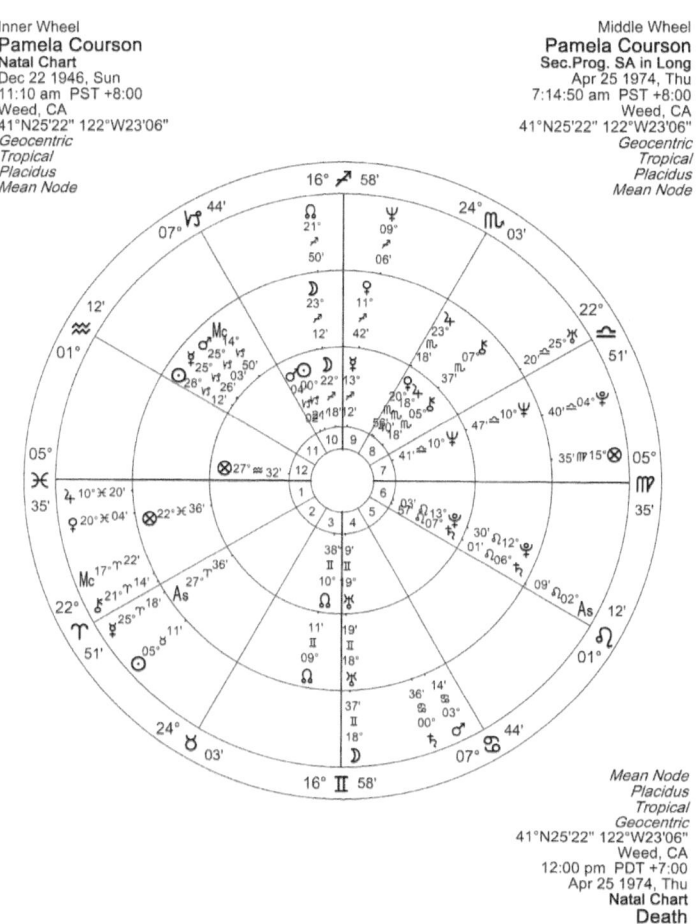

Pamela Courson

Pamela Courson was Jim Morrison's long-time girlfriend and common-law wife. She died three years after Morrison, on April 25, 1974, of a heroin overdose, in Los Angeles at age twenty-seven.

Morrison had left Courson his estate, but after her death, a battle ensued between Morrison's and Courson's parents over who had legal claim to the substantial estate. The families reached an out-of-court settlement, with each receiving a portion of the estate.

Yod One: transiting Chiron at 21 Aries 15 in the first house; natal retrograde Uranus at 19 Gemini 20 in the fourth house; progressed retrograde Uranus at 18 Gemini 19 in the fourth house; transiting Moon at 18 Gemini 38 in the fourth house; and natal Venus at the critical degree of 20 Scorpio 56 in the eighth house.

It appears that healing from Morrison's death was difficult for Courson. She may have blamed herself for his overdose. Her drug dependency is indicated by Pisces in the first house with Saturn in the sixth house ruling her health.

Yod Two: natal Ascendant at 5 Pisces 35; natal retrograde Saturn at 7 Leo 57 in the sixth house; progressed retrograde Saturn at 6 Leo 01 in the sixth house; and natal Mars at 4 Capricorn 03 in the tenth house.

Additionally, transiting Saturn at the critical degree of 0 Cancer 36 in the fourth house ruled the end of life. Transiting Saturn opposed the natal Sun, ruling self, at the critical degree of 0 Capricorn 21 in the tenth house.

Janis Joplin

Janis Joplin was known as "The Queen of Rock and Roll" as well as "The Queen of Psychedelic Soul." She was also a painter, a dancer, and a music arranger. In 2004, *Rolling Stone* magazine ranked her as number forty-six of its list of the 100 Greatest Artists of All Time and number twenty-eight on its 2008 list of 100 Greatest Singers of All Time.

Joplin battled drugs and alcohol for years and died October 4, 1970 from acute heroin-morphine intoxication; she was age twenty-seven.

Yod One: natal Moon at 8 Cancer 49 in the fifth house; natal Midheaven at 7 Sagittarius 15 at the Midheaven; and natal retrograde Mercury at the critical degree of 9 Aquarius 29 in the twelfth house.

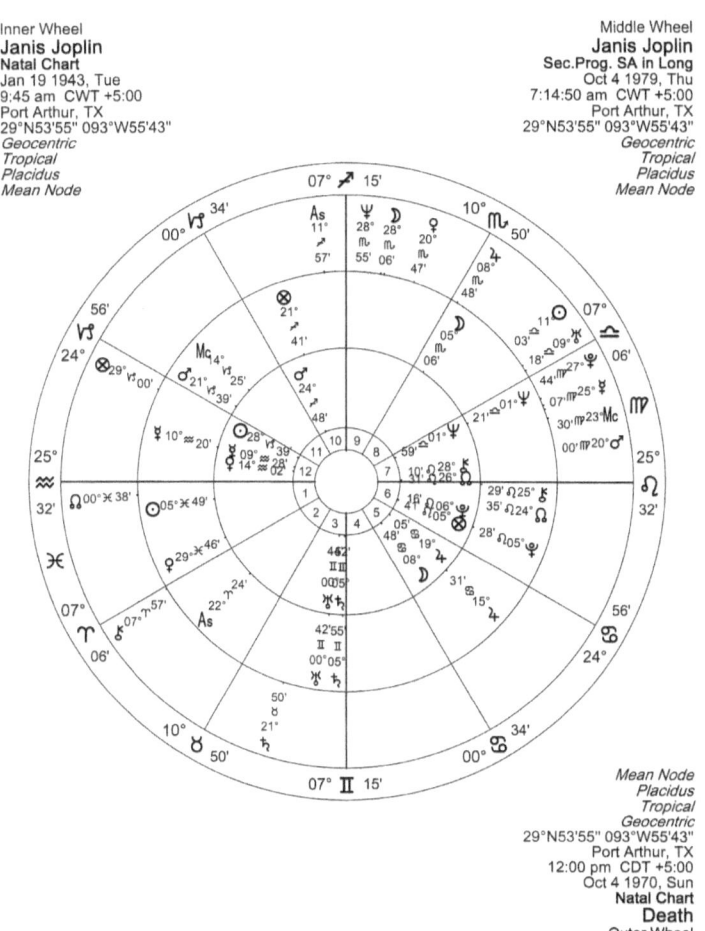

Joplin's natal Mercury is at the critical degree of 9 Aquarius 29 in her twelfth house, ruling bad habits and self-undoing.

Yod Two: natal retrograde Saturn at 5 Gemini 53 in the third house; transiting Saturn at 5 Gemini 41 in the third house; natal Part of Fortune (Misfortune) at 5 Leo 41 in the sixth house; natal retrograde Pluto at 6 Leo 16 in the sixth house; progressed retrograde Pluto at 5 Leo 39 in the sixth house; and progressed Midheaven at 5 Capricorn 22 in the eleventh house.

Joplin's natal and transiting Saturn were in her third house of routine activities. The Part of Fortune (Misfortune) and natal and progressed Pluto in Leo were in her sixth house. Leo ruled Joplin's having fun and the sixth house ruled her health and work.

Homicides

The keywords in the following yods may also give clues as to what occurred in each death. Each of the following three deaths were the result of a gunshot wound to the head.

Carol Stuart

On October 23, 1989, Carol Stuart and husband Charles were driving through a Boston neighborhood after attending childbirth classes. According to Charles' statement, a black gunman forced his way into their car at a stoplight, ordered them to drive, and robbed them. He then shot Charles in the stomach and Carol in the head, after which Charles drove away and called 911.

This case received national attention when Carol died hours after the shooting and their son, who was delivered by caesarean two months premature, died seventeen days later. Charles' brother subsequently identified him as Carol's killer. Hours after his brother revealed the truth, Charles committed suicide. His body was found in the Mystic River the next day.

Yod One: transiting Saturn at 8 Sagittarius 44 in the sixth house; transiting retrograde Neptune at 9 Capricorn 59 in the sixth house; natal Part of Fortune (Misfortune) at the critical degree of 9 Aquarius 15 in the eighth house; and progressed Mars at 8 Cancer 59 in the twelfth house.

Second Yod: natal retrograde Uranus at 12 Leo 29 in the second house; progressed Uranus at 12 Leo 14 in the second house; transiting Neptune at 9 Capricorn 54 in the sixth house; natal Descendant at the critical degree of 13 Capricorn 48; and progressed Venus at 13 Gemini 22 in the twelfth house.

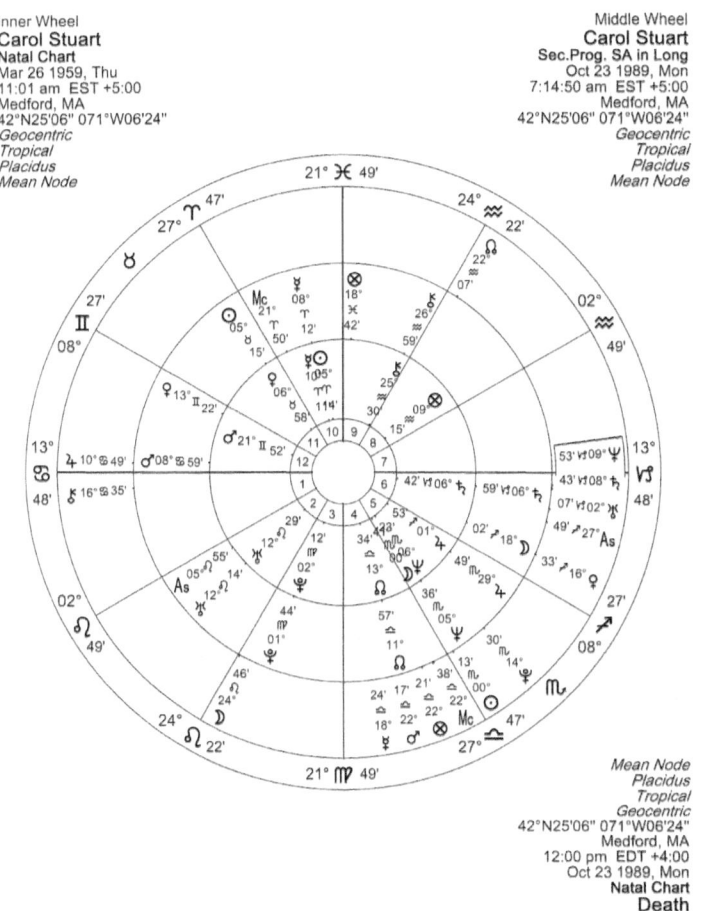

Bonnie Lee Bakley

Bonnie (Bonny) Lee Bakley was the wife of actor and *Baretta* star Robert Blake. She was shot once in the back of the head at about 9:45 p.m. on May 4, 2001 while waiting in Blake's car outside a restaurant in the Los Angeles area.

In 2002, Blake was charged with Bakley's murder, solicitation of murder, conspiracy, and special circumstance of lying in wait. A jury found Blake not guilty of the crimes. However, months lat-

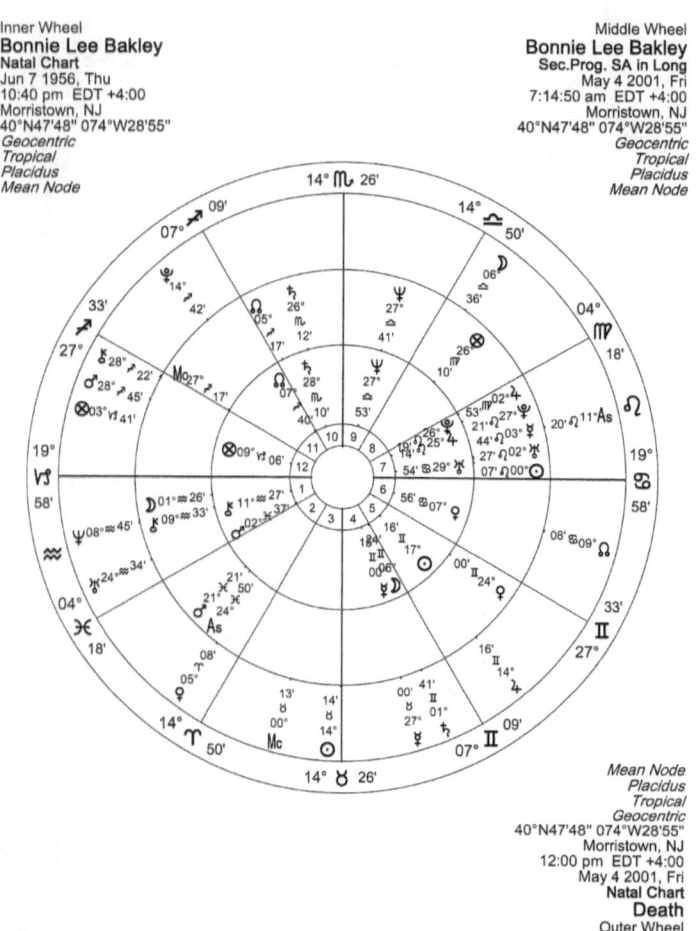

er, Blake was found guilty in a wrongful death civil suit brought against him by Bakley's children. Bakley's murder officially remains unsolved.

Yod One: natal Mars at 2 Pisces 38 in the first house; natal Uranus at 29 Cancer 54 in the seventh house; progressed Sun at 0 Leo 07 in the seventh house; progressed Uranus at 2 Leo 28 in the seventh house; progressed Mercury at 03 Leo 44 in the seventh house; transiting retrograde Chiron at 28 Sagittarius 23

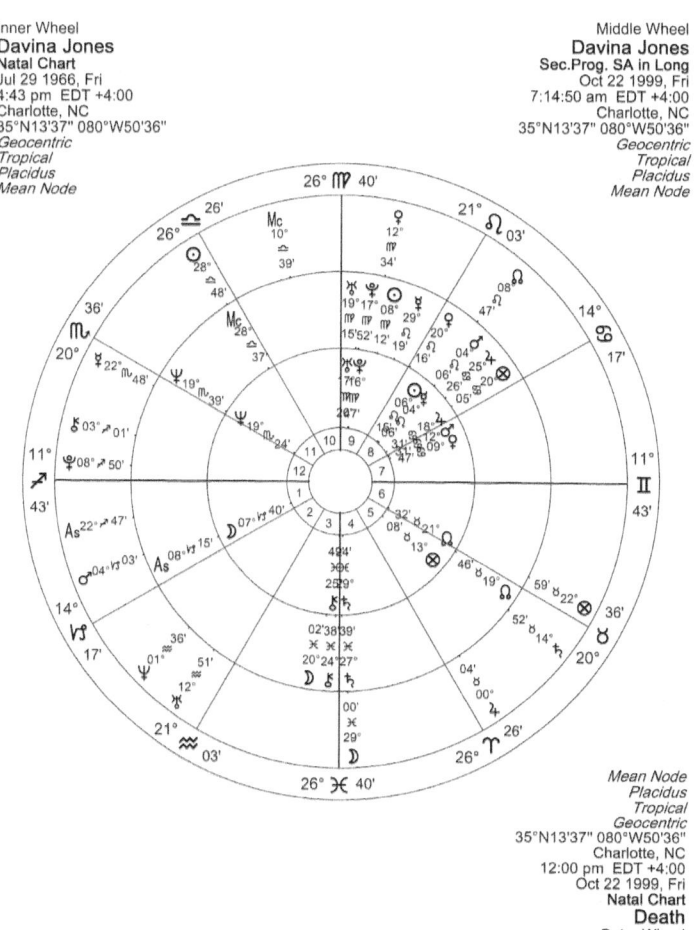

in the twelfth house; and transiting Mars at 28 Sagittarius 45 in the twelfth house.

Yod Two: progressed Ascendant at 24 Pisces 51 in the second house; natal Jupiter at 25 Leo 14 in the seventh house; natal Pluto at 26 Leo 20 in the seventh house; progressed Pluto at 27 Leo 22 in the seventh house; natal retrograde Neptune at 27 Libra 54 in the ninth house; progressed Neptune at 27 Libra 42 in the ninth house.

Davina Buff Jones

Davina Jones was a police officer on Bald Head Island, South Carolina. She died while on duty on the night of October 22, 1999 and her death was ruled a suicide from a self-inflicted gunshot. Reportedly, her partner was not with her at the time of her death.

Prior to her death, Jones had mentioned that she was planning to do a drug raid on the island. In July 2006, the official cause of Jones' death was changed to homicide and is still listed as under re-investigation and unsolved.

Yod One: natal Moon at 7 Capricorn 40 in the first house; progressed Midheaven at 8 Capricorn 15 in the first house; natal Venus at 9 Cancer 48 in the seventh house; progressed Sun at 8 Virgo 12 in the ninth house.

Yod Two: transiting retrograde Uranus at 12 Aquarius 52 in the second house; natal Mars at 12 Cancer 32 in the seventh house; and transiting Venus at 12 Virgo 34 in the ninth house.

Yod Three: natal retrograde Saturn at 29 Pisces 25 in the fourth house; progressed Mercury at 29 Leo 19 in the ninth house; progressed Midheaven at 28 Libra 37 in the eleventh house; and transiting Sun at 28 Libra 48 in the eleventh house.

Questionable Deaths

The following deaths have been ruled either accidental or suicide; however, they remain questionable:

Princess Diana of Wales

The world was saddened by the death of Princess Diana on Sunday, August 31, 1997. She was fatally injured in a car crash in the Pont de l'Alma road tunnel in Paris. The accident also caused the deaths of Diana's companion, Dodi Fayed, and the driver, Henri Paul.

An inquest in London that started in 2003 and continued

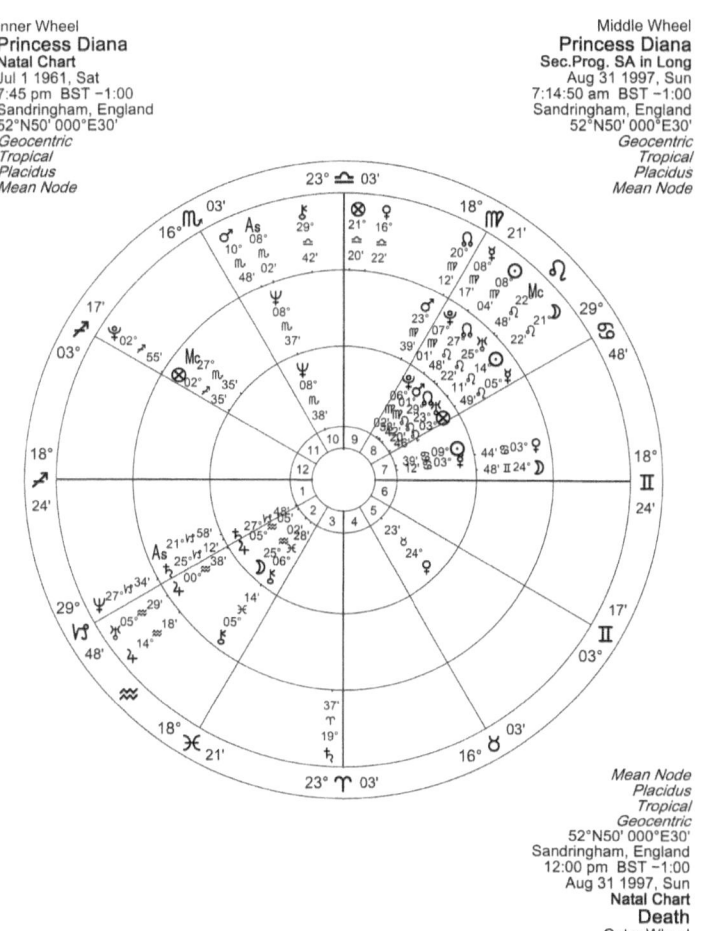

through 2007-08 stated the accident was a result of gross negligent driving by Henri Paul and the pursuing paparazzi. On April 7, 2008, the jury return a verdict of "unlawful killing." After the final inquest verdict, Al-Fayed stated, for the sake of the Princess's children, that he would end his ten-year campaign to establish that these deaths were murder rather than an accident.

Let's look at one yod from Princess Diana's chart: natal retrograde Jupiter at 5 Aquarius 06 in the second house; transiting retrograde Uranus at 5 Aquarius 29 in the second house; natal retrograde Mercury at 3 Cancer 12 in the seventh house; progressed Venus at 3 Cancer 45 in the seventh house; natal Pluto at 6 Virgo 03 in the eighth house; progressed Pluto at 7 Virgo 02 in the eighth house; transiting Sun at 8 Virgo 04 in the eighth house; and transiting retrograde Mercury at 8 Virgo 17 in the eighth house.

The activation point of this yod was progressed Mercury at 5 Leo 49 in the eighth house.

Below are keywords for each of the yod planets and houses; they are from *The Rulership Book* by Rex E. Bills:

Jupiter: Friendships, government and officials, millionaires, nobility, restaurants and workers, royalty and travel.

Aquarius: Acquaintances and motion picture producers (Dodi Fayed was a movie producer).

Second House: Death of partner and public enemies.

Uranus: Accidents, assassination attempts, automobiles and drivers, aviators, sudden deaths, foreigners, mechanics, motion picture producers, passengers, pilots and propellants.

Mercury: Automobiles, bisexuality, cabs and drivers, gasoline stations and owners, investigators, perjury and witnesses.

Cancer: One's family, restaurants and workers, and women in general.

Seventh House: Children in general, deaths, divorces, enemies, one's husband, lovers, marriage partner, opponents and public enemies.

Venus: Companions, courtships, crown jewels, engagement to be married, females in general, fiancées, happiness, love, marriage and wealth.

Pluto: Ambushes, assassins, betrayal, corruption, criminals, death, homicide, laser beams, liars, murder, crimes of violence and wrecks and wreckers.

Virgo: August, one's inferiors, Paris, France, police, restaurants and workers.

Eighth House: Manner of one's death, estates of marriage and wills.

Sun: Government and officials, one's husband, kings, men in general, nobility, politics, position of prominence, princes and princesses, queens, relatives rich and powerful, royalty, sons and Sunday.

Natalie Wood

The circumstances surrounding Natalie Wood's death have remained questionable since she drowned on November 29, 1981. She died after a night of partying while on their yacht, Splendor, with her husband, Robert Wagner, and their friend, Christopher Walken. There were conflicting versions of what occurred, but her death was ruled an accident.

In 2011, thirty years after Wood's death, Los Angeles investigators heard from potential witnesses who were not included in the original investigation and who provided some new information. The autopsy report revealed that Wood had bruises on her body and arms as well as an abrasion on her left cheek. In June 2012, her death was reclassified as "drowning and other undetermined factors."

Yod One: transiting Uranus at 0 Sagittarius 49 in the second house; natal Moon at 0 Taurus 59 in the seventh house; and natal Chiron at 5 Cancer 02 in the ninth house.

Yod Two: progressed Ascendant at 16 Scorpio 17 in the second house; natal Saturn at 17 Aries 58 in the seventh house; progressed retrograde Saturn at 17 Aries 08 in the seventh house; natal Neptune at 19 Virgo 03 in the twelfth house; progressed Neptune at 20 Virgo 26 in the twelfth house; progressed Part of Fortune (Misfortune) at the critical degree of 21 Aquarius 06 in the fifth house; progressed retrograde Jupiter at 25 Aquarius 43 in the fifth house; transiting North Node at 24 Cancer 53 in the

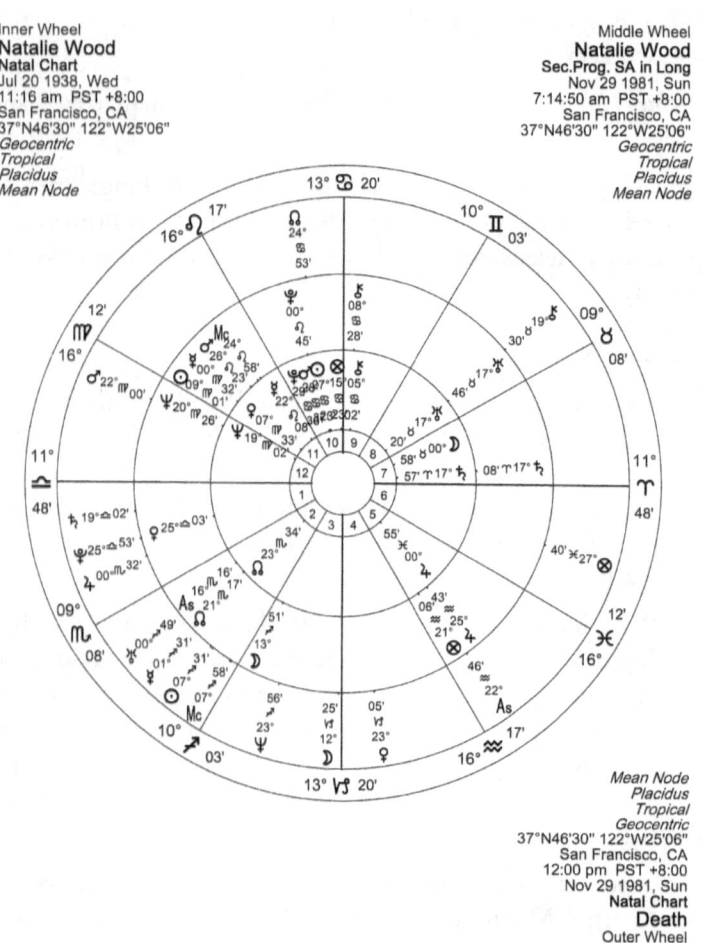

tenth house; natal Neptune at 19 Virgo 03 in the twelfth house; progressed Neptune at 20 Virgo 26 in the twelfth house; and transiting Mars at 22 Virgo 01 in the twelfth house.

The activation point of the above yod was the progressed Midheaven at 24 Leo 59 in the eleventh house and progressed Mars at 26 Leo 23 in the eleventh house.

The yod was triggered by an inconjunct to Jupiter at the foot of the yod to progressed Venus at 25 Libra 04 in the first house and transiting Pluto at 25 Libra 53 in the first house.

Let's look at some keywords for this yod:

Aquarius: Ankles, fractures of, body fluids, lower legs, Los Angeles, and motion pictures.

Fifth House: Courtships, entertainers, films, filmdom, friends of one's partners, love affairs, motion pictures, pleasures, promiscuity, risks and romance.

Jupiter: Carelessness, excesses, facts, friends, millionaires, morality and Splendor.

Cancer: Boating, boat trips, restaurants and workers and women in general.

Ninth House: Voyages especially by water.

Neptune: Abnormal behavior, actors, actresses, alcoholic beverages, bartenders, bays, cheaters, crimes, drowning, drugs in general, hidden side of life, infidelity, fictitious names, scandal, the deep sea, swimming, swimmers and yachts.

Virgo: Los Angeles.

Twelfth House: Cheaters, crimes, drugs in general, secret love affairs, scandal and suicides.

Mars: Accidents, aggressors, anger, assault, bladders, crime, deaths by accident or violence, sudden deaths, fights, injuries by violence, liquors, males in general, manslaughter, murder, perjury, quarrels and violence.

Marilyn Monroe

Marilyn Monroe's death on August 5, 1962 remains one of the most mysterious and controversial in Hollywood history. Monroe was found dead at age thirty-six in the bedroom of her Brentwood, California home by Eunice Murray, her live-in housekeeper.

At the time, there was talk of Monroe being involved with the

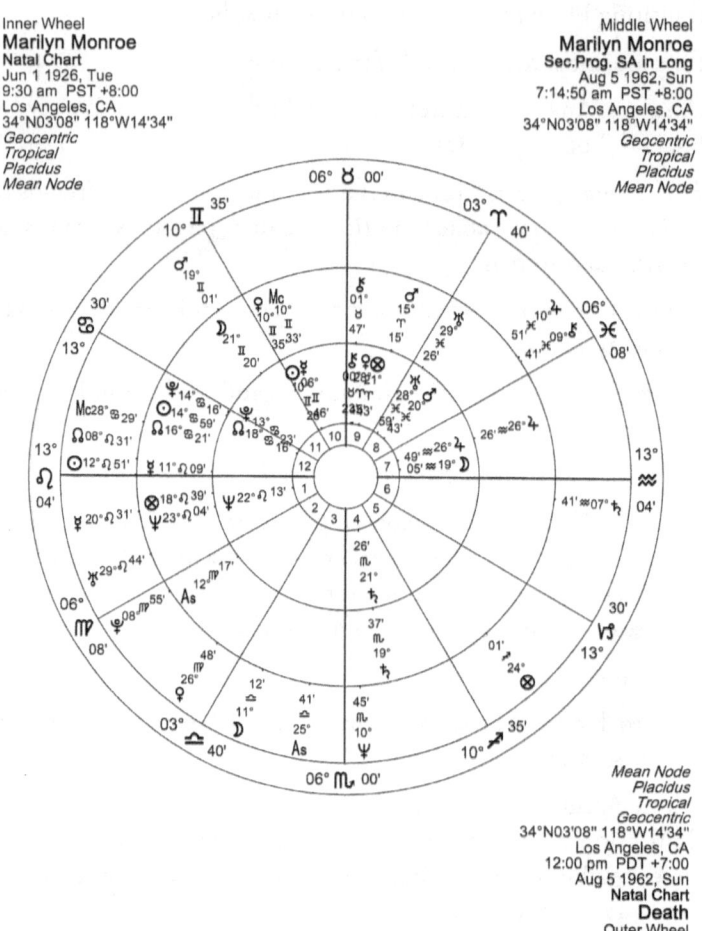

Kennedys, Frank Sinatra, and others. She was also planning to remarry Joe DiMaggio on August 8, the date of her funeral. Monroe's death was ruled a "probable suicide" as a result of acute barbiturate poisoning. However, there were no drugs in her stomach and no needle marks found on her body.

Using repetitive keywords, we will go through the whole interpretative process of one of Monroe's yods to see what it reveals about her death:

Yod One: natal retrograde Saturn at the critical degree of 21 Scorpio 26 and progressed retrograde Saturn at 19 Scorpio 38, both in the fourth house; natal Part of Fortune (Misfortune) at 21 Aries 44 in the ninth house; progressed Moon at 21 Gemini 19 and transiting Mars at 19 Gemini 02, both in the natal eleventh house.

Saturn keywords: death, common people, employment, depression, emotional, deceit, deceiver, enema, elderly person, grudges, secret or private enemy, habits, jealousy, keepers, men in general, punishment, sedative

Scorpio keywords: autopsy, colon, death, druggist, drug store, organs of elimination, hate, jealousy, psychiatrist, reproductive organs, resentment, sex, Washington, DC

Fourth house keywords: one's death, government activity, one's home, midnight, people residing in your home, older people

Aries keywords: coma, common people, head, insomnia, physiotherapist, therapist

Ninth house keywords: secret enemy, friend of a friend, stranger who plays an important part in one's life

Moon keywords: bowels and bowel troubles, domestic servant, evening, females in general, fluids, dealer in fluids, functions of the body, one's home, female housekeeper, insomnia, laundry, nurse, sleeping potion, servant, washing, washing machine, women in general

Mars keywords: aggressor, anger, argument, assailant, assassination, assassin, crime of passion, sudden death, death by accident or violence, diarrhea, druggist, drug store, execution, executioner, head in general, injury by violence, males in general, murder, needle, sharp pains, perjury, rectum, resentment, sex, struggles, struggling, thieves

Gemini keywords: neighbor, secretary, telephone

Eleventh house keywords: acquaintance, companion, counselor, friends, senate, senator

Working with these keywords and putting them into possible categories applicable to Monroe's death, and comparing these words with known facts and/or possible solutions, results in:

Perpetrators of Monroe's Death: Secret enemies, keepers, elderly persons, men in general, druggists, psychiatrists, persons sharing home, friends of a friend, females in general, domestic servants, female housekeepers, nurses, pharmacists, acquaintances, counselors, companions, friends, liquids and those who use liquids.

It was known that Monroe had hired a live-in housekeeper at the recommendation of her psychiatrist, but was ending her relationship with both because of her upcoming remarriage to Joe DiMaggio.

Reasons for Monroe's death: Punishment, grudges, jealousy, hates, resentment, aggression, arguments and anger.

All of the above could have been possible in connection with Monroe's death.

Cause of Death: Habits, sedatives, fluids and dealers of fluids, sleeping potions, murder and sudden death.

As with many actresses of that day, it was Monroe's habit to take an enema for hygiene and dietetic purposes. Monroe's housekeeper administered the enemas. It is also thought that the fatal dose of barbiturates was administered by enema.

Where and When: One's home, evening and midnight.

The above accurately depicts where and when Monroe's death took place.

Miscellaneous Keywords: Sedatives, death, colons, organs of elimination, rectum, comas, insomnia, laundry, washing and washing machines, perjury.

When police arrived at Monroe's home and found her dead in the bedroom at 4:35 a.m., they noted that the housekeeper was washing the sheets from Monroe's bed. It has been questioned as to why she was washing at that hour unless the bedding had become soiled as a result of administering the drugs. Perjury was prevalent in the events surrounding Monroe's death and including the time of death.

Yod Two: natal retrograde Saturn at critical degree of 21 Scorpio 26 in the fourth house; progressed retrograde Saturn at 19 Scorpio 38 in the fourth house; natal Part of Fortune (Misfortune) at 21 Aries 44 in the ninth house; progressed Moon at 21 Gemini 19 in the eleventh house; transiting Mars at 19 Gemini 02 in the eleventh house

Yod Three: transiting Venus at 26 Virgo 48 in the second house; natal Jupiter at 26 Aquarius 50 in the seventh house; progressed retrograde Jupiter at 26 Aquarius 26 in the seventh house; natal Venus at 28 Aries 45 in the ninth house; and natal Chiron at 0 Taurus 24 in the ninth house.

The activation points of the above yod are natal Uranus at the decisive degree of 29 Pisces 00 and progressed retrograde Uranus at the decisive degree of 29 Pisces 26, both in the eighth house.

The trigger was an inconjunct from transiting Uranus at 29 Leo 44 in the first house.

Birth Data

With the exception of Davina Buff Jones, all birth data is from AstroDataBank. Jones' birth data is from birth certificate.

References

Bills, Rex E. *The Rulership Book*. Richmond. MaCoy Publishing & Masonic Supply Co., Inc., 1971.
Oldenburg, Ann. "Whitney Houston's cause of death revealed by L.A. coroner," *USA Today*, March 22, 2012.
Serpe, Gina. "Amy Winehouse's Cause of Death: Accidental Alcohol Poinsoning, Blood Level Five Times the Legal Limit," http://www.eonline.com/news/, Oct. 26, 2011.
"Kurt Cobain Death Certificate," http://en.wikipedia.org/wiki/Death_of_Kurt_Cobain.

Sieczkowski, Cavan. "Seattle Police Reexamine Kurt Cobain's Death," *The Huffington Post*, March 20, 2014.
Doland, Angela. "New questions about Jim Morrison's death," *USA Today*, July 11, 2007.
http://www.astro.databank/ Courson, Pamela.
http://en.wikipedia.org/wiki/Pamela_Courson
http://en.wikipedia.org/wiki/Janis_Joplin
http://en.wikipedia.org/wiki/Charles_Stuart_(murderer)
King, Gary C. "Who Murdered Bonny Lee Bakley?", Crime Library, http://www.crimelibrary.com/notorious_murders/family/bakley/1.html.
WWAY3, http://www.wwaytv3.com/2013/12/17/suicide-death -of-davina-buff-jones-now-ruled-undetermined
Gonzales, Jason and Julian March. "DA - Bald Head officer's 1999 death not definitively suicide," Star News Online, Dec. 17, 2013, http://www.starnewsonline.com/article/20131217/ARTICLES/131219748?p=2&tc=pg
http://en.wikipedia.org/wiki/Death_of_Diana,_Princess_of_Wales
McCarthney, Anthony. "Probe of Wood's death reopened," *Albany Times Union*, Nov. 19, 2011.
Associated Press. "Report: Wood's body was bruised," *Albany Times Union*, Jan. 15, 2013.
Spoto, Donald. *Marilyn Monroe: The Biography*. New York: Harper Collins Publishers, 1993.

9/56 Year Cycle: U.S. Presidential Assassinations

By David McMinn

ABSTRACT: This paper examines the prospect of a 9/56 year cycle in the timing of successful and attempted assassinations of US presidents and vice presidents. Strangely, 18/56 and 36/56 year cycles could be correlated with these events. Why these grids were so important in the timing of such threats remains unknown. Lunisolar tidal harmonics are fundamental in solving the mystery, but that is all that can be stated. The 9/56 year cycle was also assessed in relation to the deaths of U.S. leaders, but no significance could be achieved.

A 56-year cycle in U.S. financial activity was first proposed by Funk (1932). McMinn (1986, 1993, 1996) expanded upon the concept and presented a 9/56 year cycle in the timing of major U.S. and Western European financial panics since 1760. This cycle was then extrapolated to major earthquakes (McMinn, 2011a, 2011b, 2011d), Category 5 Atlantic hurricanes (McMinn, 2011c) and volcanic eruptions (McMinn, 2011d, 2012). Firm correlates could be produced with the 9/56 year grid, after assessing historic catalogs in each of the respective disciplines. The 9/56 year grid can be intimately linked with Moon Sun cycles, as several lunisolar cycles aligned very closely at 9.0 and

56.0 solar years (McMinn, 2011a). Moon Sun tidal harmonics were therefore believed to activate critical events that clustered within 9/56 year patterns.

McMinn (2010) established various anomalies in the timing of the deaths and births of U.S. presidents and vice presidents. Strangely, seasonality and lunar phase were significant in the timing of these events in U.S. history. Given the strong luni-solar influence, a 9/56 year effect was hypothesized to be important in cycles of U.S. presidential deaths. Alas, no correlates could be achieved, despite an extensive assessment. However, significance could still be realized between the 18/56 and 36/56 year grids and successful and attempted assassinations of U.S. leaders. The 9/56 year cycle consists of a grid repeating the intervals 56 years vertically (called sequences) and 9 years horizontally (called subcycles). The 56-year sequences have been numbered in accordance with McMinn (1993), with 1817, 1873, 1929, 1985 being designated as Sequence 01; 1818, 1874, 1930, 1986 as Sequence 02 and so forth. McMinn (Appendix 2, 2002) presented the full numbering. In this paper, the term season denotes any interval during the solar year and does not pertain to the traditional seasons—spring, summer, autumn and winter. In the tables, the year of best fit was taken as the year ending September 30. The list of attempted assassinations was sourced from Wikipedia (see Appendix 1), because it gave the most comprehensive coverage.

9/56 Year Grid

This cycle was considered in relation to the deaths of U.S. presidents and vice presidents, but no correlates could be produced. The data for the 66 leaders who have died to date was considered by season and by era and still the outcome was negative. Additional grids were considered with 18, 36 and 54 years on the horizontal—denoted as 18/56, 36/56 and 54/56 year cycles respectively. Again nothing could be achieved.

36/56 Year Grid

Of the 33 successful and attempted assassinations listed in Appendix 1, some 16 appeared in the 36/56 year grid in Table 1 (see below), which compared with an expected 8.25 (significant $p < .01$). Unusually, three of the four successful U.S. presidential assassinations clustered in Sequences 49, 29 and 09.

18/56 Year Grid

Of the 33 events in Appendix 1, 24 showed up in the complete 18/56 year grid in Appendix 2 (significant $p < .01$).

Discussion and Conclusions

A few correlates do not make a theory and the finding of 18/56 and 36/56 year assassination cycles must be considered in context. Thus, the original article by McMinn (2010) is recommended background reading to appreciate more fully the cycles of death and assassination for U.S. presidents and vice presidents. In the 2010 paper, numerous correlates were established supporting a strong seasonal and lunar phase influence in the occurrence of the deaths and births of U.S. leaders. Assassinations were also found to fall selectively in 18/56 and 36/56 year patterns. Grids based on 56 years and multiples of 9 years can be strongly linked to Moon Sun cycles (McMinn, 2006, 2011a). These two luminaries may explain how the 9/56 year effect actually functioned in relation to a range of phenomena, such as earthquakes, volcanoes and financial panics.

Grids based on 56 years and multiples of 9 years correlate perfectly with Moon Sun cycles (see Appendix 3). Any events occurring in the same 56 year sequence will have the lunar ascending node (LAN) sited a narrow sector of the ecliptic, WITH NO EXCEPTIONS (1st harmonic). Any events clustering in the 9/56 year layout will have the LAN in two sectors approximately 180 degrees opposite in the ecliptic WITH NO EXCEPTIONS (1st and 2nd harmonics). For any events clustering in

Table 1 36/56 Year Grid: Successful & Attempted Assassinations of U.S. Leaders 1830-2013 Year ending September 30							
Sq 05	Sq 41	Sq 21	Sq 01	Sq 37	Sq 17	Sq 53
					1833	1869
				1853	1889	1925
		1837	1873	1909	1945	**1981** 0330
1821	1857	1893	1929 **1928** 1119	1965	**2001** 0207	
1877	1913 **1912** 1014	1949	1985	2021		
1933 0515	1969	**2005** 0510				
1989	2025					
Sq 33	Sq 13	Sq 49	Sq 29	Sq 09	Sq 45	Sq 25
						1841
					1861	1897
				0223		
			1845	**1881** 0702	1917	1953
		1865 0414	**1901** 0906	1937	1973	**2009** 04??
1849	1885	1921	1957	**1993** 0413		
1905	1941	1977	**2013** 0420			
1961 **1960** 1211	1997 **1996** 1022					
2017						

> The 56-year sequences are separated by intervals of 36 years on the horizontal. Includes successful and attempted assassinations of presidents and vice presidents as listed in Appendix 1.
> Dates of various assassination attempts, plots, and murders are highlighted in **bold**.
> *Source of Raw Data*: Wikipedia. List of United States Presidential Assassination Attempts and Plots.

the 9/56 year grid and occurring around the same time of year will have apogee sited in three sectors 120 degrees apart on the ecliptic WITH NO EXCEPTIONS (3rd harmonic). These patterns arise due to the very close alignment of several Moon Sun cycles at 9.0 and 56.0 solar years (see Appendix 4).

For successful and attempted assassinations of U.S. leaders, various grid patterns were considered based on 56 years and multiples of 9 years. The 18/56 and 36/56 year grids yielded significance at the $p < .01$ level and thus they do not occur randomly. No connection could be established between the death of US leaders and the 9/56 year grid. There were two options to account for this failure. 1) There is no link between these two factors. 2) A relationship does exist but it has yet to be established. Only further research will confirm which proposal is valid.

Numerous correlates can be produced to support the non-random hypothesis for deaths of US leaders. However, making accurate forecasts from the 9/56 year grid is impossible, based on current understanding. How the cycle actually functioned is completely unknown. The mathematics associated with lunisolar tidal harmonics will need to be deciphered, a formidable task given its inherent complexity. Hopefully, other researchers will explore this theme more fully and ultimately solve the mystery.

References

about.com. American History. Presidential Assassinations and Assassination Attempts.
http://americanhistory.about.com/od/uspresidents/a/assassinations.htm

Funk, J M. 1932. The 56 Year Cycle in American Business Activity. Ottawa, IL.
LA Times. 2012. Presidential Assassinations and Attempts. Jan 22. http://timelines.latimes.com/us-presidential-assassinations-and-attempts/
McMinn, David. 1986, The 56 Year Cycles & Financial Crises. 15th Conference of Economists. *The Economics Society of Australia*. Monash University, Melbourne. 18p. Aug 25-29.
McMinn, David. 1993. Financial Crises & The Number 56. *The Australian Technical Analysts Association Newsletter*. p 21-25. September.
McMinn, David. 1996. Financial Crises & The Number 56. *Cycles*. The Foundation For The Study of Cycles. p 11-17. Vol 46, No 1. August.
McMinn, David. 2002. 9/56 Year Cycle: Financial Crises. http://www.davidmcminn.com/pages/fcnum56.htm
McMinn, David. 2006. Market Timing by The Moon & The Sun. Twin Palms Publishing. 163p.
McMinn, David. 2010. Lunar Phase, Seasonality and US Presidential Deaths. Today's Astrologer. *American Federation of Astrologers*. Vol 72, No 11. p 4-12. November 6.
McMinn, David. 2011a. 9/56 Year Cycle: Californian Earthquakes. *New Concepts In Global Tectonics Newsletter*. No 58. p 33-44. March.
McMinn, David. 2011b. 9/56 Year Cycle: Record Earthquakes. *New Concepts In Global Tectonics Newsletter*. No 59. p 88-104. June.
McMinn, David. 2011c, 9/56 Year Cycle: Hurricanes. *New Concepts In Global Tectonics Newsletter*. No 59. p 105-111. June.
McMinn, David. 2011d. 9/56 Year Cycle: Earthquakes in Selected Countries. *New Concepts in Global Tectonics Newsletter*. No 60. p 9-37. September.
McMinn, David. 2012. 9/56 Year Cycle: World Mega Volcanic Eruptions. *New Concepts in Global Tectonics Newsletter*. No 64. p 7-18. September.
Wikipedia. List of United States presidential assassination attempts and plots. http://en.wikipedia.org/wiki/List_of_United_States_presidential_assassination_attempts_and_plots

Appendix 1
Assassinations of U.S. Presidents & Vice Presidents 1800-2013

Successful Assassinations

Date	U.S. Leader	Comment
Apr. 14, 1865	Abraham Lincoln	Shot by John Wilkes Booth
July 2, 1881	James Garfield	Shot July 2; died Sept. 19
Sep. 6, 1901	William McKinley	Shot Sep. 6; died Sept. 14
Nov. 22, 1963	John Kennedy	Shot by Lee Harvey Oswald

Assassination Attempts and Plots (Wikipedia)

Date	U.S. Leader	Comment
Jan. 30, 1835	Andrew Jackson	Shot at by Richard Lawrence; pistols misfired
Feb. 23, 1861	Abraham Lincoln	Baltimore Plot
Aug. ??, 1864	Abraham Lincoln	Shot at while horse riding
Apr. 14, 1865	Andrew Johnson VP	Attempted assassination
Oct. 14, 1912	Theodore Roosevelt	Shot in chest by John Schrank
July 2, 1915	Thomas Marshall VP	Bomb exploded prematurely in Marshall's office
Nov. 19, 1928	Herbert Hoover	Attempted railroad bombing in Argentina
May 15, 1933	FDR	Assassination attempt by Guiseppe Zangara
Summer 1947	Harry Truman	Mail tainted with ricin poison
Nov. 22, 1950	Harry Truman	Attack by Puerto Rican pro-independence activists
Dec. 11, 1960	JFK	Threatened by Pavlick in Palm Beach Florida

Nov. 2, 1963	JFK	FBI thwarted a 4-man conspiracy
Apr. 13, 1972	Richard Nixon	Assassination attempt by Arthur Bremer
Feb. 22, 1974	Richard Nixon	Assassination attempt by Samuel Byck.
Sept. 5, 1975	Gerald Ford	Assassination attempt by Lynette Fromme
Sept. 22, 1975	Gerald Ford	Assassination attempt by Sara Jane Moore
May 5, 1979	Jimmy Carter	Assassination attempt by Raymond Harvey
Mar. 30, 1981	Ronald Reagan	Assassination attempt by John Hinckley Jnr
Apr. 13, 1993	George H.W. Bush	Unsuccessful plot in Kuwait
Jan. 21, 1994	Bill Clinton	Barbour plotted to kill Clinton
Sept. 12, 1994	Bill Clinton	Corder crashed a plane in the White House gardens
Oct. 29, 1994	Bill Clinton	Duran fires shots at the White House
Nov. ??, 1996	Bill Clinton	Assassination plot foiled in Manila
Feb. 7, 2001	George W. Bush	Robert Pickett shoots at the White House
May 10, 2005	George W. Bush	Live hand grenade attack in Georgia
Aug. 28, 2008	Barack Obama	Plot to attack Obama at Democratic convention
Apr. ??, 2009	Barack Obama	Plot to assassinate Obama in Istanbul
Oct. 22, 2009	Barack Obama	White supremacists' assassination plot
Apr. 20, 2013	Barack Obama	Letter spiked with ricin poison

Abbreviation: VP—Vice President.
Various conspiracy theories have arisen claiming that Presidents Taylor and Harding were murdered and did not die from natural causes. There is no firm evidence to support these claims and thus their deaths are not included in the listing. In June 1991, President Taylor's remains were exhumed and small samples were tested for excessive arsenic levels. Nothing was found to indicate death by poisoning. Taylor most probably died of a combination of cholera and bad medical care.
Source of Raw Data: Wikipedia. List of United States Presidential Assassination Attempts and Plots. All events listed have been included in the appendix.
Data not from Wikipedia: All successful assassinations; VP Andrew Johnson attempted assassination; bomb exploded premature in VP Thomas Marshall's office

Appendix 2
Complete 18/56 Year Grid: Successful & Attempted Assassinations of U.S. Leaders 1830-2013, Year Ending September 30

Sq 05	Sq 23	Sq 41	Sq 03	Sq 21	Sq 39	Sq 01
						1761
			1763	1781	1799	1817
1765	1783	1801	1819	1837	1855	1873
1821	1839	**1857** 0302	1875	1893	1911	1929 **1928** 1119
1877	1895	1913 **1912** 1014	1931	1949	1967	1985
1933 0515	1951 **1950** 1122	1969	1987	**2005** 0510	2023	
1989	2007	2025				
Sq 19	Sq 37	Sq 55	Sq 17	Sq 35	Sq 53	Sq 15
			1833	1851	1869	1887
1835 0130	1853	1871	1889	1907	1925	1943
1891	1909	1927	1945	1963	**1981** 0330	1999
1947 summer	1965	1983	2001 0207	2019		
2003	2021					
Sq 33	Sq 51	Sq 13	Sq 31	Sq 49	Sq 11	Sq 29
					1771	1789 1845
			1847	**1865** 0414	1883	**1901** 0906
1849	1867	1885	1903	1921	1939	1957

1905	1923	1941	1959	1977	1995	**2013**
					1994	0420
					1029	
1961	**1979**	1997	2015			
1960	0505	**1996**				
1211		11??				
2017						
Sq 47	Sq 09	Sq 27	Sq 45	Sq 07	Sq 25	Sq 43
					1841	1859
		1843	**1861**	1879	1897	**1915**
			0223			0702
1863	**1881**	1899	1917	1935	1953	1971
	0702					
1919	1937	1955	1973	1991	**2009**	
					04??	
1975	**1993**	2011				
0905	0413					
1975						
0922						

The 56-year sequences are separated by intervals of 18 years on the horizontal. Includes successful and attempted assassinations of presidents and vice presidents as listed in Appendix 1.
Dates of various assassination attempts, plots and murders have been highlighted in **bold**.
Source of Raw Data: Wikipedia. List of United States Presidential Assassination Attempts and Plots.

Appendix 3 Moon-Sun Background Information

Apogee

Apogee is the point in the lunar orbit where the Moon is the greatest distance from Earth, while perigee is the least distance. In the lunar apse cycle, the apogee-perigee axis (apsides) rotates counter-clockwise around the ecliptic circle, with apogee passing from spring equinox to spring equinox every 8.8474 tropical years. The apsides axis is very important in oceanic tides on Earth. When the Full/New Moon is at apogee, the amplitude of tides in New York Harbor is 50 percent lower than when the Full/New Moon is at perigee. Apogee could be expected to play a key role in any Moon-Sun seismic effect.

9.0 divided by the 8.8474 year apse cycle yielded 1.02, while 56.0 divided by the apse cycle gave 6.33 (6 plus one third). Thus, every 9.0 years in the 9/56 year grid, apogee will be sited about 6 degrees further anti-clockwise on the ecliptical circle. Every 56.0 years, apogee will be located 120 degrees further anticlockwise on the ecliptical circle. In the 9/56 year grid, apogee will therefore always located in three segments approximately 120 degrees apart on the ecliptical circle. For example, Table A gives the apogee position as on July 1 of those years in a 9/56 year grid. Apogee is always located in the following three segments 120 degrees apart 335–013 E; 095–135 E and 215–250 E with no exceptions.

Apogee takes 5.995 tropical years to complete one cycle ascending node to ascending node. The 18.0 year Saros eclipse cycle divided by 6 produced the integral number three and the 9 year Half Saros divided by 6 gave 1.5 (one plus a half). The 56 year cycle divided by 6 gave 9.3333 tropical years (9 plus one third). Thus the angle between the ascending node and apogee oscillates by about 180 degrees every 9.0 years and by about 120 degrees every 56.0 years. This is illustrated on the same date in Table B, which gives ascending node—apogee angles grouping 60o apart in the angular circle with no exceptions.

Table A Appendix 3 9/56 Year Cycle & the Position of Apogee, Ecliptic Degree of Apogee on July 1					
Sq 32	Sq 41	Sq 50	Sq 03	Sq 12	Sq 21
			1763 000 E	1772 007 E	1781 013 E
1792 100 E	1801 106 E	1810 113 E	1819 119 E	1828 126 E	1837 131 E
1848 219 E	1857 225 E	1866 231 E	1875 237 E	1884 244 E	1893 250 E
1904 337 E	1913 344 E	1922 350 E	1931 356 E	1940 002 E	1949 008 E
1960 096 E	1969 102 E	1978 108 E	1987 115 E	1996 121 E	2005 127 E

The 56 year sequences are separated by an interval of 9 years.
Abbreviation: E = Ecliptic degrees.

Table B Appendix 3 9/56 Year Cycle: Angle Between Lan & Apogee, Angle Between LAN and Apogee on July 1					
Sq 32	Sq 41	Sq 50	Sq 03	Sq 12	Sq 21
			1763 341 A	1772 162 A	1781 342 A
1792 282 A	1801 102 A	1810 283 A	1819 103 A	1828 283 A	1837 103 A
1848 044 A	1857 224 A	1866 044 A	1875 224 A	1884 046 A	1893 225 A
1904 165 A	1913 346 A	1922 166 A	1931 346A	1940 168 A	1949 346 A
1960 287 A	1969 107 A	1978 287 A	1987 108 A	1996 288 A	2005 108 A

The 56 year sequences are separated by an interval of 9 years.
Abbreviation: LAN—lunar ascending node. A—angular degrees.

Table C Appendix 3 9/56 Year Cycle & the Position of LAN Ecliptical Degree of LAN on July 1					
Sq 32	Sq 41	Sq 50	Sq 03	Sq 12	Sq 21
			1763 019 E	1772 205 E	1781 031 E
1792 178 E	1801 004 E	1810 190 E	1819 016 E	1828 202 E	1837 028 E
1848 175 E	1857 001 E	1866 187 E	1875 013 E	1884 199 E	1893 025 E
1904 172 E	1913 358 E	1922 184 E	1931 010 E	1940 196 E	1949 022 E
1960 169 E	1969 355 E	1978 181 E	1987 007 E	1996 193 E	2005 019 E
The 56-year sequences are separated by an interval of 9 years. *Abbreviation*: LAN—lunar ascending node. E—ecliptic degrees					

Equinoxes

These points are sited where the plane of the Earth's equator projected out into the sky (celestial equator) cuts the plane of the Earth's orbit around the Sun (ecliptic). At these points, the equatorial ascending node is where the Sun crosses the celestial equator from south to north the celestial equator at 0 E (0 Aries vernal or spring equinox at around 20 March). The equatorial descending node is where the Sun crosses the celestial equator from north to south at 180 E (0 Libra, autumnal equinox at around 22 September).

Lunar Ascending Node

The lunar nodes are imaginary points in the heavens, where the plane of the Earth's orbit around the Sun (the ecliptic) is cut by the plane of the Moon's orbit around the Earth. The ascending (north) node is where the Moon crosses the ecliptic from south to north, where as the descending (south) node is where the

Moon crosses from north to south. In the lunar nutation cycle, it takes 18.62 years for the ascending node to complete one cycle from spring equinox to spring equinox.

Table C shows the ecliptical position of the lunar ascending node as on July 1 in a 9/56 year grid. This point is always found in two segments approximately 180 degrees apart in the ecliptical circle with no exceptions.

Appendix 4 9 & 56 Year Lunisolar Cycles		
18.0 Year Saros		
Days	Years	Lunisolar Cycles
6,574.36	18.00	18.0 Tropical Years
6,585.78	18.03	19.0 Nodical Years
6,585.32	18.03	223.0 Synodic Months (one Saros)
6,584.51	18.03	241.0 Tropical Months
6,585.35	18.03	242.0 Nodical Months
6,585.55	18.03	239.0 Apogee Months
9.0 Year Half Saros		
Days	Years	Lunisolar Cycles
3,287.18	9.00	9.0 Tropical Years
3,292.89	9.02	9.5 Nodical Years
3,292.66	9.02	111.5 Synodic Months (one half Saros)
3,292.26	9.01	120.5 Tropical Months
3,292.68	9.02	121.0 Nodical Months
3,292.77	9.02	119.5 Apogee Months
112.0 Year Cycle		
Days	Years	Lunisolar Cycles
40,906.88	112.00	112.0 Tropical Years
40,901.16	111.98	118.0 Nodical Years
40,899.89	111.98	1385.0 Synodic Months (one 112-year cycle)
40,900.44	111.98	1497.0 Tropical Months
40,899.94	111.98	1503.0 Nodical Months
40,900.12	111.98	1484.33 Apogee Months
56.0 Year Cycle		
20,453.44	56.00	56.0 Tropical Years
20,450.58	55.99	59.0 Nodical Years

20,449.94	55.99	692.5 Synodic Months (one 56-year cycle)
20,450.23	55.99	748.5 Tropical Months
20,449.97	55.99	751.5 Nodical Months
20,450.06	55.99	742.17 Apogee Months

Synodic Month (or Lunar Month) is the interval between successive New Moons and is equal to 29.5306 days.

Tropical Year (or Solar Year) is the time taken for the Sun to complete one cycle of the ecliptic from spring equinox to spring equinox and is equal to 365.2422 days.

Tropical Month is the time taken for the Moon to complete one cycle of the ecliptic from spring equinox to spring equinox and is equal to 27.3216 days.

Nodical Month (or Draconic Month) is the time taken for the Moon to complete one cycle from ascending node to ascending node and is equal to 27.2122 days.

Nodical Year (or Eclipse Year) is the time taken for the Sun to complete one cycle from ascending node to ascending node and is equal to 346.6201 days.

Apogee Month (or Anomalistic Month) is the time taken for the Moon to complete one cycle from apogee to apogee and is equal to 27.5546 days.

Source: McMinn, 1995.

Wind Direction

By Kris Brandt Riske

ABSTRACT: The author tested two methods to determine wind direction: the instructions of Paul of Alexandria and the monthly lunar phases; the latter is often used to prepare weather forecasts using astrology (astrometeorology). This article presents a summary of the author's research and testing of the two methods, as well as the findings and conclusions.

Astrometeorology is an excellent tool to predict precipitation, hurricanes, thunderstorms, tornadoes, weather fronts, and cloudiness. However, its usefulness regarding temperature, precipitation levels, and wind is limited. The best an astrometeorologist can do with the current knowledge level is to forecast temperatures and precipitation using the terms average, above average, or below average; regarding wind, it is possible to forecast very windy conditions, but other wind speeds are less evident, and specific values cannot be determined.

It seems logical, however, that given the strengths and limitations of astrometeorology, it *should* be possible to forecast wind direction. My research in this area has shown some positive results but also some anomalies for which I have yet to find an explanation.

Paul of Alexandria

Paul's instructions for determining wind direction are quite simple, relying solely on the separating and applying trine aspects made by the Moon. He states that when the Moon forms a trine with a planet in a fire sign, the wind will be easterly; to an earth sign, southerly; to an air sign, westerly; and to a water sign, northerly. Paul also adds that the nature of the planet aspected by the Moon will determine whether conditions will be stormy or calm.

Alexandria, Egypt, presumably Paul's location when he wrote his treatise on astrology, was used to test his method. A noon chart was calculated for Alexandria for each of the thirty days in June 2012, and the results were compared with meteorological statistics (data from Weather Underground) for the same dates.

The prevailing wind direction throughout the month was northerly, sometimes varying to northwest. In its normal transit of the zodiac, the Moon is in a water sign (northerly, according to Paul) on only approximately twenty-five percent of the days. So Paul's theory appears to be invalid, even if one considers changes in climate and terrain during the years between the 4th century and the present day.

Although a larger sample would be necessary to confirm or deny Paul's statements about conditions being stormy or calm, there may be some truth to this. Alexandria, which had no recorded precipitation in June 2012, did experience variable cloudiness on the individual days that the Moon was in an approaching or separating trine to Venus, the Sun, and Saturn in an air sign; trine Mars in an earth sign; trine Saturn in an air sign; trine Jupiter and Venus in an air sign; and trine the Sun in a water sign. Most of the other days were clear, the exception being the dates when the Moon was in Cancer but made no aspects. On the dates when the Moon was in the water signs Scorpio and Pisces, but made no aspects, there were no clouds.

Lunar Ingress

Because wind direction based on the fast-moving Moon seems logical, another approach was tested. The results *may* be statistically significant (a larger sample is needed), but questions remain because of significant anomalies. Possibly this general approach is valid, and can be refined by incorporating other factors such as specific aspects and planets into a study.

Two charts were calculated for the time of the Moon's ingress into each sign during June 2012, one for Chandler, Arizona, and the second for Midland, Texas. The charts were then compared with meteorological statistics (data from Weather Underground) in order to determine if the Moon's placement in the chart indicated the prevailing wind direction during the succeeding two and a half days (the Moon's approximate time frame to transit a sign). There were eleven lunar ingresses during the month. (The top of the chart, the Midheaven, is south; the IC is north; the Ascendant is east; and the Descendant is west.)

The prevailing wind direction in Chandler throughout the month was westerly to southwesterly. Only one lunar ingress indicated the southwesterly direction, and six were westerly or northwesterly. Two ingresses indicated northerly winds (during one, however, the wind switched from northerly to westerly during the day), and two indicated easterly winds.

In Midland in June 2012, prevailing winds were southeasterly. Only one lunar ingress reflected this direction. Six were westerly or northwesterly, one was westerly, and three were easterly.

Conclusion

My conclusion is that neither of these methods—Paul's and lunar ingress—is valid. But it's also possible that further research may reveal other relevant factors related to the Moon's motion that could lead to a workable method to determine wind direction.

Biodynamics Agriculture: An Earth Astrology

Glen Atkinson

ABSTRACT: This essay is an overview of the correlations between traditional astrological structure and knowledge, and the indications that Austrian philosopher Rudolf Steiner gave for land, plant, and animal management. My approach has been to use the astrological formula to show how Steiner provides a very practical deepening of the astrological world view so that his contributions can be seen as a natural expression of modern astrological practice—Earth astrology. An emphasis is placed upon where the external cosmic principles become embodied by physical substances. This naturally leads to practical actions we can take to naturally and safely influence nature, thus showing the practical reality of Heaven brought to Earth.

Biodynamic agriculture was first outlined in 1924 by Austrian philosopher Rudolf Steiner as a remedy for the many problems farmers saw developing during this period. His Agriculture lectures (1) start by saying that to understand nature, we need to appreciate that everything on Earth, is a reflection of the Cosmos within which we exist. He then proceeded to describe practical mechanisms by which life organizes according to the references we are familiar with. He gave only eight lectures specifically focused on agriculture. (1) However, he also gave many related lectures to the medical community (2-7) that are very useful for understanding his difficult agricultural suggestions. The astrological formula shines through all of those lectures.

His methodology was to use the basic astrological ordering of the twelve constellations, seven planets, four elements, three modes, and polarity as the structural form for stories about the organization and functioning of nature. He therefore provides a logical "earthing" of astrology into the practical realities of creating high-quality food production and environmental sustainability. His lectures are the acknowledged beginning of the modern organic movement even though his astrological and energetic references have now been abandoned by this movement. It is a credit to his practical applications that very little real astrological knowledge is necessary to make biodynamics work. The basic techniques, if carried out faithfully, will create healthy environments. Having said this, many wonderful insights and practices emerge if one studies his astrological indications.

Ultimately, biodynamics is a world view for managing nature. Steiner went to great effort to provide the reasoning behind his suggestions, so we can do what he did. One of the gifts of his work was that it led me to see all these parts of astrology as a naturally unfolding vortex. This allows all the various energetic bits of astrology to relate to each other. In turn this allowed for Steiner's story to also fit this same ordering. Both disciplines benefited through a broadening of the reference material and simple clarification. (8)

Bringing Heaven to Earth

Amid his many insights, the most powerful understanding he provides is outlining the connection between the energetic influences of the galaxy, solar system, atmosphere, and Earth, and the chemical elements of protein, hydrogen, nitrogen, oxygen, and carbon. As an expression of "As Above, So Below" he suggested

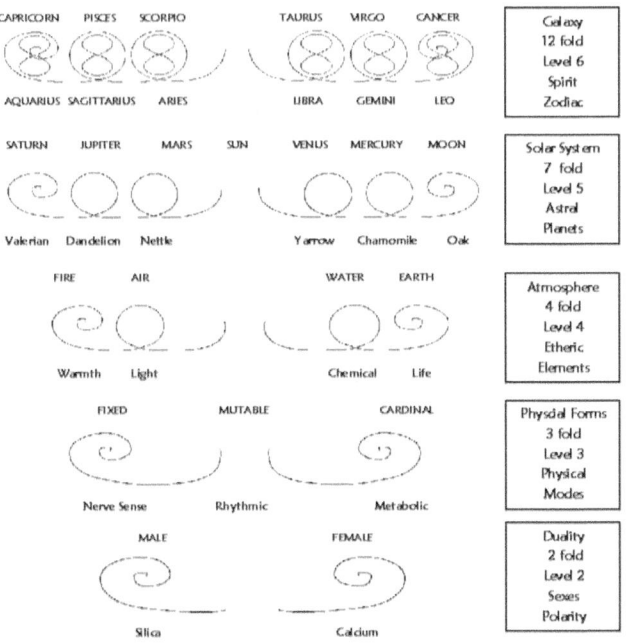

Bodynamic Vortex

that hydrogen—the element of space and the stars' fuel—is the physical carrier of the stars' activity into life processes. Nitrogen, which is found mostly in the planets' atmospheres—eighty percent in ours—is the carrier of planetary activity into matter. Similarly, oxygen, only found in our atmosphere as an excudate of life processes, carries the living activity of the atmosphere, while carbon is the element that carries the physical processes into life. He then went on to say that the chemical constitution of any environment will indicate the energetic nature of that environment. (9) In this simple truth the heavens are bound to Earth. There is no need for faith and belief. The physical matrix of matter is the carrier of cosmic influence. If we look at a chemical formula of any substance, we can determine the energetic activity of that substance. There is no separation. Astrology is not only a fact of physics but also a fact of chemistry. (10)

Energetic Activities

Steiner clearly defines the energetic difference between the stars, planets, atmosphere, and Earth. He acknowledges that each is a real energetic dimension and uses names that will be familiar to those with a Hindu world view.

Stars are the primary energy generators within creation. Their nuclear reacting centers constantly beam out their forces in all directions for billions of years. These are thus the form-givers that set the standing wave tone within our energetic environment and that provide the energetic structure upon which a species can develop. Star force is the archetypal plan that Steiner calls spirit. Paracelsus in the 1500s made a similar comment when he said, "Each species finds its source in a star."

The planets exist as virtual compost heaps of accumulated trash ejected from the activity of our star, the sun. While they are part of the Sun's energetic body and moving, the force they produce and radiate, while present, is nothing like the force of a star.

Steiner emphasized that we look not just to the planet but also to the energetic sphere within which the planet exists. The solar system is somewhat like the inside of an onion, and the planets each have their own shell within which they exist. Because of their mass they will warp the shape of that shell as they move around the sun. Thus the sun's energetic body will be altered, as will all the incoming forces of the other stars, as they move through the planetary shells. Thus the overall planetary tones will be altered as the star forces move through them and as the planets themselves continue to move. Thus the planetary effect we experience will be altered, accordingly. He is asking us to acknowledge the whole interactive nature of the electromagnetic environment we exist within. (11)

Planets Secondary to Sun

Let's go back to my earlier comment, that "the planets are a secondary manifestation of the activity of the sun." The sun does its thing and squirts out dross that is accumulated on Earth. Similarly we can look for the energetic activity of the planets in this image. Just as the sun is the center of the solar system, so is the spirit the center of our being. The part of you that is watching your body reading this article, the bit that is observing these words—that is your spirit. That is the eternal you. As you move through this life and all your other lives you accumulate experiences, just as you are reading this article now. All these experiences are accumulated in your planetary body, just as the planets accumulate star trash. This is your astral body. All these experiences are like pieces of clothing that over time form the personality, psychology, and emotions that can be read in the positions of the planets in your birth chart. Planetary astrology is indeed the study of your astral body.

Many spiritual practices will tell us that the spirit can be free because it does not have to be bound by this astral dross. Thus, spiritual awakening and spiritual enlightenment are not doing words; they are instantaneous words. We can wake up from our astral sleep and be in spirit. This allows an experience of looking back with objectivity upon the wanderings of the astral body that we know is controlled by the planetary movements. We do not truly have the spirit described in the usual Western birth chart. We only have the spirit's delusion as the sun is sitting amongst the planets. We cannot truly predict the outcome of an event. We can at best describe the question, the context, and the timing with some certainty, but not the outcome because the spirit has the option of a free will choice. Only if a person is asleep and the spirit is possessed by the astral body can events be predicted with any certainty. Indeed, if someone considers you a proficient predictive astrologer, the individual is admitting to his or her own astral possession.

The astral body, however, is our friend. As the planets are the only moving part of our cosmic environment, they provide everything else in the system with momentum, which allows these other parts to become active. Even with spirit objectivity, our karma, and the events of the life we have chosen to work through here on Earth, is brought to us by our astral body/the planets. So if we wish to live our life on Earth we need to use the astral body. The trick is our relationship to it. Does it rule us or do we rule it. Is the beast dragging us around or are we using the beast to plow the field?

Earth is the next very real thing we find. Around Earth we have a electromagnetic sphere, and between the ionosphere and Earth we have the Schumann cavity. This cavity forms the home of our atmosphere, which in turn has the unique quality of having twenty percent oxygen within it. This oxygen has been released into the atmosphere from plants. As oxygen became available, so the vast diversity of lifeforms we have on Earth prospered. Life has thus created further life. Interestingly, the Schumann cavity has an energetic resonance of 7.8 hertz, which is the same as we and most other lifeforms have. Thus we can conclude that our internal life and growth functions are energetically connected to and supported by the external atmosphere of Earth. It is within the atmosphere that we find the four elements. These life activities are called the etheric body.

The forces we receive directly from Earth are related to our carbon-based physical body.

The Kingdoms of Nature

These activities are the four major active players in our game of life. It is these external activities that can be traced as internal bodies in all physical manifestations within the four kingdoms of nature. The mineral kingdom only manifests the physical body, while the plant kingdom internalizes the etheric into the physical. This provides the life processes that lift the carbon out of Earth and into a living form. It is worth noting that plant chemistry is all based upon carbohydrates. The animal kingdom takes the living form and internalizes the astral body, thus bringing in nitrogen, to form real proteins and provide the form with internalized sensation and movement. It is only the human kingdom that internalizes the spirit, and we stand upright and have a sense of our individuality. Rational thought is also a byproduct of a properly incarnated spirit.

While the lower kingdoms may not internalize an activity, these activities still work upon them from the outside. Hence the animal kingdom finds "spirit individuality" as a collective such as a flock of sheep or a school of fish. So while the spirit is not fully incarnated, the star forces do still work on and through the incarnated bodies, and this secondary influence can be seen in many aspects of their form and other internal processes. These four processes are active in all living, but not in exactly the same manner. (Visit www.garudabd.org to see Steiner's image of how the bodies sit in a healthy human.) Illnesses in all kingdoms arise when any one of these bodies moves out of this natural order.

Going Inside: Two-fold

When Steiner talks of Earth he starts by describing the Earth itself and how we have "above the soil" and "below the soil" realms. In the pattern of polarity, he calls what comes from above "cosmic" and what comes from the Earth as "earthly." In another of his unique observations he shows how silica, which is a great carrier of electrical energy and makes up seventy percent of Earth's crust, is the primary carrier of the cosmic activities into substance. Calcium, which accumulates as a residue of life forms and is an essential element of life, is the primary carrier of the earthly processes. This is an image of the Male Heaven and the Female Earth stories of most cultures, from which a body will develop. He suggests the elements of the above, warmth and light, are the physical carriers of the great spheres of the spirit and the astral, respectively. The earthly elements of earth and water are the carriers of the physical and etheric activities.

Physical Body: Three-fold

Once the body has formed, we move to the three-fold nature astrology described as the modes. Looking at Earth and the plants that live upon it, Steiner identifies an expansive "above" process we call cardinal and a contractive "below" process we call fixed, with a mutable middle being the process that manifests as a result of the two active poles. This organization has application to the bodies of all life forms. In the human the head is the most contracted form, while our digestion and reproductive organs are where all the cooking, digestive, and procreation processes take place, representing an expansive processes. Our chest with the rhythm between our heart and lungs is the manifestation of the middle. Like the Hindus, Steiner identifies that the human and the plant sit in opposite positions. Our head, which is the center of our nerve sense activity, is similar to a plant's roots, which is the most condensed part. The flowers and seeds are the image of our digestive and reproductive organs (metabolic). Thus the cosmic activity of our heads is found below in the soil in the roots, while the above parts of the plant correspond to our belly.

These two poles do not exist in isolation. The activities of the head work down into the belly, and those of the belly work up into the head. Therefore, within the head we can find normal contractive processes as an expression of the activity of the spirit and astrality, and also an expansive process coming from the belly as an expression of the physical and etheric activities. Likewise in the belly the normal process is expansive; however, contractive processes from the head are also present. This image is the same as that presented by the yin-yang symbol of the Chinese, where within the yin (metabolism) there is a little bit of yang (nerve sense) and so on.

So within the overall structure of a three-fold physical body there is a four-fold process taking place. Steiner outlines this concisely by saying, "Although the three major systems intermingle, they are distinctly different from one another. The physical, etheric, astral, and I-organizations work differently in our sensory nervous system, for example, than they do in our rhythmic or metabolic-limb systems. All four members of the human constitution—physical, etheric, astral and I—are present in each of the three spatially somewhat separate systems, but affect each one in very different ways." (12)

The Atmosphere and the Etheric Body: Four-fold

The three-fold story identifies the areas of spatial activity; however, it is the four activities, sourced from the four world spheres working within them that "does the business." Luckily, these four activities can be controlled. Steiner again anchors these activities into substances. With the silica processes he tells a story of the spirit and astral working through the light and warmth in the atmosphere in autumn. This is drawn down into the soil with the in-breath of winter via the silica sand. This activity is crystallized there through the winter in the quartz that may be present. The following spring, with the help of clay (aluminium silicate), this cosmic process moves upward and heads toward going to seed. This is the big push out of the earth in the spring flush, which eventually comes to an end with ripe seed and fruit, which falls back to earth again, with the autumn in breathing. If this upward moving silica process is held back, then plants do not go off to seed. (22) This is seen in the difference between the first and second year growth of biennial plants such as carrots.

The earthly process works a little differently. Calcium (and other cation elements) in the soil hitch a ride on the upward moving silica "train," and bring minerals and water to the plant so it can grow and photosynthesize. In this process the water and minerals spiral through the plant into ever smaller channels. The minerals are held in the plant while the water, now essentially a homeopathically potentized mist, is transpired into the atmosphere. This homeopathic water is then either drawn back into the plant or falls to Earth as dew or rain. The humus content of the soil acts as the attracting sponge of these life giving forces. While the upward moving physical calcium provides tissue integrity, the inward moving watery atmospheric calcium provides the life activity to make fruit larger. It is the light and warmth of the atmospheric silica process that ripens this large fruit to increase its nutritive quality.

In this story we have a very practical image of how the four elements of the atmosphere work. In practical terms these four activities can be influenced by the amount of sand, clay, humus, and cations that are in the environment, just as any alteration in the amount of light, warmth, or water we provide the plant will also have a direct impact upon its growth.

Seven-fold Planets and the Astral Body

Steiner's use of the planets is very informative. First, he only uses the six visible planets. He considers these to be the primary influence upon physical forms. We know the outer planets are those of the collective unconscious and of a different nature to the personal planets. Steiner makes this a clear demarcation and it does provide a neat ordering. The three planets beyond the Sun are associated with the cosmic, air/fire pole, while the three inner planets are associated with the earthly earth/water pole. With this ordering comes an interesting observation and clarification for astrology. We know that each planet rules two zodiacal signs, while the Sun and Moon, which have a natural polarity, rule one sign each.

Earlier I described the manifest growth cycle of the plant according to the four elements, which are processes influencing the etheric body. Now we can talk of the planets' astral influences upon plant growth. I mentioned earlier how the stars are the ones who have the plan. They are the architect of the build-

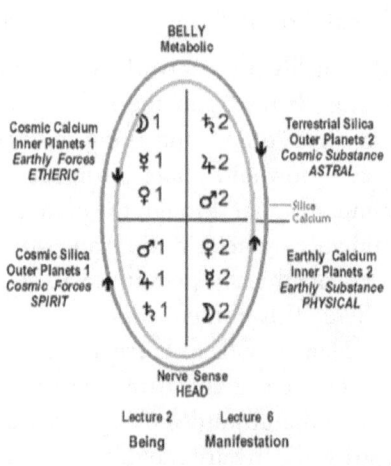

Planets' Astral Influences

ing. So the spirit plan comes from the stars and enters into the astral realm through Saturn. Thus Saturn/1/Aquarius becomes the holder of the plan within the astrality, and Jupiter/1/Pisces provides a mutability that allows this plan to change, to fit into the needs of the time and environment in which it will grow. Mars/1/Aries provides the astrality inspired active inner will desire to incarnate, while Venus/1/Taurus begins to incorporate this movement into the developing life processes by accumulating activities that will nourish the plant. Mercury/1/Gemini connects the life processes of the atmosphere with the physical form, while the Moon/1/Cancer shows as the reproductive processes that lead to the germination of the plant. From here the plant sprouts and moves in an outward journey to the setting of the seed. The Moon/2(Sun)/Leo processes show in the quality and growth potential of the plant tissues, Mercury/2/Virgo provides organs for the plant to grow leaves and begin to photosynthesize, while the Venus/2/Libra processes raise the plant to a readiness for fertilization by bringing the plant to flower. But it is only when Mars/2/Scorpio engages that we have fertilization and the beginning of the formation of proteins within the plant. Jupiter/2/Sagittarius provides light and warmth so that oils can be produced from the basic carbohydrates, while Saturn/2/Capricorn brings the ripening and hardening processes needed to have fertile seed that will keep until next season. (13) The Sun activity on plant growth is seen in the effects of the overall seasons, with the extremes being the contractive winter and expansive summer processes.

In reality all the processes described here take place in coordination with the four-fold processes more connected to the environment. Indeed, in the final analysis of all these activities, lower levels have to be working properly for those above to have their full influence. So the state and ratio of the mediating physical elements, at the bottom of it all, ultimately control how things happen. Biodynamic agricultural tasks should start from the bottom of the vortex and work upwards.

Biodynamic Preparations

One of Steiner's greatest gifts from the planets was his suggestion for eight mineral, plant, and animal based preparations used to control all of the energetic activities. They are essentially an expression of sympathetic magic principles. He suggested getting a herb that is an expression of a particular planetary influence; for example, chamomile, known for use on the digestion and so related to Mercury. He placed the flowers inside the intestines of a sheep. Sheep, like cows, are dominated by their digestive processes. These "chamomile sausages" are then buried in the ground throughout the winter, to make use of the natural crystalizing processes of that time. This "composting" of these two Mercury activities—the herb and the animal parts—produces a Mercury preparation called 503. Similarly, the calcium based oak bark (505) is composted under water for the winter and is used for the Moon preparation; yarrow (502) for Venus; stinging nettle (504) for Mars; dandelion (506) for Jupiter; and valerian (507) for the Saturn preparation. Usually these preparations are applied to the soil and compost heaps to help harmonize the digestive processes. However, they are much more than that; there are two other preparations. One, related to the summer sun processes, is made of quartz crystals, and another related to the winter sun processes is made from cow manure.

Steiner, in 1924, Leivegoed in 1951, and myself in 1989, each made the correspondences of two of these preparations to the way they influence the four primary energetic bodies. This means these six remedies have now become a complete set of substances that influence the way the four world activities (spirit, astral, etheric, and physical) and their internal counterparts work with each other. The valerian incarnates the spirit, the dandelion helps connect the spirit to the physical body, the Mars preparation harmonizes the astrality, the Venus yarrow preparation helps the etheric and astral bind together, the Mercury chamomile preparation strengthens the etheric, and the oak bark preparation helps the etheric and physical bind together. Within this matrix, all of the manifestations of life can be controlled.

Controlled Experiment

While I have carried out many controlled experiments during the past thirty years, the one trial (and now commercial product) that stands monumentally above the rest is one carried out by New Zealand's premier research center, HortResearch, in 2001. This trial showed that my bird control product reduced high levels of bird damage on ripe grapes by fifty percent. (16) This product is made from a selection of the biodynamic preparations that have been homeopathically diluted to more than one part per trillion. The aim of this remedy is to be an energetic mirror of several types of bird so that the energetic imbalance that allows them to eat the fruit is adjusted; thus, the birds can no longer be in that environment.

One way to understand this phenomenon is to refer to the fact that any two sound waves of the same frequency but opposite phase, when played at each other, will cancel each other out and there will be silence. My homeopathic copy of the birds cancels out the energetic resonance that allows them to be present and so they have no choice but to leave. Interestingly, this product enhances the ripening of the fruit, which we would expect would make the fruit more palatable, but this is not the case.

The key to this effect is the identification of the energetic make-up of the pest. This is achieved via the zodiacal based animal species organization mentioned earlier, plus an assessment of the energetic, planetary, and elemental influences that help to shape the form of the particular. This information is all contained within the biodynamic literature.

Planets and Plants

Another example of the way the planets show their formative imprint is seen in the plant families. Initially there is a division between the annual plants and those that live longer than one year. The softer annual plants are ruled by the inner planets, while perennial plants are ruled by the outer planets.

The Moon, because of its quick, watery nature, governs the vegetables and succulents. Mercury plants are those that move about, namely the cucurbits, pumpkin, cucumber, and all climbing plants that require external support to rise above the ground. Venus governs plants that are dominated by their flowering, such as the bulbs and flowering annuals. Once we move to the perennials, Mars is the controller of the shrubs, especially those with thorns, and any tree that has a dieback element within its growth process; that is, when the terminal bud dies and side shoots give the new growth. Jupiter governs deciduous trees and fruit trees that provide so much abundant fruit. Saturn trees are the conifer family that are generally evergreen, live in harsh environments, and provide hardly any living environment under their canopy. (17)

Within any of these large groupings there will be sub-groups showing the characteristics of the other groups. Within the Jupiter deciduous trees we thus find the Moon in the willows, Mercury in perennial climbers such as kiwifruit and grapes along with the clematis and wisteria, and so on through all the sub-groups this species.

Beyond this the element influences are identified in the shapes of plants and their parts. Fire and warmth makes for spherical shapes as seen in fruit, and air and light make for sharp pointy forms such as the sun-loving grasses. Water leads to round and wavy forms, while the earth forces appear as square forms often seen in roots and some plants such as the stems of the peppermint and sage, Labiate family.

The Sun influence is identified as those plants that have an even focus upon all the various plant parts, such as the clover plant that has strong roots, ample leaves, lots of flowers, and very viable seeds.

By observing a plant's or animal's form, habit, and nature within this framework, it is possible to gather an image of how the four energetic activities have worked to create this unique being. All these considerations can be translated into a biodynamic preparation "copy" of any organism. It is as if each natural being is a musical tune comprised of all the parts we identify in astrology. Within the biodynamic world view and accumulated knowledge this tune can be recreated, and when played back at nature, imbalances are harmonized and pest and disease cannot carry on in that environment. This is practically applied and scientifically proven astrological knowledge.

Twelve-fold Zodiac and Spirit

The earlier story about the planets' influence on plants highlights a practical use of the dual planetary rulership of the zodiac. This order has led me to question why we use the Aries-Pisces zodiac when there is no inherent planetary symmetry? The answer clarified for me that the Aries-Pisces zodiac is a seasonal based zodiac and thus an "external" zodiac, while the zodiac just described describes more archetypal processes standing one step behind manifest nature. (14)

Steiner makes good use of the Cancer-Leo zodiac by looking at the evolution of the animal species we have on Earth. This story is enlarged by his student, Eugen Kolisko (15). He begins his story at Cancer, with the single-celled protozoa and runs backward through the zodiac until he reaches the mammals in Leo. A homeopath friend did some trials of these suggestions by using the animal remedy for strong-signed people, with good results.

Cancer	Protozoa	Cellular system developed.
Gemini	Coelenterata	Digestive system developed.
Taurus	Echinodermata	Rhythmic system developed.
Aries	Tunicata	A harmony of all the organs occurs; however, it is still at an embryonic stage.

Pisces	Mollusca	Reproductive system dominates.
Aquarius	Vermes	Digestion is dominant process.
Capricorn	Insecta	Respiration is dominant feature.
Sagittarius	Pisces	Blood circulation is developed; early stages of the heart exist.
Scorpio	Amphibia	Reproductive system highly developed.
Libra	Reptilia	Digestive process emphasized.
Virgo	Aves (birds)	Respiratory system further developed.
Leo	Mammalia	Animals that have a true heart, warm blood.

Planting by the Moon

One of the more obvious applications of astrology by biodynamics is planting by the Moon. Steiner indicated the effect of the using the waxing and waning cycle; however, further research has been conducted by several people into the five Moon cycles. (18,19,20) These can be summarized by their influence on plants according to their expanding and contracting influences. The expanding side of the cycle enhances above-ground jobs such as sowing activities and grafting, while the contracting part of the cycle enhances groundwork and the effectiveness of transplanting and pruning jobs. The main cycles are the waxing and waning Moon, and the ascending and descending paths of the Moon and planets. This last set is reversed in the different hemispheres. Apogee tends to overdraw the plants upward, while the perigee pushes plants into the ground. The node days are considered to be generally negative and ones when no work should be done.

It was through the investigations of the Moon through the zodiac that biodynamic research by Lily Kolisko (20) and Agnes Fyfe (18) showed plants respond most to the sidereal zodiac. This is not surprising given they are the stars and plants have not yet internalized the star realm (spirit) into their bodies in the manner that humans have. So they do not display the same degree of emancipation from the direct cosmos that humans do. Maria Thun (19) has done many years of plant trials regarding the Moon and the zodiac and concluded that the elemental ruler of the zodiacal constellation has a marked effect upon particular parts of the plant. Work done on the soil and plants on the earth constellations affects the root of the plant, water constellations enhance leaf growth, air constellations enhance flower growth, and fire constellations enhance fruit production. This work has its critics, as well as a legion of loyal followers.

In my own garden I use the principle that "a job is better done on the wrong day than not done on the right day," and so apart from one or two tasks such as sowing seeds, I just do a job when I get to it. This is nice knowledge, but in practice it can drive you nuts, if you are dealing with large areas.

However, in practice, many benefits can arise. If you are cutting wood for furniture and burning, it is best to do it on the contracting cycles—New Moon, waning period, descending period. For food crops for immediate use, picking them in the morning of the expansive cycles is good; however, if for storage, use the opposite contractive cycles. Seed sowing is best done during times of tension, most notably just before the Full Moon, or if plants are to experience drought conditions, just before a Moon-Saturn opposition.

Chemistry

In Steiner's medical lectures (2-7) he tells an intricate story of how all the pieces of his puzzle fit together to manifest as various diseases. Similarly, he tells of the remedies that can be discovered and used to find their solutions. Amid these texts are references to the planets' classic relationship to the metals and how they relate to the three-fold story of the nerve sense, rhythmic and metabolic systems of physical organisms, and thus to the alchemical processes of fixed salt and the element sodium, the mutable Mercury, and the cardinal sulphur pole with the element phosphorus being prominent. From his indications I have been able to extend this story into work I have done on the periodic table of chemical elements, which then provides an avenue into an astrological chemistry. (10)

For those interested in the details of this process it can be seen on my Web site (www.garudabd.org). In biodynamic chemistry/ glenological chemistry I have reorganized the Periodic Table into a circular and then spherical order. This allows it to be related to Steiner's energetic bodies from which the energetic activity of all the chemical elements can be determined.

In the second stage of alchemical chemistry, Steiner's medical lectures are incorporated in a more practical manner so that chemistry can be practically applied. Alchemical astrology is then opened up within this framework, and the picture on my Web site is a summary of the associations.

This final union of chemistry, the very structure of matter, with Steiner's energetic and astrological indications, provides a real expression of Heaven brought to Earth. "As Above" is indeed "So Below." Just as we can work in precise detail with humans through astrology, so Steiner has allowed us to use the very same principles to work with the other kingdoms of nature.

Bibliography
1. Steiner, Rudolf. *Agriculture*. Junction City, OR, Bio-Dynamic Farming and Gardening Association, Inc., 1993
2. Steiner, Rudolf. *Spiritual Science and Medicine*. Dornach, Switzerland, 1920.
3. Steiner, Rudolf. *Anthroposophical Spiritual Science and Medical Therapy*. Lectures, April 11-18, 1921.
4. Steiner, Rudolf. *Spiritual Relations in the Human Organism*. Lectures Oct. 20-23, 1922.
5. Steiner, Rudolf. *Fundamentals of Anthroposophical Medicine*. Lectures Oct. 26-28, 1922.

6. Steiner, Rudolf. *The Healing Process*. Lectures Aug. 28, 1923-Aug. 29, 1924.
7. Steiner, Rudolf. *Pastoral Medicine*. Lectures, Sep. 8-18, 1924.
8. The Garuda Trust. *Biodynamics Decoded*. 2000.
9. Reference for chemical construction, energetic activity 1920.
10. The Garuda Trust. *Glenological Chemistry*.
11. Rudolf Steiner. *The Astronomy Course*, Jan. 1-18, 1921.
12. Steiner, Rudolf. Lecture 6 of *The Healing Process*, Nov. 16, 1923.
13. Lievegoed, C. B.J. *The Working of the Planets and the Life Processes in Man and Earth*. 1951.
14. The Garuda Trust. *Biodynamic Questions, Astrological Answers*.
15. Kolisko, E. *The Twelve Groups of Animals*. Clunies Ross Press, 1977.
16. Hortresearch bird research document
17. Grohmann, G. *The Plant*. Biodynamic Assocation. 2009.
18. Fyfe, Agnes. *Moon and Plant*. Verlag Freies Geistesleben 1.
19. Thun, Maria. *Working on the Land with the Constellations*. Lanthorn Press, 1979.
20. Kolisko, E. *Agriculture of Tomorrow*. UK: Kolisko Archive Publishers.
21. www.garudabd.org
22. http://garudabd.org/node/27

Homosexuality Signature in Vedic Astrology

By Indranil Ray

ABSTRACT: The purpose of this paper is to determine the astrological significators of homosexuality. Brihat Prajapatya, Skandahora refers to homosexuality combinations. A few planetary positions were also cited by Dr. B. V. Raman. Mars and Venus are the main planets that indicate sexual behavior, and Venus-Uranus and Venus-Neptune aspects are also significant. Squares, conjunctions, and oppositions are the important aspects to look for, and outer planets in angular placement is also seen. The significators for homosexuality include Mars and Neptune, and these planets in certain houses and aspects can indicate openness to homosexuality. A powerful Uranus or Neptune influence in the fifth or eighth house is often an indication of a person's nontraditional sexual expression. Male planets in female signs and vice-versa often indicate an affinity with people of same gender.

On December 2013, Queen Elizabeth II granted a posthumous pardon to Alan Turing for "a sentence we would now consider unjust and discriminatory." Prime Minister David Cameron said the World War II code-breaker's work had saved "countless lives." Often called the father of modern computing, Turing's pivotal role in breaking Germany's "Enigma" code is thought to have brought an earlier end to World War II. Turing took his own life in 1954 by eating a cyanide poisoned apple after being convicted of the then-crime of homosexuality, which was decriminalized in Britain in 1967.

Discrimination against the LGBT (lesbian, gay, bisexual and transgender) community in Russia was a flash point at the 2012 Winter Olympics in Sochi. President Barack Obama named openly gay athletes to represent the U.S. at the opening and closing ceremonies: tennis champion Billie Jean King ice hockey player Caitlin Cahow. The White House said that the delegation "represents the diversity that is the United States."

Hindu views of homosexuality are varied. Although some Hindu dharmic texts ban homosexuality and sexuality is rarely discussed in Hindu society, a number of Hindu mythic stories depicted homosexual experience as common. There are several Hindu temples that portray same-sex sexuality through carvings that show both men and women engaging in homosexual sex. Third sex was referred to in ancient texts such as Narada-Smriti, Sushruta Samhita (a highly appreciated Hindu medical text that dates to at least 600 B.C), and Kama Sutra.

Some editions of the popular Bengali text Krittivasa Ramayana, on the pastimes of Lord Rama, tell about two queens that conceived a child together. When the renowned king of the Sun Dynasty, Maharaja Dilip, died, the demigods become concerned that he did not have a son to continue his lineage. Lord Shiva appeared before the king's two widowed queens and ordered them to make love. The two wives, with immense love for each other, executed Lord Shiva's order until one of them conceived a child. A boneless child was born, but by the blessing of sage Astavakra the child was reinstated to full vigor and sustained the line. Astavakra so named the child "Bhagiratha"—he who was born from two vulvas. Bhagiratha later became an emperor and is credited with bringing the Ganges River down to earth through his asceticism. There are also other antique Sanskrit texts that refer to homosexuality.

Brihat Prajapatya, Skandahora references homosexuality combinations useful for astrologers:

- Mutual aspect between Venus and Saturn placed in the Navamsha of each other.
- Navamsha of both Venus and Saturn in Aquarius; in Rashi chart their placement in Taurus/Libra.
- Venus and Saturn in Taurus Navamsha; in Rashi chart, placed in Capricorn/Aquarius.
- In a conjunction or aspected by Saturn, Mars in the seventh indulges in homosexuality. (Bhrigusutra, Ref SakndaHora)

Other combinations found in classics are:

- Mars, Muthaseela[1] with Venus. (Prasna Tantra by Neelakanta Daivagnya, sloka 82)
- Mercury and Ketu are in seventh from karkamsha.
- Unisex planet Saturn is in another unisex planet's (Mercury) sign, or vice versa or they are both in trine aspect to Ascendant/the seventh house; this confers gay inclination, independent of male or female.
- Influence of Saturn and Mercury on Ascendant and/or the seventh house indicates homosexual tendencies.
- Aspect of Mercury and Saturn to the seventh house/situated in the seventh and Mars and Saturn both aspect the seventh, the native is gay. (Jyotish Kalpadruma)

A few planetary positions[2] cited by B. V. Raman are:

- Saturn in depression/in a watery sign in the sixth/twelfth, devoid of benefic aspects.
- Saturn in the sixth/eighth from Venus (emotions, taste, happiness).
- Mercury in an odd sign and the Moon in an even sign and

both being aspected by Mars.
- Occupancy of odd Navamsha of Lagna, Venus, and the Moon.
- Mars in an even sign and the Lagna in an odd sign.
- Seventh lord and Venus in the sixth.

From Aries, the alternate signs are outwardly masculine (fire and air, alternatively) and the others (earth and water, alternatively) are inwardly feminine. Venus, ruler of Taurus, spots inward light on standards, aesthetics, and individual property and is therefore feminine. Venus, ruler of Libra, is masculine, defining self through others. Mars, ruler of Aries, is externally directed, busy in a free life and wandering, and revolutionary and self-governing. Mars, as a ruler of Scorpio, sign of transformations, looks inner-directed.

In many horoscopes, male planets in female signs and vice-versa generate the propensity of pulling attraction among the people of similar gender. Afflicted Moon and Venus by Mars, Rahu, Saturn, and Mercury may generate homosexual inclination. All combinations must be seen in Rasi/Navamsha/Bhava charts. Close interpersonal relationships are being judged from the fifth and seventh houses. Mars represents the sexuality in aggressive and piercing men. The Moon combined with Mars brings seduction and becomes forceful. Afflicted Mars turns a male's conventional interest in females to other males.

The aspectual relationship of Uranus, Neptune and Pluto with the Sun, Moon, Mercury, Mars, Jupiter, and Saturn indicate an edgy nature. These can become means for spiritual expansion, mainly from the individual's standpoint. The harmful side of Uranus is about personal control, that of Neptune is about free or clandestine fantasies, and Pluto is about having power. These traits are found in most sexual relationship. Squares, conjunctions, and oppositions are the strongest aspects between the planets, and the trine can also indicate some of these divergences.

The angular position of the outer planets also have a dominant role if they affect the Ascendant (own point of view), twelfth house (fascination), seventh house (relationship), or tenth house (early days and insensible insist). The fifth house indicates secret love affairs, and the eighth house indicates deviations. A powerful Uranus or Neptune in the fifth or eighth house is a good indication of a person's non-traditional sexual expression. The fifth house and aspects are a good preliminary point for examining anyone's sexual propensity. For example, an angular Neptune or in Neptune in the fifth house indicates a desire to be injured or dominated. An angular Saturn or Saturn in the fifth indicates a desire to harm and rebuke. Angular Pluto indicates a desire to take someone into custody (many kidnapping cases show strong Plutonian energies).

Outer Planet Influence

The subtle influence of the outer planets—Uranus, Neptune, and Pluto—in sexual deviation is interesting. It is subtle because in each of these planets there is a spiritual breadth that the majority of human beings cannot alter and find difficult to bring into positive or creative expression.

The angularity of the planets in the natal chart brings the decision about the sexual type and compatibility. The variation relies on the communication of soft and hard planets either by transit or from the natal chart. For example Mars-Uranus is hard and depends on the gender balance of Venus or Neptune. Additionally, Saturn and Jupiter communicate fear of losing control and excesses. Saturn and Mars stand for a positive reevaluation of the sex drive, and Saturn and Venus denote inconsistency in age and the learning of lessons in love.

However, Saturn with Uranus or Jupiter-Uranus represents activity out of the norm, Saturn-Neptune indicates a vicious spite or masochistic inclination in sex, and Jupiter-Neptune indicates an idealized romantic liaison tied with charm and seduction. In developed human beings these energies often manifest as religious gifts responsible for raising human realization beyond the matter into the celestial plane. In unevolved human beings these higher planetary energies discover other avenues in social and personal behavior.

Love and relationship are indicated by Venus and Mars. These planets, their aspects, and house placements give a hint of lovemaking (Venus) and sex (Mars), representing the internal feminine and masculine, passion (Venus), and lust (Mars).

In a woman's chart, Venus can signal how she relates to her own femininity. Mars in a woman's chart tells how she utters her masculine energy and what she is attracted to in a man. In a man's chart, Mars tells what makes him feel male, and gives clues about his communication with his own inner vigor. Venus in a man's chart points to the feminine qualities a man may assign to a woman, what he's looking for in women and his relationship with his own feminine plane. Although "she" is used for Venus and "he" is used for Mars, this is only for easiness. We can look at a man's Venus and a woman's Mars, or the Venus and Mars residency for the partners in a same-sex couple. Venus in hard aspect to Uranus is often associated with homosexuality.

Other Indicators

A study of homosexuality in the astrological chart was completed by Karl Heimsoth in Germany in 1928. He assumed that homosexuality is astrologically linked with Uranus hard aspects to the inner planets. Derek and Julia Parker state that aspects between the Sun and Moon and Uranus are often found in the charts of homosexuals.

Francis Sakoian and Louis Acker, authors of *The Astrologer's Handbook* and *The Astrology of Human Relationships*, portray the strong aspects of Venus-Neptune and Mars-Neptune as indicating homosexuality. Regarding Venus square Neptune, they said that it can indicate covert sexual relationships. Venus opposition

Neptune is mentioned as sexual seduction. Mars square Neptune indicates sexual deviation. But the authors also said that fifth house involvement is necessary. Venus-Uranus and Venus-Neptune aspects are important. Venus trine Uranus and Mars trine Uranus indicate acceptance of unconventional sex. They mention that Venus-Uranus hard aspects indicate sudden, exhilarating, but unbalanced and non-enduring infatuations.

In *Astrology, Karma and Transformation*, Stephen Arroyo writes about natal aspects in relation to homosexuality, citing Venus-Uranus, Venus-Neptune, and Venus-Pluto aspects with hard Mars-Neptune aspects. He suggests a powerful link between Mars and Uranus as an indication of homosexuality, and also mentions a higher probability of sexual experimentation if Venus is in sensual sign such as Scorpio or Taurus.

Astrology and Homosexuality by Wim van Dam mentions that aspects between the Moon and Saturn, either in the natal or navamsha chart, are frequent. He also uses conjunctions in the ninth harmonic chart and the twelfth harmonic chart with regard to the Moon and Saturn, and the "debilitating" house cusps six and twelve. *Astrological Insights into Personality* by Betty Lunsted cites difficult aspects between the Moon and Venus as indicative of female homosexuality.

In summary, according to the above referenced authors, the following hard planetary aspects are associated with homosexuality:

- Stephen Arroyo—Venus-Pluto, Mars-Uranus, Mars-Pluto, Mars-Neptune, Venus-Uranus
- Francis Sakoian and Louis Acker—Mars-Neptune, Venus-Uranus, Venus-Neptune, Sun-Uranus
- Betty Lunsted—Moon-Venus
- Derek and Julia Parker—Moon-Uranus
- Betty Lunsted—Venus-Mars
- Liz Greene—Venus-Saturn

Generally, men express the dynamism of the male planets in their charts through Mars and the Sun. Women express the energies of Venus and the Moon, the female planets. The interesting thing is that men also have womanly vigor because they also have Venus and the Moon. Women have the Sun and Mars, so they also have a male factor. These differing sexual energies within each of us are called the animus and the anima. Men with a prominent Venus sign can be gay, and the same is true for women with a prominent Mars sign. A Mars affliction can indicate fanatacism in sexual activities, as can Rahu. The animus (male) side could have an unconscious influence, as could the feminine side in a homosexual man. These unconscious male components are then projected on to other men. Some of this nature can be observed by the sign, house, and aspects of the Sun and Mars in the natal chart. In a lesbian relationship the Moon and Venus are operative.

The hard aspects (square, opposition, and sometimes conjunction) between Mars-Venus and the outer planets are more likely to be linked to homosexuality than heterosexuality. A Mars affliction makes one fervent in sexual activities, as does Rahu. Male planets in female signs and vice-versa generate an affinity between the people of the same gender seen in many charts, along with affliction to Moon and Venus by Saturn, Mars, Rahu, or Mercury.

Navamsha Chart

In the navamsha, Saturn and Mercury in odd houses or in mutually reception indicates gay tendencies. However, this is negated by a strong Jupiter in an odd house. Saturn and Mercury are the gay planets because they don't produce offspring like the other planets, especially Venus and Jupiter, which represent wife and husband. This is dependent upon an aspect such as Venus-Uranus, Moon-Uranus, Moon-Venus aspect, rather than planetary placement. The eighth house (sex and mystery) is an even greater authority than Uranus alone. Either Venus in the eighth or Venus and Mars in the eighth could entail bisexuality or homosexuality. This is confirmed with affable aspects with Venus-Mars and other planets, mainly the Moon and Uranus. Mars in the eighth is not only one significator. Uranus in the eighth is also an important factor that signifies a tendency toward homosexuality. The opposition aspect generates an ongoing struggle relating to that. Males are often outer-directed than females, although it can differ within any one individual.

The Moon, highly private and allied with the Earth, is indicative of conduct. After that, going outward from the Sun, next in order of emergence are Mercury, Venus, and Mars. Mars, in the majority of the signs, represents purpose and states most commonly outer-directed and forceful energy and is thus masculine. Mars with the Sun indicates the important men in a woman's chart. However, women can be aggressive, whether openly or secretly, and certainly modern women are more likely to convey their own Mars and their own Sun. When women are forceful, their Mars and its sign and aspects represent their animosity. However, their sexuality is usually represented by Venus. Venus is friendly. Venus plus the Moon is alluring and seductive and, above all, amenable. The sexuality of men is indicated by Mars in their chart, its astrological state, and its residency by house, sign, and aspect. Mars is piercing, leading, forceful, aggressive, and forceful. Mars draws sharp lines amid the individual's ego and that of others. Mars plus the Moon is forceful, seductive, and overjoyed. This does not mean men cannot be amenable.

In looking to mark the astrology of homosexuality, we are mostly interested in the condition of one planet: Mars. Mars tells a good deal about aggression, the outside push of the ego, and sexuality. In parallel, we are looking for a condition in addition to Mars that they all have in common and that influences the fifth house of sexuality and the seventh house of association, the two houses that govern close interpersonal relationships. For a man to be more interested in other men, there must be other planets that make men sexually more attractive to him. The influence of Neptune in certain houses and when configured with Mars initiates openness to homosexuality, as follows:

- If Mars-Neptune aspects an angle, a light (Sun, Moon, or Nodes) is not needed because the angle itself performs like a light [one with a two-degree orb].

- If Mars-Neptune does not aspect an angle, then there must be a light involved, or a planet involved that rules an angle.

Examples

Alan Turing, a technical genius, mathematician, logician, and scientist was behind Britain's successful efforts to break German Enigma code in World War II .His Computable Numbers, written in 1937, is a blueprint for the digital computer, and his Universal Turing Machine is an ancestor of the information age. When a robbery occurred at his house he told police that the robber was known to his homosexual partner. Turing was later convicted of homosexuality, a crime in Britain in 1952. On June 7, 1954, he committed suicide by eating an apple laced with cyanide.

In Turing's chart the seventh house lord, Mars, and vargottama Neptune, lord of the third house (lower mind) are in Cancer. They are is aspected by Saturn, lord of the ninth and tenth houses and Uranus in the tenth Retrograde powerful vargottama Jupiter's aspect from seventh house (Scorpio, natural lord of the eighth house) inflames the aspect. The Moon and Ketu (secret) are in Mars' star, Chitra, in the fifth house. Combust Venus and afflicted Moon (by Rahu) reinforce the pattern.

In the navamsha chart (not shown) the Moon and Ketu are in the fifth house, aspected by Mars. Mars and Neptune are in opposition (conflict). The Moon (with Ketu) is aspected by Mars and Rahu, adding to the seriousness. Saturn and Mercury are trine to the seventh house. Venus with retrograde Jupiter is in the eighth, aspected by Saturn.

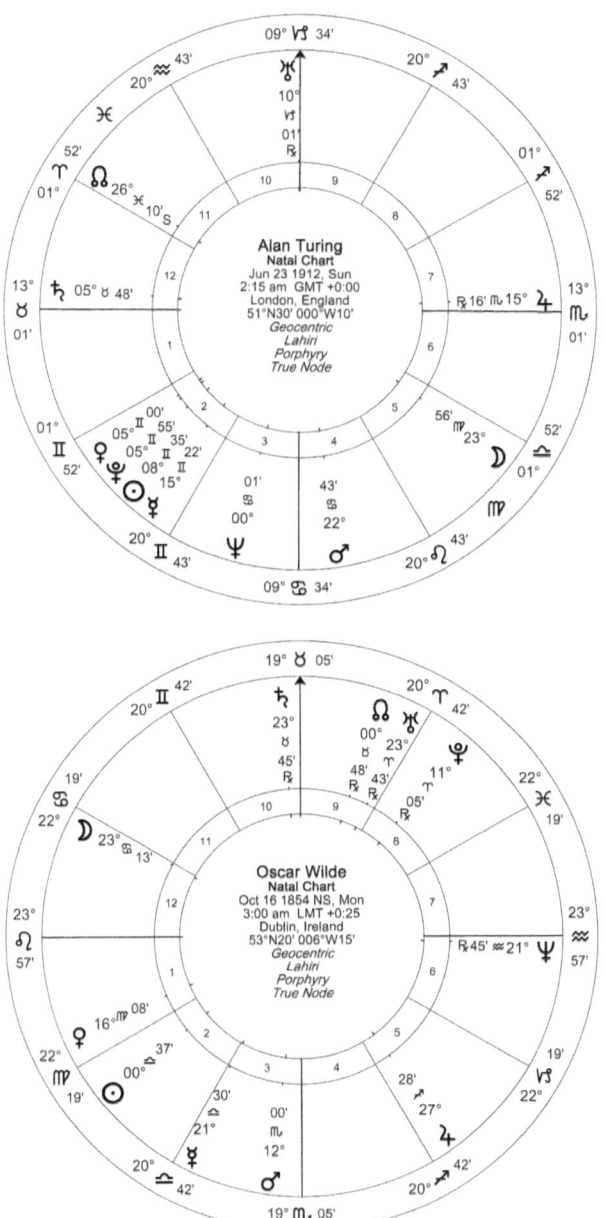

Oscar Wilde, a noted Irish-British writer, poet, and dramatist, was accused of having a homosexual affair at the peak of his career. He was convicted and spent two years in prison.

In Oscar Wilde's chart, Mars, lord of the fourth and ninth houses, is with Ketu in the fourth and aspected by Saturn and Rahu from Taurus. Mars also aspects Neptune on the seventh house cusp, which is also aspected by Saturn. Venus, dispositor of Saturn, is debilitated, and Mercury is afflicted by Uranus and Pluto.

In the navamsha chart (not shown), the Moon is in an even sign, Mercury is in an odd sign, and both are aspected by Mars. The seventh lord, Venus, is aspected by Saturn, Mars (with the Sun), Rahu (with the Moon), and Uranus. The Ascendant lord, Mars, and the tenth lord, Sun, are aspected by Saturn. Mars with the Sun is opposition Neptune and Mercury.

John E. Boswell was an American writer, a Yale University professor, and the author of *Same Sex Unions in Pre-modern Europe*.

In Boswell's chart, Mercury and all of the outer planets except Uranus are retrograde. Neptune is in aspect with the Sun, the Ascendant lord; Mars in the seventh house, lord of the fourth and ninth houses; Saturn from the twelfth house; and Rahu in the tenth house. Mars aspects Rahu and Uranus. Afflicted Venus (by Rahu) and Saturn (in Cancer) are in oppsition. The twelfth lord, the Moon, is afflicted by vargottama Mercury and conjunct Mars in the seventh house in Rahu's star. Jupiter, the fifth house lord, is in the fourth house with Ketu. The dispositor of the fourth lord is Mars in the seventh house with the Moon and Mercury.

In the navamsha chart (not shown), Saturn and Mars are badly influencing the lagna along with their mutual aspect. Ketu is in the fifth. From Ascendant, the seventh lord is retrograde (Jupiter). The seventh house is aspected by Rahu, whose dispositor is Mars in the tenth in Pisces and Jupiter in the third house with Uranus, Venus, and the Sun.

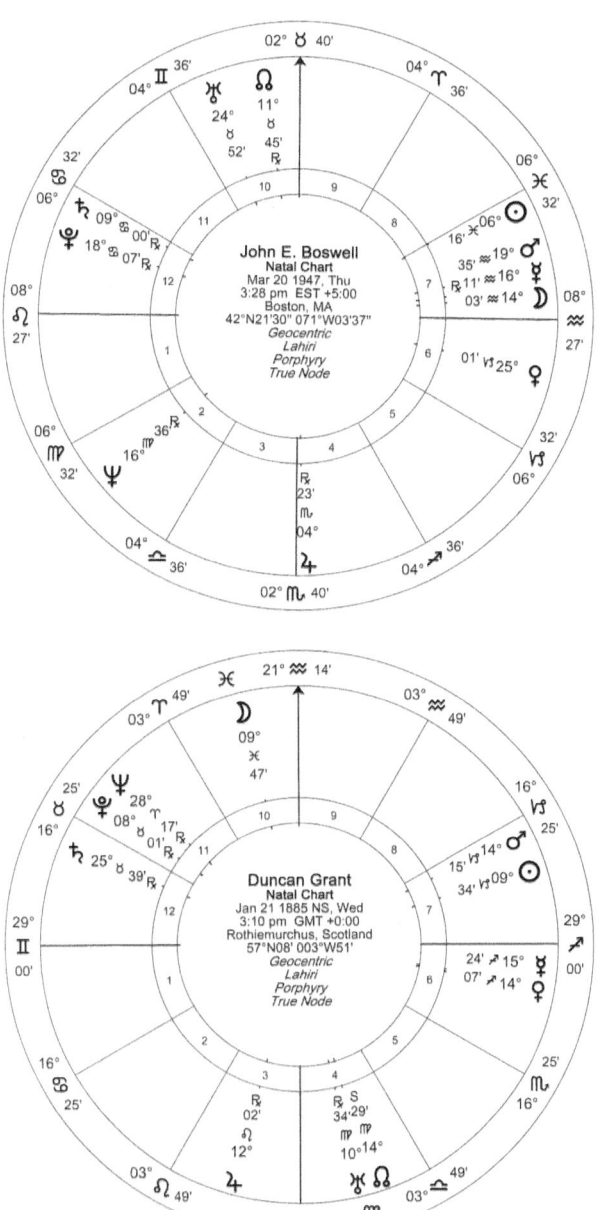

Duncan Grant was a British painter, designer, and decorator, and a lover of economist John Maynard Keynes.

In Duncan's chart, Venus is in the sixth house and Saturn in the twelfth. Mars (with the Sun) aspects Neptune and Jupiter, seventh house lord, from the eighth. Rahu and Uranus afflict the Moon. Mars is also in aspect with Rahu in the fourth house.

In the navamsha chart (not shown), Mars is in an even sign and the vargottama lagna is in an odd sign. Lagna and fourth house lord Mercury, eighth and ninth house lord Saturn, and fifth house lord Venus are aspected by Mars (afflicted by Rahu) from the twelfth. Neptune is in aspect to Ketu in the sixth. Mars with Rahu and Neptune is in 6/8 relation. The dispositor of the Moon in the fourth house is in the third, indicating liberal thinking.

Data Source

All data is from AstroDataBank.

Endnotes

[1] An lthasala yoga is caused when a faster planet with lesser longitude is behind a slower planet with greater longitude. This is a benefic yoga. When the lthasala occurs within half a degree, it becomes Muthaseela.
[2] How to Judge a Horoscope, vols. I and II, in chapter on the seventh house. Some other combinations are occupancy of odd Navamsha of Lagna, Venus and the Moon; Mars in an even sign and the Lagna is in an odd sign; and seventh lord and Venus in the sixth house.

Antikythera Mechanism: A 2000-year-old Astro-Computer

By Demetra George

ABSTRACT: The Antikythera Mechanism is a recently discovered multi-geared device found in fragments in an ancient shipwreck. It functions as an astronomical computer, calculating and displaying dates for eclipses and a range of other celestial phenomena. This paper explores the various speculations as to its origin and proposes that it, and possibly other similar devices, played a critical role in the rapid development of Hellenistic astrology in the early centuries BCE.

The Antikythera Mechanism, a 2000-year old astronomical computer, is one of the most important current discoveries from the ancient world and it sheds light on a critical era of our own astrological history. This sophisticated multi-geared device, which is now dated to the late 3rd century BCE, is the world's first known analog computer and its purpose was to calculate and display precise positions of solar, lunar, stellar, and planetary phenomena. It was an eclipse predictor, an astrological tool for erecting charts, and an astronomical teaching device. Tracking the mystery of this astronomical computer – how does it work,

The Antikythera Mechanism.
http://en.wikipedia.org/wiki/Antikythera_mechanism.

who built it, when, and for what purpose provides a glimpse into the misty origins of Hellenistic astrology.

Discovery

About 65 BCE a ship set sail from Asia Minor, its cargo overloaded with looted Greek treasures from the Roman conquests of Eastern kingdoms. It carried coins from Pergamum and Ephesus, and stopped at the islands of Kos and Rhodes picking up vessels filled with oil and wine. As it rounded the tip southern Greece, it was caught up in a severe storm and sank near the tiny island of Antikythera. Its treasures remained buried beneath the sea, lost and undisturbed until 1900-01 when the cache was accidently discovered by Greek sponge divers. Among the trove of glassware and marble and bronze statues were a number of pieces of a bronze geared mechanism, encrusted by two millennia of seashells and limestone accumulations. The fragments of the mechanism were placed in various boxes in the basement of the National Archaeological Museum of Athens and a few pieces eventually went on display with little explanatory commentary.

Over the next century various museum curators, academics, historians, and researchers were intrigued with this mysterious device and some even became obsessed for decades of their careers with the attempt to unravel its secrets.[1] In 1974 Derek de Solla Price described the antikythera mechanism as the cornerstone of computer's technology and wrote that "it must surely rank as one of the greatest basic mechanical inventions of all time."[2] A group of international scientists[3] was formed in 2005 to further study the device's significance and functions. Using state of art x-ray and imaging techniques, the 82 fragments of the 32 known gears revealed evidence of the machine's architecture engineering that incorporated the state of the art astronomical knowledge of its era, and even a user's manual.

The advanced technology of this machine would not be evident again in Western culture for another thousand years until the sophisticated clockwork of 14th century Europe. Instead, like many of the other Greek sciences, it would take an obscure and circuitous route through 6th century Byzantium, the Arabic world of the 11th century al-Biruni, and the 13th century Moorish Spain before reappearing in the wave of translations from Arabic to Latin in 12th century Medieval Europe.

How Did it Work

The antikythera mechanism was enclosed in wooden box about the size of a shoebox and driven by a handle on the side. On the front face was a fixed ring dial representing the ecliptic, marked off by equal 30-degree sectors bearing inscriptions of the Greek names of the twelve zodiacal signs. Outside that dial was a rotatable ring with the months of the Sothic calendar having the Egyptian names of the months transcribed into the letters of the Greek alphabet. Turning a hand crank moved the date pointer on the front dial giving the position of the Sun which would then be set to the correct Egyptian calendar day. The action of turning the crank also caused all the other interlocked gears to rotate, calculating and displaying the positions of the Sun,

Moon, moon phase, specific stars longitudes with their morning and evening risings, solar and lunar eclipses according to day of month, hour of day or night, direction, and color, and tentatively the locations of the planets and/or their first and last appearances and changes in direction. The device was calibrated to compensate for the extra quarter day in the solar year and the Moon's faster and slower motions over the course of the month.

In order to determine precise eclipse times, the many gears include dials that tracked the Saros, Metonic, Exeligmos, and Callippic cycles according to the sidereal, synodic, and draconic months of the soli-lunar cycle.[4] The Olympiad dial gave a civil calendar for the year dates for the pan Hellenic games of Isthmia, Olympia, Nemea, Pythia, and the lesser games at Dodona and Rhodes that were all used to keep political and religious chronologies. Astronomical calculations helped the Greeks to follow their traditions of sacrifices to the gods at the appropriate times of the year.

When, Where and Who Built It?

The answers to these questions are still shrouded in mystery with several different contenders vying for the credit of the invention, including several of the premiere geniuses of antiquity—Archimedes, Hipparchus and Poseidonius.

The Case for Rhodes: An initial examination of the inscriptions dated them to around 150-100 BCE, and this coupled with the evidence that the ship had stopped at the island of Rhodes suggested that the device might have been made there or was added to the cargo. At that time, Rhodes was famed for its astronomical school over which the great Greek astronomer Hipparchus presided from 140 to 120 BCE. Hipparchus employed geometry in the study of astronomical phenomena, invented trigonometry, predicted eclipses, and compiled the first star catalog by which he discovered the precession of the constellations. The initial reports in 2006 stated that the technology of the device mirrored his work.[5] Another possibility considered by scholars was the Stoic philosopher Poseidonius (135-51 BCE) who succeeded Hipparchus as head of the school on Rhodes. The Roman orator Cicero, who studied under him, reported that Poseidonius had constructed a planetarium sphere that showed the movements of the sun, stars, and planets, by day and night, just as they appear in the sky.[6] Also in the running was the 1st century BCE astronomer Geminos, a student of Poseidonius, who included ideas in his Introduction to the Phenomena that resemble the inscriptions on the anikythera mechanism regarding the details of the names and numbers of the days of the months.

The arguments for Rhodes as the place of invention or manufacture were that Rhodes was a center of astronomy and engineering at that time; the calculations used in the prediction of eclipses on the antikythera mechanism were derived from the trigonometric methods developed by Hipparchus or his students; and the Olympiad dial on the antikythera mechanism included the name and dates for a minor athletic event that was held on Rhodes.[7]

The Case for Syracuse or Corinth: In 2008, researchers discovered that the month names used in the Olympiad dials are from a local calendar used only in western Greece by colonies associated with Corinth, including Syracuse.[8] This pointed to the possible manufacture of the mechanism in the powerful city state of Syracuse, home to the most brilliant engineer and mathematical genius of the ancient world, Archimedes (287-212) who pioneered the use of gear wheels in his many inventions. Archimedes studied in Alexandria in his youth and his father Phidias was an astronomer. He wrote a lost treatise on the construction of Sphere-Making and built a planetarium which showed the motions of the sun, moon, and five planets which was taken to Rome after his death. More than a century later during the time of Cicero, Archimedes' planetarium was described as an eclipse predictor:

"When Gallus moved the globe, it happened that

the Moon followed the Sun by as many turns on that bronze contrivance as in the sky itself, from which also in the sky the Sun's globe became to have that same eclipse, and the Moon came then to that position which was its shadow on the Earth, when the Sun was in line.[9]

The Syracuse/Corinth connection is based upon the local calendar names, astronomical calculations indicating observations that are thought to only be made in Corinth area, but most of all, the heritage of Archimedes unique genius in building geared mechanical devices that reflected his astronomical knowledge.

The Latest Findings: Several weeks ago, in November 2014 historian of astronomy Christian Carman and physicist James Evans published their latest findings after further analysis of the eclipse dial.[10] Their evidence suggests that the device works best if the full moon of month 1 of the Saros dial corresponds to May 12, 204 BCE with the Exeligmos dial set at 0. Carmen and Evans pointed out the epoch date is not necessarily the same as the manufacture date, but that it would be surprising if they were widely separated. Furthermore, they concluded that the Babylonian arithmetic scheme for predicting eclipse times matches the evidence better than does the trigonometric model. And finally that the longitudes for eclipses on the Saros dial encompassing the 18-year cycle from 204-186 BCE fit best for the Aegean Sea area.

While Evans remains cautious about attempting to identify the mechanism, his findings indicate that the device was likely built shortly after the death of Archimedes but almost a century before the flourishing of Hipparchus and his trigonometry methods for prediction of astronomical phenomena. And that Rhodes is located in the Aegean Sea while Syracuse is not. Alexander Jones, specialist in the history of ancient mathematical sciences at New York University places his bets on Rhodes as the site of manufacture.[11]

At this point in the inquiry as to origins, we can speculate that it was Archimedes' advanced science, mechanics, engineering, and prototype astronomical planetarium that provided the foundational models (and possibly even Corinthian month names for the Olympiad games dial) for the invention of the antikythera mechanism. In the late third century when the device was built, Rhodes was a thriving intellectual center of technology and astronomy and it stood at the crossroads of trade and cultural exchange between Mesopotamia, Asia Minor, Greece and Rome. The time and place were conducive for some theorist in Rhodes to merge the arithmetic predictive methods of the Babylonians which were accompanied by lists of actual observations with the models of Archimedes in order to design the many interlocking gears of the mechanism. It could then be built according to specifications by the local technicians.

Implications for History of Hellenistic Astrology: Historians of astrology have long been perplexed by the seemingly sudden emergence of a highly complex and sophisticated Hellenistic astrology over the course of a few generations. Its predecessor, Babylonian celestial divination had quite simpler interpretative texts and at this time there is no evidence of any transitional texts documenting a gradual development of advanced techniques from Babylonian to Hellenistic astrologies. The antikythera mechanism may provide the missing key.

Babylonia had a long and rich history of celestial observations and corresponding omen divinations that were recorded on cuneiform clay tablets spanning the first two millennia BCE. Shortly before Alexander's conquests of the lands of the ancient Near East in the late 4th century BCE, their astrology had culminated in the first horoscopes detailing the character and destiny of an individual based upon the planetary positions at the time of birth. Just a few simple interpretive texts have been discovered, which contain guidelines such as "If a child is born when Jupiter comes forth and Mercury had set, it will go excellently for that man, his oldest son will die."[12] Their astronomy included hundreds of ephemerides, almanacs, goal year texts and diaries that represented the systematic computation of daily planetary motions with risings, settings, visibility and direction changes, ingresses into different zodiacal signs, eclipses, and periodic planetary returns for predictive purposes.

Babylonian astronomical and astrological knowledge became available to the Greeks in the aftermath of Alexander's conquests. Strabo tells us of Chaldean astrological schools at Babylon, Borsippa, Sippar and names of Chaldean astrologers Kidenas and Naburanos.[13] Berossus, a Babylonian priest, opened first school of astrology in Greece in 290 BCE on the island Kos, adjacent to Rhodes.[14] Greek astrologers such as Sudines (fl. 250 BCE), astrological advisor to Attallus I in Pergamon; Apollonius of Myndos[15] (fl. 225 BCE on the Carian coast of Asia Minor), Epigenes of Byzantium[16] and Critodemus[17] were all cited by ancient authors as having learned directly from Babylonian sources.

The Babylonian school for Greek astrologers on Kos was a short sail from Rhodes to the next island over and Kos had strong political ties with the Ptolemaic kingdoms whose center was in Alexandria, Egypt. Within the next half century, the comprehensive astrological textbook of Nechepso and Petosiris appeared in Egypt circa 150 BCE. It contained significations of planets, four zodiacal rulerships systems, elements, modalities, sect, houses, aspects, time lord systems, fixed stars, elaborate algorithms for determining length of life, critical periods, and analysis of the various topics of life such as marriage, children, wealth, rank, and health. This unique work established the foundation for the subsequent development of Hellenistic astrology and the Western tradition.

The invention and availability of a device such as the antikythera mechanism could have fostered this rapid advance of astrological practice—with a crank of the hand astrologers could compute planetary positions for charts much like we do today with a click of a finger or a mouse.

Jo Marchant points out that geared models that were similar

to the antikythera mechanism were still being made in both Syracuse and Rhodes during the time of Cicero a century later. She speculates that Archimedes original design continued to updated by the latest astronomical knowledge from Rhodes and elsewhere, and was shipped across the Greek-speaking world.[18] In the 4th century CE the Alexandrian mathematician Pappus includes in his discussion of the mechanical arts of his time that of sphere-makers who construct models of the heavens.[19] The antikythera mechanism is our first material evidence of this tradition that may have revolutionized the practice of astrology.

A colophon to this story emerged in my research for this essay: Robert Schmidt and others have struggled with the correct translation for the Greek word zoidion. While most astrologers refer to this word as a zodiacal sign and teach the zodiac as circle of animals, the Greek lexicon entry includes "a small figure, painted or carved." Schmidt settled upon "image" (of a small living creature) for his translation of zoidion.

It turns out that when Archimedes was in Alexandria, he was friends with the engineer Ctesbius who specialized in modelling living creatures such as people, animals, and birds as automated figures that were used on water clocks powered by steam, hot air, or water. This was a parallel tradition to Archimedes who modelled planets in the heavens with geared devices, and small images of the zodiac animals might have been included upon the ecliptic ring of the planetariums. Zoidion, one of the most important words for astrologers, can possibly be traced back to the youthful friendship of two ancient sages making moving models and images of the heavens and living creatures, one of whose later work would lead to the invention of the antikythera mechanism which in turn precipitated a quantum leap of astrology.

For the latest findings on the AntiKythera Mechanism, visit http://www.antikythera-mechanism.gr/

Endnotes
[1]Naval historian Konstantinos Rados (1905), German philologist

Albert Rehm (1907), Greek admiral J. Theophanides (1920s), British physicist and historian of science Derek de Solla Price (from 1953 -1984), British museum curator of mechanical engineering Michael Wright (from 1983 to present)

[2]Derek de Solla Price, "Gears from the Greeks: "The Antikythera Mechanism–A Calendar Computer from ca. 80 BC," in *Transactions of the American Philosophical Society*, 1974, 64.

[3]British professor of astronomy Mike Edmunds, British mathematician and film-maker Tony Freeth, Greek professors of astronomy J. Seiradakis and Xenophon Moussas.

[4]The Saros Cycle is 223 synodic months equal to about 18 years; the Exeligmos cycle is 54-year triple Saros cycles; the Metonic cycle is 235 synodic months equal to about 19 tropical years; the Callippic cycle is 76 years equal to 4 Metonic cycles.

[5]Tony Freeth, et al. "Supplementary Notes" in Calendars with Olympian display and eclipse prediction on the Antikythera Mechanism," *Nature*, 31, July 2008, 458, pp. 614-17.

[6]Cicero. *The Nature of the Gods*, 2.87-89.

[7]Paul Iverson, https://www.youtube.com/watch?v=NrV4A8o7NAk

[8]Tony Freeth, Alexander Jones, John M. Steele & Yanis Bitsakis "Calendars with Olympic display and eclipse predictions on the Antikythera Mechanism," *Nature*, 454, 614-617 (31 July 2008)

[9]Cicero. *The Rebublic*, 1.14

[10]Christian C. Carman and James Evans. "On the epoch of the Antikythera mechanism and its eclipse predictor," in *The Archive of History of Exact Sciences*, 68, Nov. 2014, 693-774.

[11]"On the Trail of an Ancient Mystery" in *The New York Times*, Nov. 24, 2014.

[12]From A. Sachs. "Babylonian Horoscopes," in *Journal of Cuneiform Studies*, 6 1952, 68-75.

[13]Strabo. *Geography*, 16.1–6.

[14]Vitruvius. *On Architecture*, 9.6.2.

[15]Vettius Valens. *The Anthology*, 9,11.

[16]Seneca. *Natural Questions*, 7.30.

[17]Neugebauer and Van Hoesen. *Greek Horoscopes*. Philadelphia: The American Philosophical Society Vol. 48, 185.

[18]Jo Marchant. *Decoding the Heavens*. Cambridge, MA: Da Capo Press, 2009, 288.

[19]Pappus of Alexandria. *Mathematical Collection*, Book 8.

About the Authors

Ana Andrade

Ana Andrade is Peruvian and after ten years in Argentina, returned to her native country. She earned an M.S. in organization development at Pepperdine University. Ana belongs to the Fundación Centro Astrológico de Buenos Aires, is a memmber of its committee, graduated from the Posgrade Programme, and led the Seminar Intuition and Astrology. She earned the ISAR CAP designation and leads workshops, provides consultation, and prepares candidates for the ISAR competency exam. A former professor in ISAA (Instituto Superior de Astrología), she is the author of several published articles. Contact Ana at anaastrologer@yahoo.com.

Glen Atkinson

Glen has had an interest in astrology since 1974, and has applied it to many fields. He wrote a women's magazine column for ten years, gave readings for twenty-five years, traded financial futures for thirty years, and predicted the weather. Astrology's application to understanding Rudolf Steiner's agricultural and medical work has been an underlying endeavor since 1976, and it has been invaluable in the development of a remedial system for all kingdoms of nature.

José Luis Belmonte

A telecommunications engineer, publisher, writer, international lecturer and author of four books, José Luis Belmonte's interest in astrology began more than thirty years ago. He studied at Kepler College, where he earned a master's degree in astrology. Currently he conducts astrological research on the history of astrology, paganism, gnosticism, mythology, symbolism, archetypes, and Jungian psychology. Apart from being a guest on radio and TV shows, he conducted a weekly radio show on astrology in Miami from 2013 until early 2014. He currently lives in Barcelona, Spain, with his wife and daughter and works as an astrologer, writing papers and lecturing on astrology, and teaching astrology at Marilo Casals school of astrology.

Michael Bergen

Michael Bergen was born in Brooklyn, New York on May 27, 1971 at 3:35 p.m. After attending New York City public schools and graduating from Brooklyn Technical High School, he earned a B.A. in applied math from Brown University and an M.S. in math education from Brooklyn College. He has six years experience in the research department of Merrill Lynch and four years experience as a high school teacher. He has been studying astrology since 1993, and lives in Brooklyn with his wife and kids. For further information on The Astrology Code, visit www.AstrologyCode.com. Michael can be contacted at michael_bergen@msn.com.

Arlene DeAngelus

Arlene has been involved in astrology for about forty years and has practiced as a professional astrologer since 1980. She has a Certificate of Merit in Astrology from Ivy Goldstein-Jacobson (CA 1982) and a Certificate of Proficiency from The Mayo School of Astrology (London 1985). She lectures nationally and is the author of *Astrological Crime Charts*, published by American Federation of Astrologers (2000). She is certified by the National Spiritualist Association of Churches at Lily Dale, New York as both a Spiritualist Medium and Healer (1982-2015). Additionally, Arlene worked for the New York State Dormitory Authority as a contract administrator for more than thirty years. She also has a B.A. from The College of Saint Rose in Albany, New York and a Certification of Completion from the Albany Police Department's Citizen Police Academy. Contact Arlene at www.yourstarsite.com.

Pamela Fernsler

Pamela Joy Fernsler was born April 5, 1950, 12:46 a.m. local time, Reading, PA. A metaphysician through the AMORC and Rosicrucian Fellowship, she studied through the Rosicrucian Fellowship and many other resources. Pamela has a preference for metaphysical chart interpretation, and says she "has an embarrassment of riches concerning psi abilities, especially transentience, chronosentience and empathy." Pamela loves cats, science, including archaeology, and skillset in groupbuilding. She says she "has a brain that just won't stop."

Demetra George

Demetra George, M.A., PMAFA has been practicing astrology for more than forty years, specializing in archetypal mythology and ancient techniques. She is the author of *Astrology For Yourself, Asteroid Goddesses, Mysteries of the Dark Moon, Finding Our Way Through the Dark*, and *Astrology and the Authentic Self.* She lives in Oregon, lectures internationally, and leads pilgrimages to the sacred sites in Greece, Egypt, and India. Her forthcoming works include a translation and commentary of *Ancient Hermetic Medical Astrology* and a workbook entitled *Traditional Astrology for Yourself.* She offers astrological consultations, mentors individual students in all levels of astrological education, and currently gives monthly webinars adapting ancient techniques for contemporary practitioners. Demetra serves as a director on the AFA Board of Directors. Contact her at www.demetrageorge.com.

Sue Kientz

Sue Kientz began studying the astrological signs in 1977 to learn more about symbolism in literature. Eventually she learned to calculate and analyze charts, and became intrigued by the results. Kientz has always included the large asteroids in her chart work, and sees the dwarf planets as the finishing touches astrology needs to show that Time has actual (and often very beautiful) patterns and features. Sue's forthcoming book *More Plutos* will introduce astrologers to the Dwarf Planets of the Kuiper Belt. She has also contributed articles to the *Astrological Journal of Great Britain* and *Mountain Astrologer*. Contact her at www.moreplutos.com and Twitter, @moreplutos

David McMinn

David McMinn completed a B.Sc at the University of Melbourne in 1971 and subsequently worked as a mineral economist in the ANZ Banking Group Ltd. (a major Australian financial institution). Since leaving this position in 1982, he has conducted private research on cycles, with his main interests centering on the 9/56 year grid and Moon Sun cycles. This was found to be applicable to a range of phenomena–financial panics, earthquakes and volcanoes. McMinn has published numerous papers and articles in the fields of technical analysis and seismology, as well as three books on market timing.

Silvia Mendez

Silvia, an Argentinean has a degree in human relations from the Universidad del Salvador in Buenos Aires. A professional civil servant since 1971, her speciality is public administration. She graduated from Fundación Centro Astrológico de Buenos Aires, and since then has worked as a professional astrologer, providing consultation, leading seminars, and doing research with special emphasis on geneathlic and mundane. Since 2009, she has been co-moderator of the Siderum Nuntium List, a forum dedicated to mundane astrology. Contact ilvia at snmendez@gmail.com.

Peter Meyer

Peter Meyer studied mathematics and philosophy and has an M.Phil. in computational physics from the University of Derby. He became interested in planetary transits in 2010 after reading Richard Tarnas' *Cosmos and Psyche*, and was inspired to write the Windows software Planetary Aspects and Transits and Your

Planetary Transits, both available via his Web site at http://www.planetary-aspects.com. He is also the author of several computer programs and articles dealing with calendars and calendrical science, file and email encryption, word and phrase counting and other subjects, all of which can be seen at his Hermetic Systems Web site at http://www.hermetic.ch.

Indranil Ray

Indranil Ray has degrees in information technology, and pioneered computer education in West Bengal. He currently runs a computer training center in Kolkata. Indranil also has a degree from Viswa Jyotish Vidyapith, teaches astrology classes, and works with clients. He is a regular contributor to *The Express Star Teller* magazine, and received the EST Nostradamus Award in 2014.

Kris Brandt Riske

Kris Brandt Riske, M.A., PMAFA is executive director of the American Federation of Astrologers and a professional member of the organization. She writes an annual weather forecast for *Llewellyn's Moon Sign Book* and is the author of *Predicting Weather Events with Astrology*, *Llewellyn's Complete Book of Astrology*, and *Llewellyn's Complete Book of Predictive Astrology*, among others. In addition to an M.A. in journalism, Kris earned a Certificate of Achievement in Weather Forecasting from Penn State University. An avid NASCAR fan, she forecasts the weather for NASCAR races and other weather events throughout the year. Contact Kris at www.astroweathervane.com.

Pamela Rowe

Pamela Rowe, LPMAFA, FMFAA, Diploma Cosmobiology (Hons) is one of the most highly qualified astrology teachers in Australia. She holds a diploma in cosmobiology and professional certification from the American Federation of Astrologers, where she served on the AFA Board of Directors for more than 18 years, and received the Catharine T. Grant Award for Outstanding Education/Research Achievements in Astrology. She is also a Fellow Member of the Federation of Australian Astrologers, and has served as FAA Victorian Branch president, national secretary and national vice president. Pamela has practiced astrology professionally since 1977, and lectured throughout Australia, U.S., and New Zealand. Her involvement in popular astrology includes periods at Channel 10 Television and 3AW Radio Melbourne plus four years scripting and recording Dial-a-Horoscope for Telecom Australia, broadcast nationwide. She was also the astrological columnist for the widely distributed Australian *Sunday Herald-Sun*. Her articles on astrology have been published in Australia, U.S., and Germany, and her research interest is health. She is the author of The Health Zodiac and Practical Guide to Astrology.

Joe Simon

Joe Simon has studied astrology since the 1970s, when he was introduced to the subject by Isobel Hickey. Later, he studied with Rob Hand, learned cosmobiology, and also studied psychological astrology with Zipporah Dobyns. After a long interlude to rear a family, he was introduced to the classical revival and started studying the work of Robert Zoller. His focus now is on medieval astrology and especially medieval Arabic astrology, which is the wellspring of rennaisance and modern astrology.

www.ingramcontent.com/pod-product-compliance
Lightning Source LLC
Chambersburg PA
CBHW020759230426
43666CB00007B/766